Advanced Splunk

Master the art of getting the maximum out of
your machine data using Splunk

Ashish Kumar Tulsiram Yadav

[PACKT] enterprise
PUBLISHING professional expertise distilled

BIRMINGHAM - MUMBAI

Advanced Splunk

First published: June 2016

Production reference: 1030616

Published by Packt Publishing Ltd.
Livery Place
35 Livery Street
Birmingham B3 2PB, UK.

ISBN 978-1-78588-435-1

www.packtpub.com

Credits

Author
Ashish Kumar Tulsiram Yadav

Reviewer
Randy Rosshirt

Commissioning Editor
Veena Pagare

Acquisition Editor
Manish Nainani

Content Development Editor
Viranchi Shetty

Technical Editor
Ravikiran Pise

Copy Editors
Karuna Narayanan
Neha Vyas

Project Coordinator
Izzat Contractor

Proofreader
Safis Editing

Indexer
Rekha Nair

Graphics
Abhinash Sahu

Production Coordinator
Manu Joseph

Cover Work
Manu Joseph

About the Author

Ashish Kumar Tulsiram Yadav is a BE in computers and has around four and a half years of experience in software development, data analytics, and information security, and around four years of experience in Splunk application development and administration. He has experience of creating Splunk applications and add-ons, managing Splunk deployments, machine learning using R and Python, and analytics and visualization using various tools, such as Tableau and QlikView.

He is currently working with the information security operations team, handling the Splunk Enterprise security and cyber security of the organization. He has worked as a senior software engineer at Larsen & Toubro Technology Services in the telecom consumer electronics and semicon unit providing data analytics on a wide variety of domains, such as mobile devices, telecom infrastructure, embedded devices, Internet of Things (IOT), Machine to Machine (M2M), entertainment devices, and network and storage devices.

He has also worked in the area of information, network, and cyber security in his previous organization. He has experience in OMA LWM2M for device management and remote monitoring of IOT and M2M devices and is well versed in big data and the Hadoop ecosystem. He is a passionate ethical hacker, security enthusiast, and Linux expert and has knowledge of Python, R, .NET, HTML5, CSS, and the C language.

He is an avid blogger and writes about ethical hacking and cyber security on his blogs in his free time. He is a gadget freak and keeps on writing reviews on various gadgets he owns. He has participated in and has been a winner of hackathons, technical paper presentations, white papers, and so on.

Acknowledgements

I would like to take this opportunity to thank my wonderful mom and dad for their blessings and for everything. I would sincerely like to thank Karishma Jain and Apurv Srivastav for helping me with examples, test data, and various other required material that enabled me to complete this book on time. I would also like to thank my friends, team, and colleagues at L&T TS for their support and encouragement. Special thanks to Nate Mckervey and Mitesh Vohra for guiding and helping me in various stages of writing this book. Last, but not least, a big thanks to Manish, Viranchi, Ravikiran, and the entire Packt Publishing team for their timely support and help.

About the Reviewer

Randy Rosshirt has had a 25-year career in technology, specializing in enterprise software and big data challenges. Much of his background has been in the healthcare industry. Since he started working with Splunk in 2012, his focus has been to introduce Splunk into the healthcare informatics community. While working at Splunk, Randy was involved with creating Splunk solutions for HIPAA privacy, clinical quality indicators, and adverse events data. He also spoke on behalf of Splunk at the 2014 HIMSS event on the topic Mining Big Data for Quality Indicators. He continues to provide private consulting to solve healthcare problems with Splunk.

For more, look at `www.rrosshirt.com`

> I would like to thank Packt Publishing, especially the project coordinator and the author for inviting me to participate in this project.

www.PacktPub.com

eBooks, discount offers, and more

Did you know that Packt offers eBook versions of every book published, with PDF and ePub files available? You can upgrade to the eBook version at www.PacktPub.com and as a print book customer, you are entitled to a discount on the eBook copy. Get in touch with us at customercare@packtpub.com for more details.

At www.PacktPub.com, you can also read a collection of free technical articles, sign up for a range of free newsletters and receive exclusive discounts and offers on Packt books and eBooks.

https://www2.packtpub.com/books/subscription/packtlib

Do you need instant solutions to your IT questions? PacktLib is Packt's online digital book library. Here, you can search, access, and read Packt's entire library of books.

Why subscribe?

- Fully searchable across every book published by Packt
- Copy and paste, print, and bookmark content
- On demand and accessible via a web browser

Instant updates on new Packt books

Get notified! Find out when new books are published by following @PacktEnterprise on Twitter or the *Packt Enterprise* Facebook page.

Table of Contents

Preface

Big data: the term itself suggests a large amount of data. Big data can be defined as high-volume, high-velocity, and high-variety information. Data is sometimes also referred to as logs generated from machines that can be used for the purpose of operations, engineering, business insight, analytics and prediction, and so on as the case may be.

Now, as we have a large amount of data, there is a need for a platform or tool that can be used to create visualizations and derive insights and patterns to make informed business decisions beforehand. To overcome all these challenges of big data, Splunk came into the picture. Splunk is a big data tool that generates insights and reveals patterns, trends, and associations from machine data. It is a powerful and robust big data tool used to derive real-time or near real-time insights, and it enables you to take informed corrective measures.

Splunk can be put to use for data generated from any source and available in a human readable format. As Splunk is a feature-rich tool, it becomes difficult for a Splunk user to start and make the best use of Splunk right away. This book takes the reader through a complete understanding of making the best and most efficient use of Splunk for machine data analytics and visualization. The book covers everything from which type of data can be uploaded to how to do it in an efficient way. It also covers creating applications and add-ons on Splunk, learning analytics commands, and learning visualizations and customizations as per one's requirements. The book also talks about how Splunk can be tweaked to make the best out of Splunk, along with how it can be integrated with R for analytics and Tableau for visualization.

This step-by-step comprehensive guide to Splunk will help readers understand Splunk's capabilities, thus enabling you to make the most efficient and best use of Splunk for big data.

What this book covers

Chapter 1, What's New in Splunk 6.3?, explains in detail how Splunk works in the backend, and also explains the backbone of Splunk, thanks to which it can process big data in real time. We will also go through all the new techniques and architectural changes that have been introduced in Splunk 6.3 to make Splunk faster, better, and provide near real-time results.

Chapter 2, Developing an Application on Splunk, talks about creating and managing an application and an add-on on Splunk Enterprise. You will also learn how to use different applications available on the Splunk app store to minimize the work by using the already available applications for similar requirements.

Chapter 3, On-boarding Data in Splunk, details the various methods by which data can be indexed on Splunk. We will also have a look at various customization options available while uploading data onto Splunk in order to index the data in such a way that trends, pattern detection, and other important features can be used efficiently and easily.

Chapter 4, Data Analytics, helps the reader learn the usage of commands related to searching, data manipulation, field extraction, subsearches, and so on on Splunk, thus enabling him/her to create analytics out of the data.

Chapter 5, Advanced Data Analytics, teaches the reader to generate reports and become well-versed with commands related to geographic and locations. This chapter will also cover advanced section of commands such as anomaly detection, correlation, prediction, and machine learning.

Chapter 6, Visualization, goes through the basic visualization options available in Splunk to represent data in an easier-to-understand format. Along with visualization, we will also discuss tweaking visualizations to make them easier to read and understand.

Chapter 7, Advanced Visualization, teaches the reader to use custom plugins and extensions to implement advanced visualizations in Splunk. These advanced visualizations can even be used by the nontechnical audience to generate useful insight and derive business decisions.

Chapter 8, Dashboard Customization, teaches the reader to create basic custom dashboards with the visualization and analytics you've learned so far. We will go through the various dashboard customization techniques that can be implemented to make the most of out the data on Splunk.

Chapter 9, Advanced Dashboard Customization, instructs the reader about the techniques that will help in developing a highly dynamic, customizable, and useful dashboard over the data on Splunk.

Chapter 10, Tweaking Splunk, talks about how we can make the best use of Splunk features so that we can get the maximum use out of Splunk efficiently. You will also learn the various management and customization techniques to use Splunk in the best possible way.

Chapter 11, Enterprise Integration with Splunk, teaches the reader to set up and use the Splunk SDK along with the integration of Splunk with R for analytics and Tableau for visualization.

Chapter 12, What Next? Splunk 6.4, discusses the features introduced in Splunk 6.4, along with how they can be put to use to maximize the benefit of Splunk for analytics and visualizations.

What you need for this book

Listed as follows are the requirements for getting through the series of tasks performed through this book:

- A Windows machine
- Splunk 6.3/Splunk 6.4, which can be downloaded from the Splunk website
- Python 2.7 and the Splunk SDK for Python
- R 3.1.0
- Tableau 9.3
- Machine data, on which analytics and visualization is to be done.

Who this book is for

This book is for anyone who wants to learn Splunk and understand its advanced capabilities and doesn't want to get lost in loads of online documentation. This book will help readers understand how Splunk can be put to use to derive valuable insights from machine data in no time. This book covers Splunk from end to end, along with examples and illustrations, to make the reader a "master" of Splunk.

Conventions

In this book, you will find a number of text styles that distinguish between different kinds of information. Here are some examples of these styles and an explanation of their meaning.

Code words in text, database table names, folder names, filenames, file extensions, pathnames, dummy URLs, user input, and Twitter handles are shown as follows: "We can include other contexts through the use of the include directive."

A block of code is set as follows:

```
[general]
parallelIngestionPipelines = 2 # For 2 Ingestion Pipeline sets
```

Any command-line input or output is written as follows:

```
./splunk check-integrity -index [ index name ] [ verbose ]
```

New terms and **important words** are shown in bold. Words that you see on the screen, for example, in menus or dialog boxes, appear in the text like this: "Clicking the **Next** button moves you to the next screen."

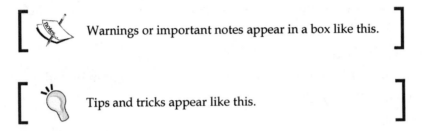

> Warnings or important notes appear in a box like this.

> Tips and tricks appear like this.

Reader feedback

Feedback from our readers is always welcome. Let us know what you think about this book—what you liked or disliked. Reader feedback is important for us as it helps us develop titles that you will really get the most out of.

To send us general feedback, simply e-mail feedback@packtpub.com, and mention the book's title in the subject of your message.

If there is a topic that you have expertise in and you are interested in either writing or contributing to a book, see our author guide at www.packtpub.com/authors.

Customer support

Now that you are the proud owner of a Packt book, we have a number of things to help you to get the most from your purchase.

Downloading the color images of this book

We also provide you with a PDF file that has color images of the screenshots/ diagrams used in this book. The color images will help you better understand the changes in the output. You can download this file from `https://www.packtpub.com/sites/default/files/downloads/AdvancedSplunk_ColorImages.pdf`.

Errata

Although we have taken every care to ensure the accuracy of our content, mistakes do happen. If you find a mistake in one of our books — maybe a mistake in the text or the code — we would be grateful if you could report this to us. By doing so, you can save other readers from frustration and help us improve subsequent versions of this book. If you find any errata, please report them by visiting `http://www.packtpub.com/submit-errata`, selecting your book, clicking on the **Errata Submission Form** link, and entering the details of your errata. Once your errata are verified, your submission will be accepted and the errata will be uploaded to our website or added to any list of existing errata under the Errata section of that title.

To view the previously submitted errata, go to `https://www.packtpub.com/books/content/support` and enter the name of the book in the search field. The required information will appear under the **Errata** section.

Piracy

Piracy of copyrighted material on the Internet is an ongoing problem across all media. At Packt, we take the protection of our copyright and licenses very seriously. If you come across any illegal copies of our works in any form on the Internet, please provide us with the location address or website name immediately so that we can pursue a remedy.

Please contact us at `copyright@packtpub.com` with a link to the suspected pirated material.

We appreciate your help in protecting our authors and our ability to bring you valuable content.

Questions

If you have a problem with any aspect of this book, you can contact us at `questions@packtpub.com`, and we will do our best to address the problem.

What's New in Splunk 6.3?

Splunk is known as the Google of machine log analytics. It is a very powerful, robust, and real-time big data analytics tool. In this chapter, we will study in detail how Splunk works in the backend and what is the backbone of Splunk due to which it can process big data in real time. We will also go through all the new techniques and architectural changes that have been introduced in Splunk 6.3 to make Splunk faster, better, and provide near real-time results.

The following topics will be covered in this chapter:

- The architecture
- Index parallelization
- Search parallelization
- Data integrity control
- Intelligent job scheduling
- The app's key-value store
- Securing Splunk Enterprise
- Single sign-on using SAML

Splunk's architecture

Splunk's architecture comprises of components that are responsible for data ingestion and indexing and analytics.

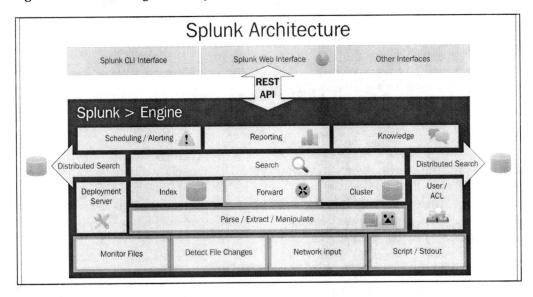

The lowest level of Splunk architecture depicts various data input methods supported by Splunk. These input methods can be configured to send data on Splunk indexers. Before the data reaches Splunk indexers, it can be parsed or manipulated, that is, data cleaning can be done if required. Once the data is indexed on Splunk, the next layer, that is, searching, comes into the picture for analytics over the log data.

Splunk supports two types of deployment: standalone deployment and distributed deployment. Depending on the deployment type, corresponding searches are performed. The Splunk engine has other additional components of knowledge manager, reporting and scheduling, and alerting. The entire Splunk engine is exposed to users via Splunk CLI, Splunk Web Interface, and Splunk SDK, which are supported by most languages.

Splunk installs a distributed server process on the host machine called **splunkd**. This process is responsible for indexing and processing a large amount of data through various sources. splunkd is capable of handling large volumes of streaming data and indexing it for real-time analytics over one or more pipelines.

Every single pipeline comprises of a series of processors, which results in faster and efficient processing of data. Listed below are the blocks of the Splunk architecture:

- **Pipeline**: This is a single-threaded configurable process residing in splunkd.

- **Processors**: They are individual reusable functions that act on incoming data passing through a pipeline. Pipelines exchange data among themselves through a queue.

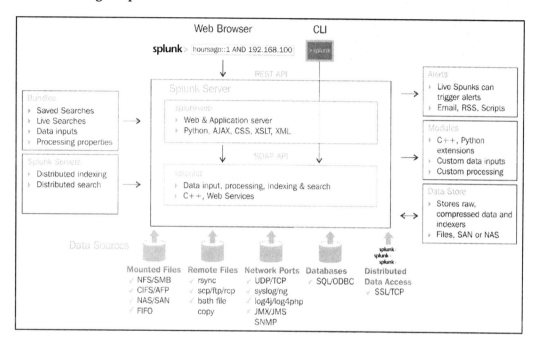

splunkd allows users to search, navigate, and manage data on Splunk Enterprise through the web interface called Splunk Web. It is a web application server based on Python providing a web interface to use Splunk. In the earlier version of Splunk, splunkd and Splunk Web were two separate processes, but from Splunk 6, both the processes were integrated in splunkd itself. It allows users to search for, analyze, and visualize data using the web interface. Splunk Web interface can be accessed using the Splunk web port, and Splunk also exposes the REST API for communication via the splunkd management port.

One of the important components of Splunk's architecture is the data store. It is responsible for compressing and storing original (raw) data. The data is stored in **Time Series Index (TSIDX)** files. A data store also includes storage and archiving based on the configurable retention policy.

Splunk Enterprise deployments can range from single-server deployments (which index a few gigabytes of data per day and are accessed by a few users who are searching, analyzing, and visualizing the data) to large, distributed enterprise deployments across multiple data centers, indexing hundreds of terabytes of data and searches performed by hundreds of users. Splunk supports communication with another instance of a Splunk Server via TCP to forward data from one Splunk server to another to archive data and various other clustering and data distribution requirements via Splunk-to-Splunk TCP communication.

Bundles are the components of the Splunk architecture that store the configuration of data input, user accounts, Splunk applications, add-ons, and various other environment configurations.

Modules are those components of the Splunk architecture that are used to add new features by modifying or creating processors and pipelines. Modules are nothing but custom scripts and data input methods or extensions that can add a new feature or modify the existing features of Splunk.

The need for parallelization

Splunk's traditional indexer had a single splunkd daemon running on a server that fetched data from different sources, which was then categorized into different indexes. Here, a traditional indexer refers to the indexers that were available in the older version of Splunk. The Splunk search queries are then processed by job queues depending on their priority. The indexer is capable of processing more searches. So, to utilize the underutilized indexer, there is need for parallelization. Parallelization leads to full utilization of the processing power of the indexer. Expanding Splunk to meet almost any capacity requirement in order to take advantage of the scaling capability of Splunk deployment requires parallel processing of indexers and search heads.

The following figure shows a traditional indexer host, where there is no parallelization and hence the indexer is left underutilized:

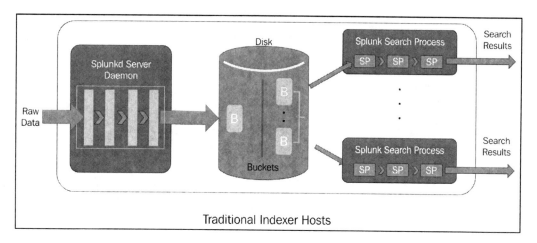

Traditional Indexer Hosts

Index parallelization

Index parallelization allows an indexer to have multiple pipeline sets. A pipeline set is responsible for processing data from ingestion of raw data, through event processing, to writing the events to a disk.

A traditional indexer runs just a single pipeline set. However, if the underlying machine is underutilized, both in terms of available cores and I/O, you can configure the indexer to run additional pipeline sets. By running multiple pipeline sets, you potentially double the indexer's indexing throughput capacity. Increasing throughput also demands disks with high **Input/output Operations Per Second (IOPS)**. So, hardware requirements should be taken into consideration while implementing parallelization.

When you implement two pipeline sets, you have two complete processing pipelines, from the point of data ingestion to the point of writing events to a disk. As shown in the following figure, there is a parallel process for each of the input method and each input is serviced by individual pipelines in the Splunk Server daemon. By enabling an indexer to create multiple pipelines, several data streams can be processed with additional CPU cores that were left underutilized earlier.

This implies that by implementing index parallelization, potentially more data can be indexed on a single indexer with the same set of hardware. It can accelerate parsing of data and writing to a disk up to the limit of indexers' I/O capacity. Index parallelization can double the indexing speed in case of sudden increase of data from the forwarders.

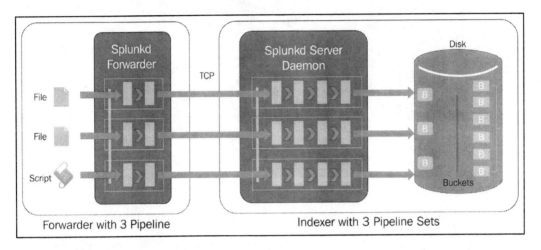

Each pipeline set has its own set of queues, pipelines, and processors. Exceptions are input pipelines that are usually singleton. No states are shared across pipelines sets, and thus, there is no dependency or a situation of deadlock. Data from a single unique source is handled by only one pipeline set at a time. Each component performs its function independently.

The following are the various components of Splunk that are enhanced in Splunk 6.3 and they function as follows to support index parallelization:

- **Monitor input**: Each pipeline set has its own set of TailReaders, BatchReaders, and archive processors. This enables parallel reading of files and archives on forwarders. Each file/archive is assigned to one pipeline set.

- **Forwarder**: There will be one TCP output processor per pipeline set per forwarder input. This enables multiple TCP connections from forwarders to different indexers at the same time. Various rules such as load balancing rules can be applied to each pipeline set independently.

- **Indexer**: Every incoming TCP forwarder connection is bound to one pipeline set on the indexer.

- **Indexing**: Every pipeline set will independently write new data to indexes. Data is written in parallel for better utilization of underutilized resources. The buckets produced by different pipeline sets could have an overlapping time range.

Next, we'll discuss how to configure multiple ingestion pipeline sets. To do that modify `Server.conf` located at `$SPLUNK_HOME\etc\system\local` as follows for a number of ingestion pipeline sets:

```
[general]
parallelIngestionPipelines = 2 # For 2 Ingestion Pipeline sets
```

 According to Splunk documents, the default value is 1.

Search parallelization

Once the data is boarded on Splunk, a search is used to create analytics over the indexed data. Here, the faster the search results produced, the more the real-time results will be. Search parallelization is the easiest and most efficient way to speed up transforming searches by adding additional search pipelines on each indexer. This helps in processing of multiple buckets at the same time. Search parallelization can also enable acceleration for a transforming search when saved as a report or report-based dashboard panel.

Pipeline parallelization

Underutilized indexers and resources provide us with opportunities to execute multiple search pipelines. Since there is no sharing of states, there exists no dependency across search pipelines among each other. Though underutilized indexers are candidates for search pipeline parallelization, it is always advised not to enable pipeline parallelization if indexers are fully utilized and don't have the bandwidth to handle more processes.

The following figure depicts that search parallelization searches are designed to search and return event data by bucket instead of time. More the search pipelines added, more the search buckets are processed simultaneously, thus increasing the speed of returning the search results. The data between different pipelines is not shared at all. Each pipeline services a single target search bucket and then processes it to send out the search results.

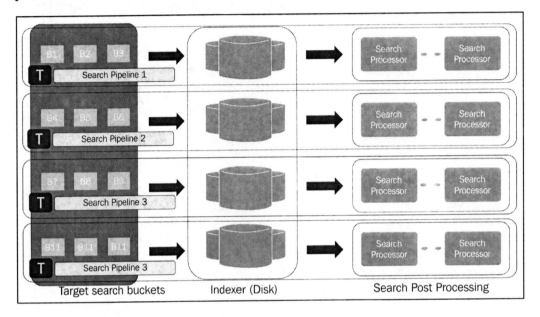

The default value of `batch_search_max_pipeline` is 1, and the maximum recommended value is 2.

Now, we'll discuss how to configure batch search in a parallel mode. To configure a batch search in a parallel mode, modify the `limits.conf` file located at `$SPLUNK_HOME\etc\system\local` as:

```
[search]
batch_search_max_pipeline = 2
```

 Note that the value should be increased in multiples of 2.

This increases the number of threads and thus improves the search performance in terms of retrieving search results.

The search scheduler

There have been tremendous improvements in the search scheduler in Splunk 6.3 to improve the search performance and for proper and efficient resource utilization. The following two important improvements were introduced in Splunk 6.3 that reduces lags and fewer skipped searches:

- **Priority scoring**: Earlier versions of Splunk had simple, single-term priority scoring that resulted in a lag in a saved search, skipping, and could also result in starvation under CPU constraint. Thus, Splunk introduced priority scoring in Splunk 6.3 with better, multi-term priority scoring that mitigates the problem and improves performance by 25 percent.

- **Schedule window**: In earlier versions of Splunk, a scheduler was not able to distinguish between searches that should run at a specific time (such as cron) from those that don't have to. This resulted into skipping of those searches from being run. So, Splunk 6.3 was featured with a schedule window for searches that don't have to run at a specific time.

We'll learn how to configure the search scheduler next. Modify the `limits.conf` file located at `$SPLUNK_HOME\etc\system\local` as follows:

```
[scheduler]
#The ratio of jobs that scheduler can use versus the manual/dashboard
jobs. Below settings applies 50% quota for scheduler.
Max_searches_perc = 50

# allow value to be 80 anytime on weekends.
Max_searches_perc.1 = 80
Maxx_searches_perc.1.when = ****0,6

# Allow value to be 60 between midnight and 5 am.
Max_searches_perc.2 = 60
Max_searches_perc.2.when = * 0-5 ***
```

Summary parallelization

The sequential nature of building summary data for data models and saved reports is very slow, and hence, the summary building process has been parallelized in Splunk 6.3.

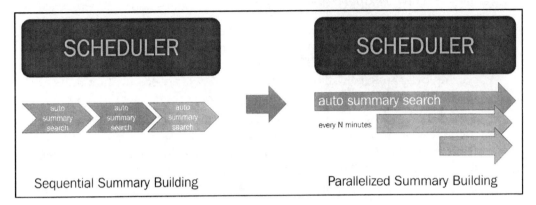

As shown in the preceding figure, in the earlier versions of Splunk, the scheduler summary building was sequential. Because of this, one after the other, there was a performance bottleneck. Now, the summary building process has been parallelized, resulting into faster and efficient summary building.

Now we're going to configure summary parallelization. Modify the `savedsearches. conf` file located at `$SPLUNK_HOME\etc\system\local` as follows:

```
[default]
Auto_summarize.max_concurrent = 3
```

Then, modify the `datamodels.conf` file located at `$SPLUNK_HOME\etc\system\local` as follows:

```
[default]
Acceleration.max_concurrent = 2
```

Data integrity control

Splunk has now come up with the data integrity managing feature in its latest version 6.3. It provides a way to verify the integrity of data that is indexed over Splunk. On enabling this feature, Splunk computes hashes on every slice of uploaded data and stores those hashes so that they can be used to verify the integrity of the data. It is a very useful feature where the logs are from sources such as bank transactions and other critical data where an integrity check is necessary.

On enabling this feature, Splunk computes hashes on every slice of newly indexed raw data and writes it to an l1Hashes file. When the bucket rolls from one bucket to another, say from hot to warm, Splunk computes the hash of contents of the l1Hashes file and stores it into the l2Hash file.

Hash validation can be done on Splunk's data by running the following CLI command:

```
./splunk check-integrity -bucketPath [ bucket path ] [ verbose ]
./splunk check-integrity -index [ index name ] [ verbose ]
```

In case hashes are lost, they can be regenerated using the following commands:

```
./splunk generate-hash-files -bucketPath [ bucket path ]  [ verbose ]
./splunk generate-hash-files -index [ index name ] [ verbose ]
```

Let's now configure data integrity control. To configure data integrity control, modify the indexes.conf file located at $SPLUNK_HOME\etc\system\local as follows:

```
enableDataIntegrityControl=true
```

 In a clustered environment, all the clusters and peers should run Splunk 6.3 to enable accurate data integrity control.

Intelligent job scheduling

This section will explain in detail how Splunk Enterprise handles scheduled reports in order to run them concurrently. Splunk uses a report scheduler to manage scheduled alerts and reports. Depending on the configuration of the system, the scheduler sets a limit on the number of reports that can be run concurrently on the Splunk search head. Whenever the number of scheduled reports crosses the threshold limit set by the scheduler, it has to prioritize the excess reports and run them in order of their priority.

The limit is set by a scheduler so as to make sure that the system performance is not degraded and fewer or no reports get skipped disproportionally more than others. Generally, reports are skipped when slow-to-complete reports crowd out quick-to-complete reports, thus causing them to miss their scheduled runtime.

The following table shows the priority order in which Splunk runs different types of searches:

Priority	Search/report type	Description
First priority	Ad hoc historical searches	• Manually run historically searches always run first • Ad hoc search jobs are given more priority than scheduled ad hoc search reports
Second priority	Manually scheduled reports and alerts with real-time scheduling	• Reports scheduled manually use a real-time scheduling mode by default • Manually run searches are prioritized against reports to reduce skipping of manually scheduled reports and alerts
Third priority	Manually scheduled reports with continuous scheduling	• The continuous scheduling mode is used by scheduled reports, populating summary indexes and other reports
Last priority	Automatically scheduled reports	• Scheduled reports related to report acceleration and data model acceleration fall into this category • These reports are always given last priority

Caution:
It is suggested that you do not change the settings until and unless you are aware of what you are doing.

The limit is automatically determined by Splunk on the basis of system-wide concurrent historical searches, depending upon the values of `max_searches_per_cpu`, `base_max_searches` in the `limits.conf` file located at `$SPLUNK_HOME\etc\system\local`.

The default value of `base_max_searches` is 6.

It is calculated as follows:

*Maximum number of concurrent historical searches = (max_searches_per_cpu * number of CPU) + base_max_searches*

So, for a system with two CPUs, the value should be 8. To get a better clarity see the following worked out example:

*Maximum number of concurrent historical searches = (1 * 2) + 6 = 8*

The *max_searches_perc* parameter can be set up so that it allows more or less concurrent scheduled reports depending on the requirement. For a system with two CPUs, the report scheduler can safely run only four scheduled reports at a time (50 percent of the maximum number of concurrent historical searches), that is, 50 percent of 8 = 4.

For efficient and full use of the Splunk scheduler, the scheduler limit can vary by time. The scheduler limit can be set to whether to have fewer or more concurrent scheduled reports.

Now, let's configure intelligent job scheduling. Modify the `limits.conf` file located at the `$SPLUNK_HOME\etc\system\local` directory. The `max_searches_perc.n` is to be set up with appropriate percentages for specific cron periods:

```
# The default limit, used when the periods defined below are not in
effect.
max_searches_perc = 50


#  Change the max search percentage at 5am every day when specifically
there is less load on server.
max_searches_perc.0 = 70
max_searches_perc.0.when = * 0-5 * * *


#  Change the max search percentage even more on Saturdays and Sundays
max_searches_perc.1 = 90
max_searches_perc.1.when = * 0-5 * * 0,6
```

There are two scheduling modes of manually scheduled reports, which are as follows:

- **Real-time scheduling**: In this type of scheduling, Splunk ensures that the recent run of the report returns current data. This means that a scheduled report with real-time scheduling runs at its scheduled runtime or not at all.

  If there are longer running reports that have not finished or there are many reports with real-time scheduling set to run at the same time, then in that case, some of the real-time scheduling reports may be skipped.

A report scheduler prioritizes reports with real-time scheduling over reports with continuous scheduling.

- **Continuous scheduling**: Continuous scheduling is used in a situation where running the report is eventually required. In case a report with continuous scheduling is not able to run due to one or other reason, then it will run in future after other reports are finished.

   All the scheduled reports are, by default, set to real-time scheduling unless they are enabled for summary indexing. In case of summary indexing, the scheduling mode is set to continuous scheduling because summary indexes are not that reliable if scheduled reports that populate them are skipped.

   If there is any server failure or Splunk Enterprise is shut down for some reason, then in that case, the continuous scheduling mode's configured reports will miss scheduled runtime. The report scheduler can replace all the missed runs of continuously scheduled reports of the last 24 hours when Splunk Enterprise goes online, provided that it was at least once on its schedule before the Splunk Enterprise instance went down.

Let's configure the scheduling mode next. To configure scheduled reports so that they are in a real-time scheduling mode or in a continuous scheduling mode, the `realtime_schedule` parameter in the `savedsearches.conf` file is to be manually changed from `realtime_schedule` to `0` or `1`. Both the scheduling modes are explained as follows:

- `realtime_schedule = 0`: This mode enables scheduled reports that are to be in a continuous scheduling mode. This ensures that the scheduled reports never skip any run. If it cannot run at that moment, it will run later when other reports are over.

- `realtime_schedule = 1`: This mode enables a scheduled report to run at its scheduled start time. If it cannot start due to other reports, it skips that scheduled run. This is the default scheduling mode for new reports.

The app key-value store

The app key-value store is a feature provided by Splunk Enterprise to manage and maintain the state of the application. Using an app key-value store, users can save and retrieve data from Splunk apps.

System requirements

The app key-value store feature is only available in the 64-bit distribution of Splunk Enterprise. It is not available in the 32-bit version of Splunk. It uses the 8191 port by default, but it can be configured from Server.conf located at $SPLUNK_HOME\etc\ system\local by modifying the [kvstore] code block.

Uses of the key-value store

The following are some of the uses of a key-value store:

- It can be used to manage the app state of the user interface by storing the session/application state information
- It creates a checkpoint of the uploaded data in case of modular inputs
- It enlists the environment variable used, accessed, or modified by users
- It is the metadata storage of the user
- It caches results from search queries

Components of the key-value store

The key-value store saves data in the collections of the key-value pair. The key-value store files are located on the search heads. The following are the various components of the key-value store:

- **Collections**: Collections are containers for data storage similar to a database table.
- **Records**: Records store the entry of data in the collection.
- **Fields**: Fields contain the value of data in the JSON format file. Fields correspond to the key name similar to columns in the database table.
- **_key**: This is the reserved field that contains a unique ID for each record. It is an autogenerated field that is not explicitly specified.
- **_user**: This is also a reserved field that is used to map the user ID of each record.
- **Accelerations**: This is used to improve search performance that contains the accelerated fields.

Let's take a look at how to create a key-value store collections via a config file. To use a key-value store, we need to create a key-value store collection using the following steps:

1. Create a `collections.conf` file in the application's `default` or `local` directory, as follows `$SPLUNK_HOME\etc\apps\APPNAME\default\collections.conf` or `$SPLUNK_HOME\etc\apps\APPNAME\local\collections.conf`.

2. Modify `collections.conf` by specifying the name of the collection and optionally, the schema of the data. Listed in the following sublist is the description of the parameters which need to be configured in `collections.conf` file:

   ○ `[collection_name]`: This is the collection name

   ○ `enforceTypes`: This is set to `True` or `False` to enforce the data types of values when inserting them into the collection.

   ○ `field.name`: This is an optional field. The available data types are string, time, Boolean, and number. If the data type is not set explicitly, then it is set to JSON.

Any change in `collections.conf` needs a restart of the Splunk instance to apply the changes on the search heads. Refer to the following example for better understanding:

```
[AndroidCollections]   #collection_name
```

The screenshot that follows shows a code snippet of the sample JSON data:

```
{
"Devicename" : "Test Device",
"DeviceID" : "9661",
"DeviceBuild" : "Test build 9661C",
"DeviceAndroidVersion" : "Marshmallow 6.0",
"DeviceIMEI" : "12345678909876",
"DeviceMAC" : "AA:BB:CC:DD:EE:FF",
"DeviceDebugBuild" : "True"
}
```

The following screenshot is the code snippet of the enforce data type for the preceding JSON data:

```
[AndroidCollections]
enforceTypes = true
field.Devicename = string
field.DeviceID = number
field.DeviceBuild = string
field.DeviceAndroidVersion = string
field.DeviceIMEI = number
field.DeviceMAC = string
field.DeviceDebugBuild = Boolean
```

The following screenshot shows the sample code snippet for hierarchical JSON data:

```
{
"Devicename" : "Test Device",
"DeviceID" : 9061,
"DeviceInfo" :
    {
    "DeviceBuild" : "Test build 9661C",
    "DeviceAndroidVersion" : "Marshmallow 6.0",
    "DeviceIMEI" : 12345678909876,
    "DeviceMAC" : "AA:BB:CC:DD:EE:FF"
    },
"DeviceDebugBuild" : True
}
```

The following screenshot shows how a data type can be enforced on hierarchical data using a dot (.) notation:

```
[AndroidCollections]
enforceTypes = true
field.Devicename = string
field.DeviceID = number
field.DeviceInfo.DeviceBuild = string
field.DeviceInfo.DeviceAndroidVersion = string
field.DeviceInfo.DeviceIMEI = number
field.DeviceInfo.DeviceMAC = string
field.DeviceDebugBuild = Boolean
```

Managing key-value store collections via REST

The Splunk REST API can be used to create, read, delete, update, and manage key-value store data and collections. The Splunk REST API accesses Splunk via the management port (by default, `8089`). The following are the REST endpoints for the key-value store:

- `storage/collections/config`:
    - GET: This fetches a list of collections in a specific app
    - POST: This creates a new collection in a specific app

- `storage/collections/config/{collection}`:
    - GET: This fetches information about a specific collection
    - DELETE: This deletes a collection
    - POST: This updates a collection

- `storage/collections/data/{collection}`:
    - GET: This fetches records from a specific collection
    - POST: This inserts a new record into a specific collection
    - DELETE: This deletes all records from a specific collection

- `storage/collections/data/{collection}/{id}`:
    - GET: This fetches records in a collection by a key ID
    - POST: This updates records in a collection by a key ID
    - DELETE: This deletes a record in a collection by a key ID

- `storage/collections/data/{collection}/batch_save`:
    - POST: This runs one or more save (insert and replace) operations in a specific collection

Examples

There are various notations used in the following examples, such as `username`, `password`, `IPAddress`, and others. Users need to replace them with their own corresponding values to execute the examples. The following are the examples:

- **Fetching a list of collections for an android app:**

```
curl -k -u username:password \
https://IPAddress:8089/servicesNS/nobody/android/storage/
  collections/config
```

- **Creating a new collection called AndroidCollections in the android app**:

```
curl -k -u username:password \ -d name= AndroidCollections \
https://IPAddress:8089/servicesNS/nobody/android/storage/
  collections/config
```

- **Defining a collection schema**:

```
curl -k -u username:password \
https://IPAddress:8089/servicesNS/nobody/android/storage/
collections/config/ AndroidCollections \
-d field.Devicename = string \
-d field.DeviceID = number \
-d field.DeviceInfo.DeviceBuild = string \
-d field.DeviceInfo.DeviceAndroidVersion = string
```

- **Adding data of the hierarchical JSON format to a collection**:

```
curl -k -u username:password \
https://IPAddress:8089/servicesNS/nobody/android/storage/
  collections/config/ AndroidCollections \
-H 'Content-Type: application/json' \
-d '{ "Devicename" : "Test Device", "DeviceID" : 9661,
  "DeviceInfo" : { "DeviceBuild" : "Test build 9661C",
  "DeviceAndroidVersion" : "Marshmallow 6.0",
  "DeviceIMEI" : 12345678909876, "DeviceMAC" :
  "AA:BB:CC:DD:EE:FF" }} '
```

- **Getting all data from the collection**:

```
curl -k -u username:password \
https://IPAddress:8089/servicesNS/nobody/android/storage/
  collections/config/ AndroidCollections
```

- **Getting a specific range of records from collections, for example, records from 10 to 15**:

```
curl -k -u username:password \
https://IPAddress:8089/servicesNS/nobody/android/storage/
  collections/config/
  AndroidCollections?sort=Devicename&skip=10&limit=5
```

- **Getting a record of a specific key ID**:

```
curl -k -u username:password \
https://IPAddress:8089/servicesNS/nobody/android/storage/
  collections/config/ AndroidCollections/KEYID
```

Where the key ID is the unique _key of collections for which the record is to be fetched.

- **Deleting the record of the specific key ID:**

```
curl -k -u username:password -X DELETE \
https://IPAddress:8089/servicesNS/nobody/android/storage/
   collections/config/ AndroidCollections/KEYID
```

- **Deleting all records of the AndroidCollections collection:**

```
curl -k -u username:password -X DELETE \
https://IPAddress:8089/servicesNS/nobody/android/storage/
   collections/config/ AndroidCollections
```

Replication of the key-value store

In case of a distributed environment, the key-value store can be replicated to a large number of search heads by enabling replication. By default, the key-value store is not replicated to indexers in distributed deployment of Splunk.

To enable replication, the `collections.conf` file is to be modified and we need to add `replicate = true` to the file.

Splunk Enterprise Security

Splunk Enterprise is connected to various data input sources, indexers, and search heads over a network, and hence, it is very important to harden the security of Splunk Enterprise. Taking necessary steps for **Splunk Enterprise Security (SES)** can mitigate risk and reduce attacks from hackers.

The following are ways to secure the Splunk Enterprise deployment:

- Setting up user authentication and creating and managing user access by assigning roles. Splunk has a built-in system for user authentication and to assign roles. Along with the built-in system, it provides integration with the **Lightweight Directory Access Protocol (LDAP)**. Splunk can be integrated with an active directory and can be used as a centralized authentication system for authentication and to assign roles. Splunk Enterprise 6.3 has been introduced with additional authentication using the **Security Assertion Markup Language (SAML)**. Splunk Enterprise can be enabled for single sign-ons using SAML, which was explained in detail in the previous section of the chapter.

- Use **Secure Socket Layer (SSL)** for secure communication of Splunk deployment. Splunk provides, by default, certificates and keys that can be used to enable SSL communication to provide encryption and data compression while communicating with different components of Splunk deployment. It secures the communication between browsers, Splunk Web, and data sent from forwarders to indexers. Splunk provisions to use your own certificates and keys to secure the communication of Splunk deployment components.

- Keep Splunk installation updated with the latest security patches and updates. Splunk continuously keeps on fixing bugs and comes up with updates on Splunk Enterprise. Splunk releases the bug fix report that has a complete description about the fixes that were updated in the next release. If there are any security-related fixes, Splunk Enterprise deployment should apply that security patch/bug fix so as to make sure that Splunk Enterprise is secure from outside threats. Continuous auditing of Splunk configuration files and Splunk audit events will result in secure Splunk deployment.

Enabling HTTPS for Splunk Web

We will see how to enable HTTPS from the Splunk Web console for all communications happening via Splunk's web channel. On enabling HTTPS, Splunk will not be able to listen over the HTTP connection, and this is the time when Splunk can be configured to either listen to HTTP or HTTPS communications only!

The following are the steps to enable HTTPS via the Splunk Web console:

1. Access the Splunk Web console via a web browser by typing the IP address followed by the port number.

    For example, `http://IPAddress:Port` or `http://localhost:8000`. Here, `8000` is a default web access port of Splunk Enterprise.

2. Go to **System Menu | System Settings**.

3. Click on the radio button to enable HTTPS. Splunk is configured to use default certificates when HTTPS is enabled. The default configuration is available at `$SPLUNK_HOME\etc\auth\web.conf`:

    ```
    [settings]
    enableSplunkWebSSL = true
    privKeyPath = etc\auth\splunkweb\privkey.pem
      #Path of Default Private Key
    caCertPath = etc\auth\splunkweb\cert.pem
      #Path of Default Certificate Path
    ```

We'll now configure Splunk Web with your own certificate and private key. We are talking about securing Splunk, so the default private key and default certificate provided by Splunk Enterprises should be changed for better authentication and security.

Certificates can be self-signed or can be purchased from third-part vendors. Once you have the certificate and private key, the following procedure is to be followed for the changes to take effect.

In our explanation, let's say the certificate filename is `TestCertificate.pem` and the private key is `TestPrivateKey.key`. The following are a series of steps to configure Splunk Web with a certificate and private key:

1. Copy `TestCertificate.pem` and `TestPrivateKey.key` to `$SPLUNK_HOME\etc\auth\splunkweb\`

2. Do not overwrite or delete the existing certificate located at `$SPLUNK_HOME\etc\auth\splunkweb\`, as the certificates are generated on every restart, and any changes made on this certificate and key will be reset

3. Configure `web.conf` located at `$SPLUNK_HOME\etc\system\local` as follows:

```
[settings]
enableSplunkWebSSL = true
privKeyPath = etc\auth\splunkweb\TestPrivateKey.key
caCertPath = etc\auth\splunkweb\TestCertificate.pem
```

Splunk needs to be restarted for the newer settings to take effect, and after the restart of Splunk Server, Splunk Web will be available only via HTTPS URL, that is, `https://localhost:8000`.

Enabling HTTPS for the Splunk forwarder

Configure `inputs.conf` located at `$SPLUNK_HOME\etc\system\local\` of the indexer, as mentioned in the following code block. In this example, port number `9000` is to be configured on the indexer:

```
[SSL]
rootCA = $SPLUNK_HOME\etc\auth\cacert.pem #Path of default Key
serverCert = $SPLUNK_HOME\etc\auth\server.pem #Path of default
  Certificate
password = password
[splunktcp-ssl:9000]
disabled=0
```

The Splunk forwarder needs to be configured to forward using the secure certificate and key. To configure the `outputs.conf` forwarder located at `$SPLUNK_HOME\etc\system\local`, place the following code block as in the following mentioned code block. In this example, `192.168.1.10` is the IP address of the indexer that was configured in the previous instance:

```
[tcpout]
defaultGroup = splunkssl

[tcpout:splunkssl]
server = 192.168.1.10:9000
sslVerifyServerCert = false
sslRootCAPath = $SPLUNK_HOME\etc\auth\cacert.pem
sslCertPath = $SPLUNK_HOME\etc\auth\server.pem
sslPassword = password
```

Similar to the previous section, even in the indexer and forwarder, the certificates and private keys can be copied to their respective folders. The path of the certificate and private key can be configured in their respective config files. Splunk must be restarted for the settings to take effect.

Securing a password with Splunk

Splunk has an in built feature of encrypting configuration files via SSH. Splunk for its first start up, creates a file named `splunk.secret`, which contains a secret key that is used to encrypt authentication information in configuration files.

The following is the list of information that is encrypted via the `splunk.secret` key:

- `web.conf`: This refers to SSL passwords of every instance
- `authentication.conf`: This refers to the LDAP password; if deployment is LDAP integrated
- `inputs.conf`: This refers to SSL passwords
- `outputs.conf`: This refers to SSL passwords

When Splunk starts and if it detects a clear-text password in any of the preceding configuration files, it creates a configuration in the equivalent local folder with the encrypted password.

In a clustered and distributed environment, when Splunk is deployed on multiple servers, a secure password mechanism of encryption can be very useful to ensure consistency across the deployment.

To apply the same settings of a secret key to all the instances, users just need to configure all the changes in the configuration files and restart Splunk to ensure that the `splunk.secret` file is updated with the latest information.

Once you have the updated file, just copy the `splunk.secret` file to all the other instances and restart the instance, and you will have the same settings you applied to all the instances.

The access control list

Splunk can be configured for high security with an access control list. Using an access control list, various restrictions on the basis of IP address to various components of Splunk deployment can be applied.

The `server.conf` and `inputs.conf` can be edited or modified to specify which IP address should be allowed and which should be restricted for various communications within the Splunk deployment.

In `server.conf` and `inputs.conf`, the [accept from] block can be added to allow communication only from a specific IP address. For example, to instruct a node to accept communication from a specific IP address, edit the [httpserver] block in `server.conf`; likewise, to restrict TCP communication using SSL to a specific IP address, edit the [tcp-ssl] block in `inputs.conf`.

Similarly, various communications of Splunk Web, forwarder, and indexers can be restricted or allowed only from a specific IP address, and thus, security can be enhanced using the access control list features of Splunk Enterprise 6.3.

Authentication using SAML

SAML is an XML standard that allows secure web domains to exchange user authentication and authorization data. It allows one online service provider to contact an identity service provider in order to authenticate users who are trying to access the secure content.

Splunk Enterprise supports the use of SAML authentication and authorization for **Single Sign-On (SSO)**. SSO can be enabled in Splunk with the configuration settings provided by the **Identity Provider (IdP)** .

SSO can be configured by Splunk Web or by modifying `authentication.conf` located at `$SPLUNK_HOME\etc\system\default` directly. At present, Splunk Enterprise supports the Ping Identity product from PingFederate® for SSO.

To configure SSO with SAML, the following is the requirement list:

- An identity provider (at present, PingIdentity) is a tested identity provider, and others can also be integrated on similar lines.
- Configuration that uses an on-premise search head.
- A user with an admin role and `change_authentication` Splunk capability. This permission allows us to enable SAML and edit authentication settings on the Splunk search head.

> SSO must be configured on all the search heads in the Splunk deployment for it to function properly.

We'll now learn how to set up SSO using SAML. Let's get acquainted with the steps of setting up SSO:

1. The following information will be required from IdP to configure Splunk in order to authenticate the user:
    - `role`
    - `realName`
    - `mail`

2. The groups returned by IdP are mapped to Splunk roles. A single Splunk role can be assigned to multiple groups.

Let's configure SSO using SAML via Splunk Web. The following are the steps to configure SSO on Splunk Web:

1. Access Splunk Web by going to `localhost:8000` from the deployment server machine or via `IPAaddress:PortNo` from a machine in the same network.
2. Go to **Settings | Access Controls | Authentication Method**.
3. Choose **SAML** as the **External Authentication Method** and click on **Configure Splunk** to use SAML.
4. In the **SAML Groups** page, click on **SAML Configuration**.
5. Browse and select the XML file provided by the IdP provider and fill in all the details and click on **Save**.

If all the settings are correct, the **SAML Groups** page will be populated with all the users and groups where specific groups and Splunk roles can be assigned.

Summary

In this chapter, we went through the architectural enhancement done by Splunk in order to speed up data ingestion and indexing to Splunk by utilizing the underutilized resources. We went through index and search parallelization and how it enhances and scales the performance of Splunk. We also went through the details of the data integrity control mechanism and intelligent job scheduling that was introduced in Splunk Enterprise 6.3. Later, we studied how the app key-value store can be used to maintain a state and other information. The last part of this chapter was concentrated on Splunk Enterprise security techniques, implementations, and configuration. We also studied in detail SSO using SAML that was introduced in Splunk 6.3. In the next chapter, we will cover how to create and manage Splunk applications and add-ons.

2
Developing an Application on Splunk

In this chapter, we will quickly go through the process of creating an application and add-on on Splunk Enterprise. You will learn how to install and manage applications and add-ons on Splunk. You will also learn how to use different applications available on the Splunk app store to minimize your work using the already available applications for similar requirements.

The following topics will be covered in this chapter:

- Splunk apps and technology add-ons
- Developing a Splunk app
- Developing a technology add-on
- Managing Splunk apps
- Splunk apps from the app store (covers examples and usage of a few apps from the app store)

Splunk apps and technology add-ons

It is very easy and simple to create a basic Splunk app or technology add-on using the Splunk Web console. We will also study how Splunk apps and add-ons can be manually created and configured in the further topics.

What is a Splunk app?

A Splunk app is basically a collection of all the dashboards, alerts, and visualizations created for a specific use case. It is a collection of an entire use case packaged in such a way that it can be installed on any Splunk Enterprise deployment to gain specific insight from the uploader, provided that its minimum requirements are fulfilled.

Splunk apps can be configured on the basis of user roles and permissions, thus providing a level of control when deploying and sharing the application across different stakeholders of the app. A Splunk app is created taking a use case into consideration and to avoid rework in case of the same use case or data sources. Splunk apps are applications that are ready to be used once the data is on board the Splunk Enterprise server.

Splunk apps make it easier for users of Splunk Enterprise to use the same deployment for different use cases; for example, the same Splunk deployment is used for network health monitoring, security and threat detection, and many more... Each Splunk application can be used for each use case, even though it is available on the same Splunk Enterprise deployment server and has the ability to assign roles where the apps will be visible and can be used only by authenticated users of each app.

Later in this chapter, you will learn how to create Splunk apps and manage and install Splunk applications on Splunk Enterprise.

What is a technology add-on?

A Splunk add-on is basically a single-component, reusable application with no user interface, and it can be used in many uses cases. A Splunk add-on can be a script that is used to fetch data from a web server and upload it to Splunk. Now, this add-on can be used along with any other application and use case where one of the requirements is to fetch and upload data from a web server. In such scenarios, Splunk add-ons can reduce the rework required to do the same task.

Splunk add-ons can be bundled with one or more Splunk apps that have similar requirements. The following are a few examples of Splunk add-ons:

- Custom data parsing and field extraction before data is uploaded on Splunk
- Custom scripts to fetch data from one or more sources and then upload it on Splunk
- Creating custom macros and sourcetypes
- Reusable JavaScript and CSS
- Custom regular expression detection and data cleaning before uploading data on Splunk

Developing a Splunk app

Developing or creating a simple Splunk application is very easy in Splunk Enterprise, but developing a Splunk app that solves a business problem specific to a use case requires the following basic process:

1. **On-boarding data on Splunk**: Using various data input methods to upload data on Splunk.

2. **Analytics**: Using the Splunk search query language to create meaningful insights into the data uploaded on Splunk.

3. **Visualization**: Creating visualizations for better understanding of the uploaded data on Splunk.

A Splunk app can include various components of Splunk Enterprise, such as data inputs, search queries, custom dashboards, macros, custom CSS, JavaScript, and many more...

Creating the Splunk application and technology add-on

The Splunk application framework works on a directory structure. All the installed and, by default, available applications are available at `$SPLUNK_HOME\etc\apps`.

The following procedure needs to be followed to create a sample Splunk app via the Splunk Web console which is accessible via `http://localhost:8000` (this address needs to be replaced with the IP address and configured port number of the Splunk instance in case it is not accessed from the Splunk Server machine.)

The procedure to create a Splunk application and Splunk technology add-ons is almost same with just a small difference in one step. The change will be highlighted in the following steps:

1. On the home screen which Splunk navigates to, after logging in, navigate to **Apps | Manage Apps**.

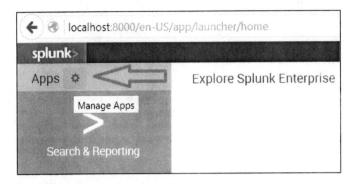

2. The screen where we navigated to after clicking on **Manage Apps**, click on the **Create App** button.

3. Splunk Web navigates to a new page called **Create App**, where textboxes are given to fill the following information:

   ° **Name**: In this field, we need to fill the name of the Splunk application or technology add-on. This will be the same name that will be visible in the app list of Splunk.

   ° **Folder Name**: Here, we need to fill the name of the folder where all the configuration files, dashboards, saved searches, and alerts will be stored with reference to the app. The folder name mentioned here will be created at $SPLUNK_HOME\etc\app. The folder name cannot have a dot (.) character in its name. Even though users are free to keep any name for the add-on, Splunk recommends you to use TA- as a prefix to the name of the add-on folder so as to uniquely differentiate Splunk applications and add-ons.

   ° **Visible**: If the application contains a UI (visualizations), then this field should be marked as **YES**. Generally, add-ons do not have a UI, so when creating an add-on, the **NO** option is marked.

   ° **Description**: In this field, we need to provide the description of the Splunk application or technology add-on. This field is required in case you plan to upload the application on the Splunk app store; otherwise, this is an optional field.

   ° **Template**: Splunk provides two templates by default: Sample_app and Barebones. The Barebones template provides a sample app directory structure, whereas Sample_app includes sample views and saved searches. In the case of a technology add-on, this is not applicable as there are no visible UIs.

- Upload Asset: This option provides users the ability to upload any custom scripts, HTML, images, CSS, or JavaScript that may be required for the application.

4. Save the settings by clicking on **Save**.

For the application to be visible in the app list of Splunk, it is required that the Splunk instance is restarted.

Now, users can navigate to the Splunk application that we created and start creating custom dashboards, visualizations, and alerts that we will be studying in the upcoming chapters in this book.

Packaging the application

Our Splunk app needs to be packed properly so that it can be redistributed to other users working on Splunk deployment. There is a specific set of instructions that needs to be followed and the app needs to be made compliant to all the instructions so that we are able to upload the Splunk app on the Splunk app store. However, making the Splunk application compliant with the Splunk app store is out of the scope of this book.

The following is the easiest and simplest method to package the Splunk app in order to install it on other Splunk deployments:

1. Make sure that all the settings are properly configured so that the application has all the configuration files updated.

2. Traverse to the `$SPLUNK_HOME\etc\app` directory on the Splunk Server and copy the `Application` folder to another path, say, your desktop. The folder name is the same that the user specified in the preceding section while creating the application.

3. For our example, the Splunk app located at `$SPLUNK_HOME\etc\app` is `TestApplication`.

4. Using any compression/decompression tool, such as 7Zip, compress the app directory into a `.zip` or `.tar.gz` file. In our case, the application after compression will become `TestApplication.zip` or `TestApplication.tar.gz`.

5. Now, the Splunk app (`TestApplication.zip` or `TestApplication.tar.gz`) is ready for redistribution and can be installed on other Splunk deployments that are running on the compatible version of Splunk.

Installing a Splunk app via Splunk Web

Installing the Splunk app via a web interface is very simple. The following steps are required for the installation of the Splunk app:

1. Log on to Splunk Web.
2. Navigate to **Apps | Manage Apps**.
3. Then, click on **Install app from file**.
4. Click on **Browse** and navigate to the folder where your compressed application is available, and then choose the Splunk app.
5. Tick on **Upgrade App** if you are installing an upgrade version of the already installed application; otherwise leave it unchecked.
6. Click on **Upload** to install the application.
7. After the successful installation, restart the Splunk Server to make it visible in the app list.

Installing the Splunk app manually

In deployments where the access to Splunk Web is not enabled or the user wants to manually install the application, the following procedure is to be followed:

1. Uncompress the compressed Splunk application package (`TestApplication.zip` or `TestApplication.tar.gz`) using any decompressing tool such as 7Zip.
2. Make sure that you have decompressed it fully so the root folder's name is that of the application's followed by the subfolders, such as `default`, `local`, and others.
3. Copy the uncompressed application folder at `$SPLUNK_HOME\etc\app`, making sure that the folder copied is the root folder of the application.

   For example, in our case, the application folder path will look like `$SPLUNK_HOME\etc\app\TestApplication`.

4. Now, restart the Splunk Server.

Yes, copying the application folder to the respective app directory and then restarting the Splunk Server installs the application on Splunk. On every restart, the Splunk Server refreshes its app list and the newly added application gets listed on the Splunk app list.

The Splunk application can be installed or updated from the command line as well. Open Command Prompt in Windows or a terminal in a Linux system and traverse to $SPLUNK_HOME\bin.

Then, run the following command to install the application for Windows users:

```
splunk install app <app_package_filename> -update 1 -auth
    <username>:<password>
```

For Linux users, run the following command:

```
./splunk install app <app_package_filename> -update 1 -auth
    <username>:<password>
```

After running this command, restart Splunk Enterprise to let the changes take effect.

Developing a Splunk add-on

It is very important to first identify the problem that the Splunk add-on will solve. On identifying the problem, the following procedure is to be followed to create an add-on.

Building an add-on

It is very important to define the need and problems that the add-on will be solving before we build it.

If the add-on will be used to add data to Splunk, then how do we get that data into Splunk?

The various methods of data input are shown in the following screenshot. An add-on can be configured to use any one of them depending on the requirement and use case.

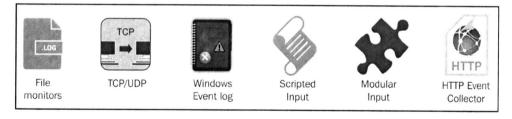

| File monitors | TCP/UDP | Windows Event log | Scripted Input | Modular Input | HTTP Event Collector |

You may wonder, what will the add-on do next? What configuration files need to be configured in the add-on for the given requirement? Add-ons can be configured for data acquisitions, data transformation, normalization, and enrichment. Add-ons can also be configured to have one or more than one features depending on the need:

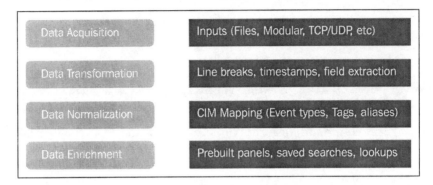

Installing a technology add-on

The steps to install technology add-ons via the Web and manually are exactly the same as the steps to install a Splunk application, as described in the earlier sections. Users need to follow the same steps and choose the add-on folder in place of the Splunk app folder specified in the preceding steps to install a technology add-on on Splunk Enterprise.

Managing Splunk apps and add-ons

Since you have learned how to create and install a Splunk application and Splunk add-on, we will now move on to how to manage apps and add-ons on Splunk Enterprise.

The following settings can be managed from the **Manage Apps** console of Splunk Web:

- **Permission management of Splunk apps and add-ons**: Splunk apps and add-ons can be applied with specific roles and permissions, and we can also decide whether the app or add-on should be shared with other applications on Splunk. From the permission section, the object created in the application or add-on can also be shared in other apps by choosing **Sharing for config file only object to all apps**.

- **Enabled and disable applications and add-ons**: All the applications and add-ons installed on Splunk Enterprise will be listed in the menu, and applications and add-ons can be enabled and disabled from this section.

- **Properties**: The name of the Splunk application or add-on can be updated from this section. Other options such as making the application visible or not and uploading customs scripts, CSS, and JavaScript can be chosen from this menu.

- **View objects**: All the objects, regex, and field extractions that are stored in the application or add-on configuration will be visible from the option. The object's permission can be modified and objects can be enabled or disabled from this option.

The application or add-on can also have other configuration options that can be enabled or disabled and configured via Splunk Web.

For example, suppose there is an add-on that fetches data from any web source and uploads to Splunk. Once the add-on is installed, since there is a data upload script defined in the **Scripts** section of **Data Upload**, the settings can be configured from the Splunk Web console.

From the Splunk Web console, go to **Settings** | **Data inputs** | **Scripts**.

In the **Scripts** section, there will be an entry of the data upload configured in the Splunk add-on. From this menu, we can enable/disable the data input script, and from this menu, we can modify the run interval of the script and define or change the source type of the data to be uploaded on Splunk.

Depending on the types of configuration defined in the Splunk app or technology add-on, different sections of Splunk settings can be configured after the installation of the application or add-on.

You must have noted that there is an option to enable and disable the application, but there is no option to uninstall the Splunk application or Splunk add-on from the web console. To uninstall, the following command needs to be run on Command Prompt or the terminal in Windows and Linux, respectively:

- **Windows users**:

  ```
  splunk remove app [appname] -auth <username>:<password>
  ```

- **Linux users**:

  ```
  ./splunk remove app [appname] -auth <username>:<password>
  ```

Another easy and clean way of uninstalling a Splunk application or add-on is to remove the application or add-on directory from `$SPLUNK_HOME\etc\apps` and restart the Splunk Enterprise server.

Splunk apps from the app store

We went through the process of creating, installing, and uninstalling applications on Splunk Enterprise. Now, we will see some examples of applications or add-ons from the Splunk app store that can be used to solve common problems:

- **The Splunk add-on for the Oracle database**: This add-on is available on the Splunk app store, and can be downloaded and installed on Splunk to connect with any Oracle database. Logs such as audit trails, trace files, incident, alert, listener, and other logs on the operating system where the Oracle database server is installed will be made available on Splunk, and thus, users can analyze, visualize, and create alerts on the uploaded data from the Splunk add-on for Oracle.

- **Browsing history analysis**: Browsing history analysis is a ready-to-use app available on the Splunk app store that can be installed and used to analyze the browsing behavior of the user on the instance on which Splunk is installed. This app scans, extracts, and analyzes history from the most popular browsers. Hence, by installing this application, users will be able to use it without any query writing and development work.

- **The Splunk add-on for Microsoft Azure**: This add-on can be used to connect to Microsoft Azure and to retrieve data from Azure Storage and Diagnostics into Splunk for analysis and visualizations.

- **The Splunk app for web analytics**: This Splunk app can generate analytics and give insight from the web logs of websites like any other analytics tools such as Google Analytics and Webtrends can. This application can be installed on Splunk Enterprise.

These were a few applications/add-ons available on the Splunk app store. There are a lot of applications and add-ons that have been created for different use cases. Splunk users can search for applications defined for various use cases, and they can download, install, and use the application as per need. The Splunk app store has applications of various categories, such as application management, IT operations, security and compliance, business analytics, and many more.

Summary

In this chapter, you learned how to create Splunk apps and technology add-ons and how to develop and manage them. We also had a look at a few examples and use cases where Splunk applications and add-ons can be used from the Splunk app store, and you can use them as per your requirements and cases. In the next chapter, you will not only learn the various methods to upload data to Splunk, but also the type of data that can be uploaded. Basically, we will be going through the in and out of on-boarding data on Splunk.

3
On-boarding Data in Splunk

This chapter will detail the most important aspect of Splunk, that is, adding data to Splunk. We will go through the newly added feature in Splunk 6.3 of JSON and REST API format of IoT event collections, HTTP Event Collector, and then, we will cover the various interfaces and options to on-board data on Splunk. We will also study how to manage event segmentation and improvise the data input process.

The following topics will be covered in this chapter:

- Deep diving into various input methods and sources
- Adding data to Splunk — new interfaces
- Data processing
- Managing event segmentation
- Improving the data input process

Deep diving into various input methods and sources

Splunk supports numerous ways to ingest data on its server. Any data generated from a human-readable machine from various sources can be uploaded using data input methods such as files, directories, and TCP/UDP scripts which can be indexed on the Splunk Enterprise server and analytics and insights can be derived from them.

Data sources

Uploading data on Splunk is one of the most important parts of analytics and visualizations of data. If data is not properly parsed, timestamped, or broken into events, then it can be difficult to analyze and get proper insight on the data. Splunk can be used to analyze and visualize data ranging from various domains, such as IT security, networking, mobile devices, telecom infrastructure, media and entertainment devices, storage devices, and many more. The machine-generated data from different sources can be of different formats and types, and hence, it is very important to parse data in the best format to get the required insight from it.

Splunk supports machine-generated data of various types and structures, and the following screenshot shows the common types of data that comes with an inbuilt support in Splunk Enterprise. The most important point of these sources is that if the data source is from the following list, then the preconfigured settings and configurations already stored in Splunk Enterprise are applied. This helps in getting the data parsed in the best and most suitable formats of events and timestamps to enable faster searching, analytics, and better visualization.

The following screenshot enlists common data sources supported by Splunk Enterprise:

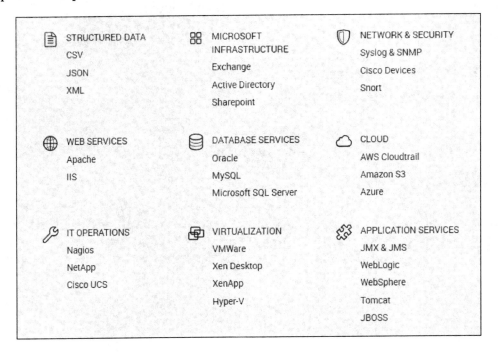

Structured data

Machine-generated data is generally structured, and in some cases, it can be semistructured. Some of the types of structured data are **EXtensible Markup Language (XML)**, **JavaScript Object Notation (JSON)**, **comma-separated values (CSV)**, **tab-separated values (TSV)**, and **pipe-separated values (PSV)**.

Any format of structured data can be uploaded on Splunk. However, if the data is from any of the preceding formats, then predefined settings and configuration can be applied directly by choosing the respective source type while uploading the data or by configuring it in the `inputs.conf` file.

The preconfigured settings for any of the preceding structured data is very generic. Many times, it happens that the machine logs are customized structured logs; in that case, additional settings will be required to parse the data.

For example, there are various types of XML. We have listed two types here. In the first type, there is the `<note>` tag at the start and `</note>` at the end, and in between, there are parameters and their values. In the second type, there are two levels of hierarchies. XML has the `<library>` tag along with the `<book>` tag. Between the `<book>` and `</book>` tags, we have parameters and their values.

The first type is as follows:

```
<note>
<to>Jack</to>
<from>Micheal</from>
<heading>Test XML Format</heading>
<body>This is one of the format of XML!</body>
</note>
```

The second type is shown in the following code snippet:

```
<Library>
  <book category="Technical">
    <title lang="en">Splunk Basic</title>
    <author>Jack Thomas</author>
    <year>2007</year>
    <price>520.00</price>
  </book>
  <book category="Story">
    <title lang="en">Jungle Book</title>
    <author>Rudyard Kiplin</author>
    <year>1984</year>
    <price>50.50</price>
  </book>
</Library >
```

Similarly, there can be many types of customized XML scripts generated by machines. To parse different types of structured data, Splunk Enterprise comes with inbuilt settings and configuration defined for the source it comes from. Let's say, for example, that the data received from a web server's logs are also structured logs and it can be in either a JSON, CSV, or simple text format. So, depending on the specific sources, Splunk tries to make the job of the user easier by providing the best settings and configuration for many common sources of data.

Some of the most common sources of data are data from web servers, databases, operation systems, network security, and various other applications and services.

Web and cloud services

The most commonly used web servers are Apache and Microsoft IIS. All Linux-based web services are hosted on Apache servers, and all Windows-based web services on IIS. The logs generated from Linux web servers are simple plain text files, whereas the log files of Microsoft IIS can be in a W3C-extended log file format or it can be stored in a database in the ODBC log file format as well.

Cloud services such as Amazon AWS, S3, and Microsoft Azure can be directly connected and configured according to the forwarded data on Splunk Enterprise. The Splunk app store has many technology add-ons that can be used to create data inputs to send data from cloud services to Splunk Enterprise.

So, when uploading log files from web services, such as Apache, Splunk provides a preconfigured source type that parses data in the best format for it to be available for visualization.

Suppose that the user wants to upload Apache error logs on the Splunk server, and then the user chooses **apache_error** from the **Web** category of **Source type**, as shown in the following screenshot:

On choosing this option, the following set of configuration is applied on the data to be uploaded:

- The event break is configured to be on the regular expression pattern ^\ [

- The events in the log files will be broken into a single event on occurrence of [at every start of a line (^)

- The timestamp is to be identified in the [%A %B %d %T %Y] format, where:

    ○ %A is the day of week; for example, Monday

    ○ %B is the month; for example, January

    ○ %d is the day of the month; for example, 1

- ○ %T is the time that has to be in the %H : %M : %S format
- ○ %Y is the year; for example, 2016

- Various other settings such as maxDist that allows the amount of variance of logs can vary from the one specified in the source type and other settings such as category, descriptions, and others.

Any new settings required as per our needs can be added using the **New Settings** option available in the section below **Settings**. After making the changes, either the settings can be saved as a new source type or the existing source type can be updated with the new settings.

IT operations and network security

Splunk Enterprise has many applications on the Splunk app store that specifically target IT operations and network security. Splunk is a widely accepted tool for intrusion detection, network and information security, fraud and theft detection, and user behavior analytics and compliance. A Splunk Enterprise application provides inbuilt support for the **Cisco Adaptive Security Appliance (ASA)** firewall, Cisco SYSLOG, **Call Detail Records (CDR)** logs, and one of the most popular intrusion detection application, Snort. The Splunk app store has many technology add-ons to get data from various security devices such as firewall, routers, DMZ, and others. The app store also has the Splunk application that shows graphical insights and analytics over the data uploaded from various IT and security devices.

Databases

The Splunk Enterprise application has inbuilt support for databases such as MySQL, Oracle Syslog, and IBM DB2. Apart from this, there are technology add-ons on the Splunk app store to fetch data from the Oracle database and the MySQL database. These technology add-ons can be used to fetch, parse, and upload data from the respective database to the Splunk Enterprise server.

There can be various types of data available from one source; let's take MySQL as an example. There can be error log data, query logging data, MySQL server health and status log data, or MySQL data stored in the form of databases and tables. This concludes that there can be a huge variety of data generated from the same source. Hence, Splunk provides support for all types of data generated from a source. We have inbuilt configuration for MySQL error logs, MySQL slow queries, and MySQL database logs that have been already defined for easier input configuration of data generated from respective sources.

Application and operating system data

The Splunk input source type has inbuilt configuration available for Linux dmesg, syslog, security logs, and various other logs available from the Linux operating system. Apart from the Linux OS, Splunk also provides configuration settings for data input of logs from Windows and iOS systems. It also provides default settings for **Log4j**-based logging for Java, PHP, and .NET enterprise applications. Splunk also supports lots of other applications' data such as Ruby on Rails, Catalina, WebSphere, and others.

Splunk Enterprise provides predefined configuration for various applications, databases, OSes, and cloud and virtual environments to enrich the respective data with better parsing and breaking into events, thus deriving at better insight from the available data. The applications' sources whose settings are not available in Splunk Enterprise can alternatively have apps or add-ons on the app store.

Data input methods

Splunk Enterprise supports data input through numerous methods. Data can be sent on Splunk via files and directories, TCP, UDP, scripts, or using universal forwarders.

Files and directories

Splunk Enterprise provides an easy interface to the uploaded data via files and directories. Files can be directly uploaded from the Splunk web interface manually or they can be configured to monitor the file for changes in content, and the new data will be uploaded on Splunk whenever it is written in the file. Splunk can also be configured to upload multiple files by either uploading all the files in one shot or the directory can be monitored for any new files, and the data will get indexed on Splunk whenever it arrives in the directory. Any data format from any sources that are in a human-readable format, that is, no propriety tools are needed to read the data, can be uploaded on Splunk.

Splunk Enterprise even supports uploading in a compressed file format such as (.zip and .tar.gz), which has multiple log files in a compressed format.

Network sources

Splunk supports both TCP and UDP to get data on Splunk from network sources. It can monitor any network port for incoming data and then can index it on Splunk. Generally, in case of data from network sources, it is recommended that you use a Universal forwarder to send data on Splunk, as Universal forwarder buffers the data in case of any issues on the Splunk server to avoid data loss.

Windows data

Splunk Enterprise provides direct configuration to access data from a Windows system. It supports both local as well as remote collections of various types and sources from a Windows system.

Local inputs

Set up data inputs from files and directories, network ports, and scripted inputs.

Type

Local event log collection
Collect event logs from this machine.

Remote event log collections
Collect event logs from remote hosts. Note: this uses WMI and requires a domain account.

Local performance monitoring
Collect performance data from local machine.

Remote performance monitoring
Collect performance and event information from remote hosts. Requires domain credentials.

Registry monitoring
Have Splunk index the local Windows Registry, and monitor it for changes.

Active Directory monitoring
Index and monitor Active Directory.

Powershell v3 Modular Input
Execute PowerShell scripts v3 with parameters as inputs.

Local Windows host monitoring
Collect up-to-date hardware and software (Computer, Operating System, Processor, Service, Disk, Network Adapter and Application) information about this machine.

Local Windows network monitoring
This is an input for Splunk Network Monitor.

Local Windows print monitoring
Collect information about printers, printer jobs, print drivers, and print ports on this machine.

Splunk has predefined input methods and settings to parse event logs, performance monitoring reports, registry information, hosts, networks and print monitoring of a local as well as remote Windows system.

So, data from different sources of different formats can be sent to Splunk using various input methods as per the requirement and suitability of the data and source. New data inputs can also be created using Splunk apps or technology add-ons available on the Splunk app store.

Adding data to Splunk – new interfaces

Splunk Enterprise introduced new interfaces to accept data that is compatible with constrained resources and lightweight devices for Internet of Things. Splunk Enterprise version 6.3 supports HTTP Event Collector and REST and JSON APIs for data collection on Splunk.

HTTP Event Collector is a very useful interface that can be used to send data without using any forwarder from your existing application to the Splunk Enterprise server. HTTP APIs are available in .NET, Java, Python, and almost all the programming languages. So, forwarding data from your existing application that is based on a specific programming language becomes a cake walk.

Let's take an example, say, you are a developer of an Android application, and you want to know what all features the user uses that are the pain areas or problem-causing screens. You also want to know the usage pattern of your application. So, in the code of your Android application, you can use REST APIs to forward the logging data on the Splunk Enterprise server. The only important point to note here is that the data needs to be sent in a JSON payload envelope. The advantage of using HTTP Event Collector is that without using any third-party tools or any configuration, the data can be sent on Splunk and we can easily derive insights, analytics, and visualizations from it.

HTTP Event Collector and configuration

HTTP Event Collector can be used when you configure it from the Splunk Web console, and the event data from HTTP can be indexed in Splunk using the REST API.

HTTP Event Collector

HTTP **Event Collector (EC)** provides an API with an endpoint that can be used to send log data from applications into Splunk Enterprise. Splunk HTTP Event Collector supports both HTTP and HTTPS for secure connections.

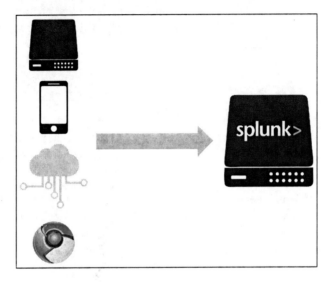

The following are the features of HTTP Event Collector, which make's adding data on Splunk Enterprise easier:

- It is very lightweight is terms of memory and resource usage, and thus can be used in resources constrained to lightweight devices as well.

- Events can be sent directly from anywhere such as web servers, mobile devices, and IoT without any need of configuration or installation of forwarders.

- It is a token-based JSON API that doesn't require you to save user credentials in the code or in the application settings. The authentication is handled by tokens used in the API.

- It is easy to configure EC from the Splunk Web console, enable HTTP EC, and define the token. After this, you are ready to accept data on Splunk Enterprise.

- It supports both HTTP and HTTPS, and hence it is very secure.

- It supports GZIP compression and batch processing.

- HTTP EC is highly scalable as it can be used in a distributed environment as well as with a load balancer to crunch and index millions of events per second.

Configuration via Splunk Web

The following are the steps to configure HTTP EC via Splunk Web:

1. **Enabling the Event Collector**:

    1. Open the Splunk Web console and go to **Settings | Data Inputs**.

    2. On the **Data Inputs** page, click on **HTTP Event Collector**.

    3. On the **HTTP Event Collector** page, in the top right corner, click on **Global Settings**.

    4. The **Edit Global Settings** page pops up after this, which is similar to the following screenshot:

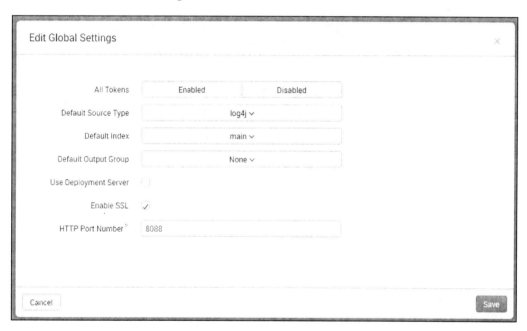

For the **All Tokens** option, click on **Enable**

    5. Depending on the source from where the data is coming or the type of data, choose your respective source type. On selecting the specific source type, relevant configuration and event parsing settings will be applied by default to the data getting uploaded through EC.

    6. If you wish to use the deployment server to configure EC tokens, then the **Use Deployment Server** checkbox needs to be selected.

7. Various other settings such as the index in which data needs to be uploaded, whether to use HTTP or HTTPS (the **SSL** option), and the port number to be used in the endpoint can be configured accordingly from the **Settings** section.

8. After modifying the relevant settings, click on **Save** to apply the settings.

2. **Creating a new token**: New tokens can be created either from the **Add Data** section of Splunk or from the **HTTP Event Collector** page from where the **Global Settings** were modified.

The following are the steps to create a new token from the **Global Settings** page:

1. Click on the **New Token** button on the top right-hand side of the **Global Settings** page. This takes the user to the **Add Data** screen with the **HTTP Event Collector** options

2. This page asks for **Name**, **Source name override**, and **Description** of the token, similar to what is shown in the following screenshot:

Configure a new token for receiving data over HTTP. Learn More ⏍

Name	
Source name override ?	optional
Description ?	optional
Output Group (optional)	None ⌄

Enter the **Name**, **Source name override**, and **Description** to identify the token. Also, users can set **Output Group** if any and then click on **Next**.

3. The next page gives users the option to choose the index and source type. If the user wants to create a new index or a new source type, then it can be created from this page itself. After selecting the index and source type, click on **Next**.

4. A review page appears, where you can verify all the inputs and settings configured for the new token, and then click on the **Submit** button to create the new token.

5. After clicking on **Submit**, the HTTP Event Collector token is generated and displayed on the screen. This token can now be used in the HTTP API to forward data on Splunk.

3. **Verifying HTTP Event Collector**: Follow the given series of steps to verify Event Collector:

1. To test and verify whether the Event Collector and token is properly configured, developers can use the following simple `curl` command:

   ```
   curl -k  https://IPAddress:PortNumber/services/collector/
   event -H "Authorization: Splunk TOKEN_GENERATED_IN_
   ABOVE_STEP" -d '{"event": "This is a test of HTTP Event
   Collector"}'
   ```

   Note that `PortNumber` refers to the port number which was configured in the **Edit Global Settings** page. In our case, we used `8088`.

   In response to the preceding `curl` command, the following response concludes that the events were successfully uploaded on Splunk:

   ```
   {"text": "Success", "code": 0}
   ```

2. The uploaded event can also be checked by logging into the Splunk Web console and using the search in the selected source type or index.

Managing the Event Collector token

Event Collector tokens can be modified by going to the **Settings** menu from the Splunk Web console and then clicking on **Data Inputs**. On the **Data Input** page, click on the **HTTP Event Collector** option. This page will list all the tokens that we created.

The tokens can be created, modified, and deleted from the **Data Input** section. Click on the respective **Edit** button of the token that needs to be modified. On doing so, various parameters such as **Source type**, **Index**, **Output group**, and others can be modified from here for the selected tokens. If any token is not in use for some time or not required at all, then it can be disabled or deleted as per the need.

The JSON API format

The HTTP Event Collector data needs to be in a specific format that is understood by Splunk Enterprise for it to parsed correctly by Splunk. Splunk HTTP Event Collector accepts the data sent from various sources in a series of JSON packets. The JSON packets comprise of two parts, one is the metadata and the other part is the data contained in the *event key*. The metadata has various parameters in a key-value format, whereas the event key has the actual data in it.

The sender of data is responsible for packaging data in the JSON format. The data can be packed either using Splunk logging libraries available for Java and .NET or using Java Apache HTTP Client or scripts or code can be written which encodes the data in the format specified in the following sections.

Authentication

The authentication is done by Splunk Event Collector using tokens. The data source needs to be authenticated and authorized first before it starts sending data to the Splunk server. The authorization is done using a client-side authorization header. Each JSON data package carries the same unique token in the authorization header. When the token is verified by HTTP EC, it consumes the data and sends a positive response to the sender. The response looks like this:

```
Authorization: Splunk 87654321-4321-1234-4321-0987654321XZ
```

Metadata

The following are the key-value pairs that can be included in the event's metadata for any set of settings that are to be overridden by what is defined in the token settings:

- `time`: The event data can be timestamped using this key-value pair of metadata. The default time format is epoch time in the `<seconds>.<milliseconds>` format.

- `host`: The hostname of the source can be defined in this key. This key can be very useful to identify the device from which the data came. In case of IoT, there can be a number of devices to uniquely identify the data of specific devices to which the hostname can be assigned.

- `source`: The source name can be specified in this key. This along with the host can be used to identify the source of the data in multiple-source deployment of Splunk.

- `sourcetype`: This key is used to identify the type of data so that the respective parsing and event processing can be done as per the data type or data source.

- index: This is the index in which the event will be uploaded on Splunk.

 All the preceding keys are optional. If it is not explicitly specified in the metadata, then the default settings are applied for a token.

An example of metadata is as follows:

```
{
    "time": 1448190998,
    "host": "192.168.10.150",
    "source": "Humiditysensor-Mumbai",
    "sourcetype": "csv",
    "index": "IoT"
}
```

Event data

Event data is associated with the event key, and it contains the actual data that needs to be uploaded on Splunk for analytics and visualization. Event data is also represented in the JSON format:

An example of event data is as follows:

```
"event":
{
    "8.00": "32",
    "12.00": "35",
    "16.00": "33",
    "20.00": "29",
}
```

The following is a complete JSON packet with metadata and event data:

```
{
    "time": 1448190998,
    "host": "192.168.10.150",
    "source": "Humiditysensor-Mumbai",
    "sourcetype": "csv",
    "index": "IOT",
    "event":
    {
        "8.00": "32",
        "12.00": "35",
        "16.00": "33",
        "20.00": "29",
    }
}
```

When a collected HTTP event receives the preceding JSON packet, it parses the data and then sends it to the indexers for event processing. It uses the metadata if any specific set of settings and configurations is applied on the uploading data by the event collected before it gets uploaded in the indexer.

Splunk introduced HTTP-based and JSON-based REST APIs to encourage the use of Splunk for IoT devices. There are various messaging and communication protocols and message brokers that are more widely used in IoT, such as CAOP, MQTT, Apache KAFKA, JMS, AMQP Broker, and the cloud streaming protocol such as Amazon Kinesis. The Splunk app store has modular input technology add-ons for all of these protocols supported by HTTP Event Collector that are ready to use. Respective modular inputs can be used along with HTTP EC to upload data on Splunk Enterprise.

Data processing

Data processing plays a very important role in parsing and enriching data to create insights faster and visualize data with the required analytics. Data processing basically includes event, timestamp, and host configuration.

Event configuration

Any data uploaded on Splunk is termed as an event. An event can be anything from a log activity, error logs, usage logs, to machine-generated data from devices, servers, or from any other sources. Events are used to create visualization and get insight about the source in the Splunk environment. So, it is required to process the events properly, depending on the data and source. The processed events' settings and configurations can be stored later in a source type.

Character encoding

Splunk supports many languages to support internationalization of Splunk Enterprise. The default character's set encoding on Splunk Enterprise is UTF-8, whereas it has inbuilt support for various other encoding available internationally. If the data is not UTF-8 or it contains non-ASCII data, then Splunk tries to convert it to UTF-8 until and unless it is specified by the user in the Splunk configuration file to not convert it.

Splunk supports various characters' sets, but it always uses UTF-8 by default. If the data is of the other encoding type, it is required to be configured in the `props.conf` file. The following line in `props.conf` forces the data uploaded from the `SatelliteData` host to be parsed using a Russian encoding character set:

```
[host::SatelliteData]
CHARSET=ISO-8859-5
```

Splunk also supports automatic detection of character set encoding. In a situation wherein the data is uploaded on Splunk to a specific source type or a specific host contains a mixture of various character sets, in that case, Splunk's powerful algorithm can automatically detect the character set encoding and apply it accordingly to the data. `Props.conf` needs to be modified with the following lines to force the source type to autoencoding, rather than using the default UTF-8 character set:

```
[host::SatelliteData]
CHARSET=AUTO
```

Event line breaking

A single event can be of a few words, a single line, or multiple lines as well. The Splunk Enterprise engine has the capability to automatically detect the events. However, since there are various types and formats of data, it may not be necessary that the events will be well detected and broken into events properly. So, manual line breaking can be required if the automatic line break does not detect multiple line events properly.

Event line breaking can be configured to be based on a regular expression, a specific word that occurs at the start of every new event, a specific word that ends the events, when a new date or time is encountered, and so on.

The following is a list of event-line breaking commands that can be configured from Splunk Web via data uploading or can be configured in the `props.conf` file:

- `TRUNCATE=<NUMBER>`: This commands accepts a number, which is in bytes, after which the lines are to be truncated. If the data is in a long line and only up to a few specific bytes, the data is useful. Using this command, data that is not required can be truncated.

  For example, `TRUNCATE=500` will truncate the line after 500 bytes of data. So, any line that has more than 500 bytes will be truncated. Generally, `truncate` is used to avoid memory leaks, search slowdown, and avoid indexing of useless data.

- `LINE_BREAKER=<REGULAR_EXPRESSION>`: This command is used to break the event at the occurrence of a specific regular expression. Whenever that specific regular expression is detected, the preceding data is termed as a new event.

- `SHOULD_LINEMERGE = [true or false]`: This command combines several lines into a single line until and unless the condition pertaining to any of the following set of attributes is satisfied:

  ○ `BREAK_ONLY_BEFORE_DATE = [true or false]`: Here, the data is marked as a new event whenever a new line with a date is detected

  ○ `BREAK_ONLY_BEFORE = < REGULAR_EXPRESSION >`: A new event is created whenever a specific regular expression is encountered in a new line

  ○ `MUST_BREAK_AFTER = < REGULAR_EXPRESSION >`: Splunk creates a new event for the next input on occurrence of a specified regular expression on the given line

  ○ `MUST_NOT_BREAK_AFTER = < REGULAR_EXPRESSION >`: Splunk does not break for a given regular expression until and unless events that satisfy the condition of `MUST_BREAK_AFTER` are satisfied

  ○ `MAX_EVENTS = <NUMBER>`: This number specifies the maximum number of lines a single event can be of.

The following is an example of configuring the event breaking in the `props.conf` file:

```
[SatelliteData]
SHOULD_LINEMERGE = true
MUST_BREAK_AFTER = </data>
```

The preceding change in `props.conf` instructs the events to be broken after the occurrence of `</data>` for the `SatelliteData` source type.

Timestamp configuration

A timestamp is one of the very important parameters of data. It is very useful in creating visualization and insight by time, that is, the number of errors and crashes occurred in one day, in the last 10 min, in the last one month, and so on. A timestamp is required to correlate data overtime, create visualizations based on time, run searches, and so on. The data that we upload from different sources may or may not have a timestamp in it. The data that has a timestamp should be parsed with a correct timestamp format, and for the data that does not have a timestamp, Splunk automatically adds a timestamp during the upload for better time-based visualizations.

The Splunk procedure of assigning a timestamp to the data is based on various parameters such as the timestamp settings in props.conf. If no settings are found in the props.conf file, then it checks for the sourcetype timestamp format in the events. If the event doesn't have a timestamp, then it tries to fetch a date from the source or filename. If it is not able to find the date, then it assigns the current time to the event. In most cases, we are not required to do any specific configuration, since Splunk checks for almost all the possible options to assign a timestamp to the data.

In some cases, if the timestamp is not properly parsed, then the timestamp can be configured during the upload of data in the **Source type Settings** page or it can be manually configured in the props.conf file as well.

The following are the attributes that can be configured in props.conf for timestamp configuration:

- TIME_PREFIX = <REGULAR_EXPRESSION>: This helps us to search for a specific regular expression that is prefixed to the timestamp. For example, if in your data, a timestamp is available after the <FORECAST> tag, then define it as TIME_PREFIX.

- MAX_TIMESTAMP_LOOKAHEAD = <NUMBER>: In this attribute, we specify the position number in the event, where the timestamp is located. Let's suppose that we have configured to break the events by every line and after every 15 words, a timestamp is found, then MAX_TIMESTAMP_LOOKAHEAD=15 needs to be configured.

- TIME_FORMAT = <STRPTIME_FORMAT>: The format of timestamp strptime().

- TZ = <TIMEZONE>: The time zone can be specified in the (+5:30) format or in the format of UTC. For example, TZ=+5:30 specifies the time zone of India.

- MAX_DAYS_AGO = <NUMBER>: These configuration settings can be very useful if you do not want to upload older data on Splunk. Let's suppose that the user is interested in uploading the data of the last one month only, then this attribute can be configured and any data older than the specified days will not be uploaded on Splunk. The default value of this parameter is 2000 days.

- MAX_DAYS_HENCE =<NUMBER>: These settings upload data that has a date less than the number of days in the future. For example, the default value for this attribute is 2, and then, from the present day, if the data has a date greater than two days, it will be ignored and not uploaded.

Let's look at an example of a timestamp extraction.

The following settings in `props.conf` will search for a timestamp after the word FORECAST. It will parse the timestamp in the following mentioned format and time zone of Asia/Kolkata, which is +5:30, and it will not allow to upload the data that is more than 30 days old:

```
[SatelliteData]
TIME_PREFIX = FORECAST:
TIME_FORMAT = %b %d %H:%M:%S %Z%z %Y
MAX_DAYS_AGO = 30
TZ= Asia/Kolkata
```

Host configuration

A hostname or host is the name used to identify the source from where the data is uploaded on Splunk. It is a default field, and Splunk assigns a host value to all the data that gets uploaded on Splunk. The default host value is generally a hostname, IP address, or path of the file or TCP/UDP port number from where the data was generated.

Let's take an example, where we have data being uploaded from four different web servers located at Mumbai, Jaipur, Delhi, and Bangalore. All the data is uploaded from web servers, so it will be available under the same source type. In such situations, it becomes difficult to get insight of only one specific location. So, a hostname can be assigned to it from where the data is getting uploaded to uniquely identify the source and also create visualizations and insight specific to that source. If a user is interested in finding the number of failures, server downtime, and other insights only specific to one web server, in that case, the hostname assigned to that specific location's web server can be used as a filter to fetch information respective to that source.

As mentioned earlier, Splunk automatically tries to assign a hostname if not already specified or configured by the user in the `transforms.conf` configuration or while defining the source type during data input configuration. In many situations, there can be a need for manual configuration of hostnames for better insight and visualizations.

The default host value can be configured from the `inputs.conf` file as follows:

```
[default]
host = <string>
```

Setting a host as `<string>` configures Splunk to keep the IP address or domain name of the source as the host.

Never include quotes (") in the host value. For example, `host=Mumbai` is valid, but `host="Mumbai"` is the wrong way of assigning a host value in the `inputs.conf` file.

In a large distributed environment, it may happen that data is uploaded via forwarders or via a directory path, and it may be required that the hostname be assigned depending on the directory in which the data needs to be classified or on the basis of events. Splunk can be configured to handle such complex scenarios, where the hostname can be either statically or dynamically assigned based on a directory structure or on the basis of the events of the data.

Configuring a static host value – files and directories

This method is useful when the data received from one specific file or directory is to be assigned a single host value. The following procedure is to be applied to define a single host value for data sourced from a specific file or directory.

Let's look at the `Web Console` method:

1. Navigate to **Settings** | **Data Input** | **Files and Directories** from **Splunk Web Console**.
2. If the settings are to be applied on the existing input, choose the respective input to update or create a new input in order to configure the host value.
3. Under the **Set host** drop-down menu, choose **Constant value**, and in the **Host filed value** textbox, enter the hostname that you wish to set for the respective input source.
4. Click on **Save/Submit** to apply the settings.

Now, Splunk will ensure that any data uploaded from the configured data input will be assigned the specified host value.

Let's see the `Config File` method. Here, static host values can also be configured manually by modifying the `inputs.conf` file as follows:

```
[monitor://<path>]
host = <Specify_host_name>
```

In case of the existing data input, just replacing the host value will ensure that any data uploaded in future will be assigned the mentioned host value. If the input method does not exist, then an entry similar to the preceding one with the path of the file/directory from where the data will be uploaded and the host value required can be configured.

Here is an example. The following settings in `inputs.conf` ensure that any data getting uploaded from the `Data` folder of the `F` drive will have the `TestHost` host value:

```
[monitor://F:\Data]
host = TestHost
```

Configuring a dynamic host value – files and directories

This configuration is useful when we are dependent on the name of the file or a regular expression from the source where the data of different hosts can be differentiated. Generally, this is useful when archived data is uploaded on Splunk and the filename has some information about the host, or this can be useful in scenarios where a single forwarder fetches data from different sources and then uploads it on Splunk.

Let me explain this with an example. Suppose that the data from the following folders is uploaded on Splunk:

- `F:\Data\Ver\4.4`
- `F:\Data\Ver\4.2`
- `F:\Data\Ver\5.1`

If for the preceding scenario, the data uploaded from the `4.4` folder has the `Kitkat` host value, the `4.2` folder has `Jellybean`, and the `5.1` folder has `Lollipop`, then a dynamic host value configuration is required.

The steps for the `Web Console` method are as follows:

1. Navigate to **Settings | Data Input | Files and Directories** from **Splunk Web Console**.

2. If the settings are to be applied on the existing input, choose the respective input to update or create a new input in order to configure the host value.

3. Under the **Set host** drop-down menu, you will find the following options:

    ○ **Regex on Path**: This option can be chosen if the hostname is to be extracted using a regular expression on the path.

    The preceding example can be implemented using this method by setting the **Regular expression** textbox as `F:\Data\Ver\(\w+)`.

    ○ **Segment in Path**: This option is useful in scenarios where the path segment can be used as a host value.

The preceding example can also be implemented by choosing this option and by setting the **Segment Number** textbox as 4, that is, `F:\Data\Ver\4.4`; in this case, `4.4` is the fourth segment of the path.

4. Click on **Save/Submit** to apply the settings.

With the `Config File` method, dynamic host values can be configured manually by modifying the `inputs.conf` file as follows. For the preceding example, `input.conf` will look like this:

- Regex on Path:

```
[monitor://F:\Data\Ver]
host_regex =F:\Data\Ver\(\w+)
```

Or, the `input.conf` file will look as follows:

- Segment in Path:

```
[monitor://F:\Data\Ver]
host_segment = 4
```

Configuring a host value – events

Splunk Enterprise supports assigning different hostnames based on the events in data. Event-based host configuration plays a very important role when the data is forwarded by a forwarder or the data is from the same file/directory where hostname classification cannot be done on the basis of files/directories. Event-based host configuration can be configured by modifying the config files, which we will look at in a later section.

The `Transforms.conf` file should have the following settings, which include a unique name using which the `props.conf` file will be updated:

```
[<name>]
REGEX = <regex>
FORMAT = host::$1
DEST_KEY = MetaData:Host
```

Now, the `props.conf` file needs to be configured accordingly in reference to `transforms.conf`. It will have a source or source type. The `TRANSFORMS` parameter will have the same name that we have used for `transforms.conf`.

For `Props.conf`, the code block should look like this:

```
[<source or sourcetype>]
TRANSFORMS-<class> = <name>
```

Let's suppose that we have data that is uploaded from the test.txt file to Splunk Enterprise, which has events from various sources, and while uploading it to Splunk, the user needs to assign different hosts based on the content of the event.

This is how the transforms.conf and props.conf files need to be configured to implement this host configuration (the host value for matching events):

```
//For Transforms.conf file
  [EventHostTest]
  REGEX = Event\soriginator:\s(\w+\-?\w+)
  FORMAT = host::$1
  DEST_KEY = MetaData:Host
//For Props.conf file
  [TestTXTUpload]
  TRANSFORMS-test= EventHostTest
```

The preceding configuration will ensure that it assigns a host based on the detected regular expression.

All the host configuration methods explained earlier need to be implemented before the data gets uploaded on Splunk. In a situation where the data is already uploaded on Splunk, the host configuration can either be done by deleting and reindexing the data or by creating tags for incorrect host values. There is also one more approach that can be useful in case when the data is already uploaded: the use of lookup tables.

Managing event segmentation

Splunk breaks the uploaded data into events. Events are the key elements of Splunk search that are further segmented on index time and search time. Basically, segmentation is breaking of events into smaller units classified as major and minor. Segmentation can be explained with the help of the following example.

The complete IP address is a major segment, and a major segment can be further broken down into many minor segments, as shown in the following screenshot:

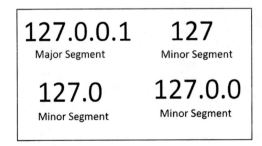

It is very important to configure event segmentation, as index-time segmentation affects storage size and indexing speed, and search-time segmentation affects the search speed and ability to create searches based on the result of searches on Splunk Web; depending on the need, specific types of segmentation can be configured. Splunk even provides the facility to apply event segmentation on a specific host, source, or source type.

The following are three types of event segmentation that can be configured for index-time and search-time segmentation:

- **Inner segmentation**: This type of segmentation ensures that the events are broken down into smallest (minor) segments. Inner segmentation leads to fast indexing and searching and less disk usage, but it also leads to the degradation in the lookahead functionality of search prediction while searching in the Splunk Web console.

  For example, the IP address `127.0.0.1` will be broken as `127`, `0`, `0` and `1` in the inner segmentation.

- **Outer segmentation**: Outer segmentation is exactly the opposite of inner segmentation. In this segmentation, major segments are not broken down into minor segments. However, it is less efficient than inner segmentation, but it is said to be more efficient than full segmentation. It also leads to restriction of the ability to click on different segments of search results while searching on the Splunk Web Console.

  For example, the IP address `127.0.0.1` will only be segmented as `127.0.0.1`. So, to search for any events having the IP address `127.0.0`, we will have to use wildcards such as `127.0.0.*` This will result in all the IP addresses starting with `127.0.0`.

- **Full segmentation**: Full segmentation is a mixture of both inner and outer segmentation. It keeps both major and minor segments. This is said to be the least efficient option for indexing and is more versatile for searching.

  For example, the IP address `127.0.0.1` will be segmented as `127.0.0.1`, `127.0`, `127.0.0`.

Splunk Enterprise is, by default, configured to the indexing type, which is a combination of outer and inner segmentation for index-time segmentation and full segmentation for search-time segmentation in `segmenters.conf` located at `$SPLUNK_HOME/etc/system/default`.

The props.conf can be configured if event segmentation is to be performed on a specific host, source type, or source. The following block can be added to props.conf for the respective event's segmentation. Inner, outer, none, and full are the values that can be configured in the SEGMENTATION attribute.

- **Index-time segmentation**:

```
[Source/Sourcetype/Host]
SEGMENTATION = <SEGMENTATION_TYPE> # SEGMENTATION_TYPE can be
Inner, Outer, None or Full
```

  For better clarity, refer the following example:

```
[TestTXTUpload]
SEGMENTATION = Outer
```

- **Search-time segmentation**:

```
[Source/Sourcetype/Host]
SEGMENTATION-<SEGMENT> = <SEGMENTATION_TYPE>
# SEGMENTATION_TYPE can be Inner, Outer, None or Full & SEGMENT
can be full,
inner, outer or raw.
```

  For example:

```
[TestTXTUpload]
SEGMENTATION-full = Outer
```

 Splunk needs to be restarted to apply the effects of changes applied for the event segment configuration.

Improving the data input process

Data input is a very important process before you generate insight and visualizations from data. So, it is very important that the data is indexed, parsed, processed, and segmented properly. It may not be the case that the first approach/setting the user applies is the best, and there may be a need for a trial-and-error method to find the best settings for the data of those types for which settings are not available, by default, in Splunk.

It is always advisable to first upload small amount of data on a test index on a development server of Splunk. Once the data is available on Splunk in the correct format of events in which queries can result in the required visualizations, then the input can be forwarded to the correct index and source on the production server.

Many times, it happens that when you are testing and trying to upload the same file more than once to try different settings of event configuration, Splunk may not index the file, as the filename or file contents are already on Splunk to avoid redundancy. In such scenarios, the index can be cleaned or the index can be deleted or disabled using the following commands, respectively:

- **Cleaning an index**: `splunk clean eventdata -index <index_name>`
- **Deleting an index**: `splunk remove index <index_name>`
- **Disabling an index**: `splunk disable index <index_name>`

If there is a stream of data directly sent to Splunk from a TCP or UDP stream, it is advisable to write that data to a file and then configure Splunk to monitor the file. This helps to avoid loss of data when Splunk or a network is down, and it can also be helpful in case you're deleting and reindexing on Splunk for some reason. Use persistent queues to buffer data in case the forwarder, TCP, UDP, or scripted data input is used. This helps us to store data in a queue in case of any issues.

It is advisable to use Splunk forwarders when data is to be uploaded on Splunk Enterprise remotely. Forwarders have a feature of sending a heartbeat to the indexer every 30 sec, and in case of connectivity loss, it will hold the data until connected again.

When the data that is to be uploaded on Splunk does not have a timestamp and Splunk is configured to use the uploaded time as a timestamp, in that scenario, timestamp searching should be disabled. Disabling timestamp searching on data that doesn't have a timestamp at all enhances the processing considerably and makes it faster. To disable timestamp searching `inputs.conf` append the `[host::SatelliteData]` block with the `DATETIME_CONFIG` attribute as `NONE`.

Refer to the following example for better clarity:

```
[host::SatelliteData]
DATETIME_CONFIG = NONE
```

Data input is a very important and crucial process of Splunk tools. The following are some of the points to be considered while setting up the input process:

- Identify how and which input methods will be used to upload data on Splunk
- Use Universal forwarder if required
- Look for the Splunk app store and utilize any technology add-on depending on the requirement, if any

- Apply the **Common Information Model (CIM)**, which specifies the standard host tags, fields, event type tags used by Splunk when processing most of the IT data

- Always test the upload on a test environment first and then proceed to the deployment server

Summary

In this chapter, we walked through various data input methods along with various data sources supported by Splunk. We also looked at HTTP Event Collector, which is a new feature added in Splunk 6.3 for data collection via REST to encourage the usage of Splunk for IoT. We studied data processing, event segmentation, and ways by which we can improve the data input process. In the next chapter, we will cover how to create analytics and provide meaningful insight over the data uploaded on Splunk.

4
Data Analytics

This chapter will help you understand how to analyze the data and get insight on the data that is uploaded on Splunk from various sources. Right from searching, sending search results over e-mail, combining search results, and accessing the data, you will be able to do basic analytics and data manipulation on Splunk Enterprise via the web console. The reader will also be able to add, extract, and modify fields and format the output as per their requirements. We will use Splunk search commands to fetch the desired the insights and statistics on Splunk Enterprise.

In this chapter, we will cover the following topics:

- Data and indexes
- Search
- Subsearch
- Time
- Fields
- Results

Data and indexes

When data is sent on Splunk Enterprise, it consumes the raw data and converts it into searchable events. This processed data gets stored in an index in Splunk. We will now go through the search commands that can be used on Splunk Web to view and manage the data and indexes.

You will now learn to use Splunk commands to analyze the data. There are many Splunk commands, and each command has many parameters. We will go through the important commands and the required parameters.

Accessing data

The following set of commands can be used to access data from indexes. These categories of commands just fetch the information and display it. They do not modify the data or indexes.

The index command

Splunk's `index` command displays the event data of the specified index. On installation, Splunk Enterprise already has the default index as `main`. It also has few other indexes names, such as `_audit`, `_internal`, `_introspection`, and so on. They can be used for Splunk error lookup, Splunk health status, and Splunk license usages and violations.

The available list of indexes can be seen by navigating to **Settings | Indexes** from the Splunk Web console. This **Indexes** page can be used to create, delete, and manage indexes.

The syntax for the `index` command is as follows:

```
index = <index_name>
```

Refer to the following example for better clarity:

```
index = _internal
index = main
```

The following screenshot shows the event data for the `_internal` index:

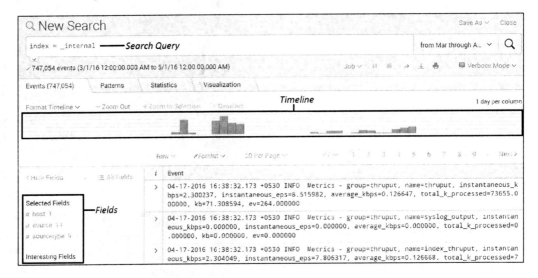

Using the index command along with index_name, you can fetch all the information of a specific index. Using index = _internal will list out the data only of the _internal index. There can be many indexes on which various sources may be forwarding data. Specifying which index to search narrows the search to a specific index only and, thus, gives faster results. The _internal index can be used to debug issues with respect to Splunk. The splunkd.log file is continuously being indexed in _internal index, and thus, any errors and issues can be searched using this index.

If, while searching, the index is not specified, then Splunk searches in the default index, that is, the main index. So, if the data is in any index other than main, it needs to be explicitly specified in Splunk CLI queries to get the desired results.

The eventcount command

This Splunk command is used to get the count of the events for the specified index or indexes.

The syntax for the eventcount command is as follows:

```
| eventcountindex=<string>
    summarize=<bool>
    report_size=<bool>
    list_vix=<bool>
```

This is the parameter description of the eventcount command:

- index: This is the name of the index or indexes whose event count is to be fetched and needs to be specified here.
- summarize: This accepts the Boolean value which determines whether to summarize events from all the peers and indexes or not.
- report_size: This accepts the Boolean value which determines whether to display the size of the index or not. The index size is reported in bytes.
- list_vix: This accepts the Boolean value which determines whether to list virtual indexes or not.

Refer to the following example for better clarity:

```
| eventcount index=* summarize=false
```

The following screenshot describes the `eventcount` command:

In the preceding example, the `eventcount` command is used to list the count of events for all the `index=*` (all indexes default or user created) and `index=_*` (all internal Splunk indexes created by Splunk Enterprise for auditing and debugging of the Splunk instance) indexes, along with the size of the `eventcount` (`report_size=true`). The event count is split by index and search peers by the `summarize=false` parameter.

The datamodel command

Splunk Knowledge Manager generates a hierarchical structured data model from one or more datasets to generate reports for pivot users. The data model has enough information to run specialized searches to create visualization as per user needs.

The syntax for the `eventcount` command is as follows:

```
| datamodel
    <data_model_name>
    <object_name>
    <search>
```

This is the parameter description of the `datamodel` command:

- `data_model_name`: This specifies the name of the specific model, and the result will be restricted to only the specified model
- `object_name`: This specifies the name of the object to be searched in the specified data model
- `search`: This specifies that Splunk should search for the specified object name and data model

Refer to the following examples of the `datamodel` command:

- **Example 1**:

  | `datamodel internal_server daily_usage`

  The following screenshot describes the `datamodel` command:

In this example, Splunk will show the data model of the `internal_server` dataset and the `daily_usage` object in the JSON format. If `data_model_name` and `object_name` are not specified, then all the data models available on Splunk will be listed.

- **Example 2**:

  | `datamodelinternal_serverdaily_usage search`

The following screenshot describes the `datamodel` command usage in the second way:

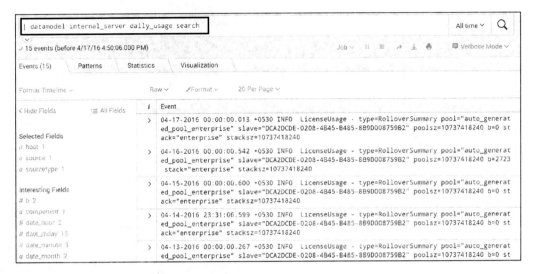

In this example, all the entries of the `internal_server` data model with the `daily_usage` as the object will be searched and displayed. In short, all the entries that satisfy the `daily_usage` object criteria defined during the creation of the data model creation will be searched and displayed.

The dbinspect command

The Splunk command—`dbinspect` enlists comprehensive information about the index, such as the bucket ID, event count, path of the database index, state of the index, and so on. This command basically helps users fetch information about the index, thus, the name `dbinspect`.

The syntax for the `dbinspect` command is as follows:

```
| dbinspect
    index=<string>
    span=<timeformat>
```

This is the parameter description of the `dbinspect` command:

- `index`: This is the name of the index whose information is required. If no index is specified, then the data of the default index is shown.

- `span`: This parameter is used to specify the length of the bucket; `span` can also be specified in the format of time.

Refer to the following examples of the `dbinspect` command:

- **Example 1**:

  ```
  | dbinspect index=_*
  ```

  The following screenshot describes the `dbinspect` command:

The `dbinspect` command of Splunk lists our detailed information about the specified index (`index=_*`). In this case, it provides information about all the internal indexes. If the index is not specified, then the default index data is shown.

- **Example 2**:

  ```
  | dbinspect index=_*span=1week
  ```

The following screenshot describes the usage dbinspect command with the span parameter:

```
| dbinspect index=_* span=1week
```

✓ 0 events (before 1/19/38 8:44:07.000 AM)

Events   Patterns   Statistics (1,162)   Visualization

20 Per Page ∨   ⁄Format ∨   Preview ∨   ‹ Prev

_time	hot-52	warm-0	warm-1	warm-10	warm-11	warm-12	warm-13
2015-10-22 00:00:00		1	2				
2015-10-22 21:40:13		1	2				
2015-11-05 00:00:00			2				
2015-11-12 00:00:00							
2015-11-19 00:00:00							
2015-11-26 00:00:00							
2015-12-03 00:00:00							
2015-12-10 00:00:00							
2015-12-17 00:00:00							
2015-12-24 00:00:00							
2015-12-31 00:00:00				11	12		
2016-01-07 00:00:00						13	14

On specifying the span (span=1week), the output shows bucket information with respect to time for the specified index.

The crawl command

The crawl Splunk command is used to index files from different sources such as a file system or from network sources as well. The default behavior of crawl can be configured in the crawl.conf file. Splunk also logs the circumstances in which the crawl command is used, which can be referred to track the usage of this command.

The syntax for the crawl command is as follows:

```
|crawl <file/Network_Path>
    <options>
```

This is the parameter description of the `crawl` command:

- `file` or `Network_Path`: Path of the file system or the network which is to be crawled to index the data to Splunk.
- `options`: Any specific settings that are to be overridden from the default `crawl.conf` file can be specified here. A few examples of `options` that can be configured here are `index`, `collapse_threshold`, `big_dir_filecount`, and so on.

Refer to the following example for better clarity:

```
|crawl
```

The following screenshot describes the `crawl` command:

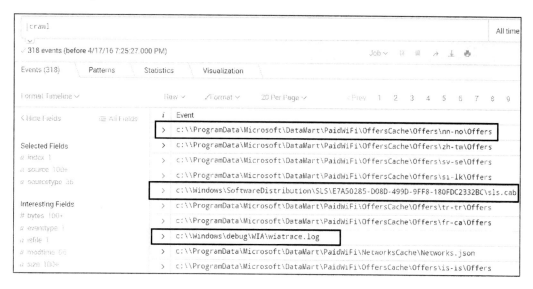

The `crawl` command of Splunk is used to crawl to all the files and folders in the specified directory or network location. In the preceding example, the file location or network path is not specified. Hence, the crawling will take place at the default path specified in `crawl.conf`. The default path is specified in `crawl.conf` is `C:\`.

If crawling is to be done at a location other than the default location, then `root=<path>` can be specified after the `crawl` command, as shown here:

```
|crawl root=d:\temp\; #for directory
|crawl host=10.20.8.47 #for network path
```

Managing data

All the preceding commands under the **Accessing Data** section were generating commands, that is, these commands do not alter the data. They just fetch and display the data. Now, you will learn about how to manage the data on indexes.

The input command

The `input` command is used to enable or disable sources from being processed in a Splunk Enterprise index. Any attributes added using the `input` command will be added to the `inputs.conf` file. The logs of the `input` command are available in the `inputs.log` file.

The `input` command is generally used along with the `crawl` command to add sources obtained from the `crawl` command in the `inputs.conf` file.

The syntax for the `input` command is as follows:

```
input add/remove
    sourcetype=string
    index=string
    string_name=string
```

The parameter description of the `input` command is as follows:

- `add/remove`: whether the input is to be added or to be removed
- `sourcetype`: specifies the source type in which the data is to be added
- `index`: specifies the index in which the data is to be added
- `string_name`: custom user fields that need to be added

Refer to the following code of the `input` command:

```
| crawl | input add sourcetype=CrawlTest index=CrawlIndex
```

The following screenshot describes the `input` command:

Sourcetype & Index ————

In the preceding example, the `input` command is used along with the `crawl` command to add as an input with the source type as `CrawlTest` and the index as `CrawlIndex`. If the index and source type are not specified, then the data will be added in the `default` index, and `automatic` source type will be classified by Splunk Enterprise, depending on the type of data.

The delete command

The `delete` command of Splunk is an irreversible command used to make events irretrievable from the indexes. This command marks the event as deleted. Hence, the deleted events will not be returned in any search result even by the user with admin privileges.

Using the `delete` command will not free up any space on the disk, and if the deleted data is required, then it has to be reindexed from the original source. This command cannot be used for real-time search.

The syntax for the delete command is as follows:

```
delete
```

Refer to the following example for better clarity:

```
sourcetype="crt-too_small" Address | delete
```

The following screenshot describes the `delete` command:

In the preceding example, all the events that had `Address` in the `crt-too_small` source type will be deleted and will be inaccessible from the Splunk index. If the address is not mentioned as in the preceding example, then all the events under the `crt-too_small` source type will be deleted.

The clean command

The `clean` command is used to delete all the events of the specified index. Generally, this command is used when using the trial-and-error method to choose the best source type and event-breaking configuration while defining new source types to empty the index. This command makes an irreversible change in the index, and the data removed can be brought back in Splunk only by reindexing it.

The syntax for the clean command is as follows:

```
splunk clean eventdata
    -index <index_name>
```

The `Index_name` parameter of the `clean` command specifies the name of index that is to be cleaned.

Following is an example of the `clean` command:

```
splunk clean eventdata -index TestIndex
```

The screenshot that follows shows the execution of a clean command instance:

```
c:\Program Files\Splunk\bin>splunk clean eventdata -index TestIndex
In order to clean, Splunkd must not be running.

c:\Program Files\Splunk\bin>splunk stop
Splunkd: Stopped

c:\Program Files\Splunk\bin>splunk clean eventdata -index TestIndex
This action will permanently erase all events from the index 'TestIndex'; it can
not be undone.
Are you sure you want to continue [y/n]? y
ERROR: Index 'TestIndex' does not exist.

c:\Program Files\Splunk\bin>splunk start

Splunk> The Notorious B.I.G. D.A.T.A.

Checking prerequisites...
        Checking http port [8000]: open
        Checking mgmt port [8089]: open
        Checking appserver port [127.0.0.1:8065]: open
        Checking kvstore port [8191]: open
        Checking configuration... Done.
        Checking critical directories...           Done
        Checking indexes...
                Validated: _audit _internal _introspection _thefishbucket histor
y main summary
        Done
        Checking filesystem compatibility...  Done
        Checking conf files for problems...
```

To run this command, the Splunk instance needs to be stopped first. The Splunk instance can be stopped by running the splunk stop command from the Command prompt. Once the Splunk instance is stopped, then the splunk clean eventdata -index TestIndex command cleans the TestIndex. If just the splunk clean eventdata command is run, then the event data of all the events are cleaned. After the index is clean, Splunk can be restarted using the splunk start command.

Summary indexing

Summary indexing is used to speed up searches that do not qualify for report acceleration. Using summary indexing commands such as sichart (the summary index version of the chart command), sitimechart (the summary index version of the timechart command), sistats (the summary index version of the stats command), sitop (the summary index version of the top command), and sirare (the summary index version of the rare command), you can compute the relevant information required to later run the non-summary indexing version of the respective commands on the summary index. The summary index is created by the collect command.

The syntax for performing a summary indexing operation is as follows:

```
|collect index=<index_name>
        File=<file_name>
        Host=<host_name>
        Source=<source_name>
        Sourcetype=<sourcetype_name>
```

The parameter description of the above summary indexing instance is as follows:

- `index_name`: Name of the summary index in which the events are to copied. The specified index name should be created before running this command.

- `File_name`: Name of the file can be specified where the summary index data will be written.

- `Host_name`: Host name can be configured using this parameter for the summary index.

- `Source_name`: Source can be specified for the summary index data.

- `Sourcetype_name`: Source type can be configured using this parameter for the created summary index.

Following this is an example of a summary indexing operation:

```
index=_internal  error | collect index=TestIndex
```

The following screenshot describes a summary indexing operation performing the `collect` action:

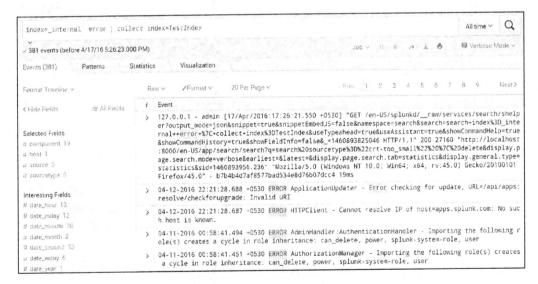

The preceding search query will export all the events of the `_internal` index that has error to index entries named `Test Index`. Similarly, the `collect` command can be used to create summary indexes for the hourly error statistics based on the host value using the following search query:

```
index=_internal |search error _time span=1h | stats count by host _time |
collect index=TestIndex
```

Also, the `sichart` command can be used to compute the necessary information to later do a `chart sum(field_name) by _time` operation on the summary indexed results:

```
| sichart sum(field_name) by _time
```

Similarly, `sistats` and `sitop` can be used to create computation for respective commands on summary indexes:

```
|sistats count(field_name) by _time
sourcetype="android_data" | sitop android_version
```

Thus, using different summary indexing commands, searches can be accelerated, and long-running search results can be obtained faster.

Search

Splunk is said to be the Google of machine data. So, searching is the most important set of actions that is performed to retrieve the exact information the user is looking for from the indexes. You will now learn how to make efficient use of search commands to fetch the relevant and required information precisely from the whole set of data.

The search command

The `search` command is used to search events and filter the result from the indexes. The `search` command, followed by keywords, phrases, regular expressions, wildcards, and key-value pairs, can be used to fetch filtered events from the indexes.

Mentioned as follows is the syntax for a `search` command instance:

```
<keywords>
    <wildcards>
    <key_value_pairs> or <fields>
    <phrases>
    <operators>
```

```
<logical_expressions>
<regular_expressions>
<time_specifiers>
```

The parameter description for the preceding parameters is as follows:

- `keywords`: A keyword can be any string or strings that are to be searched in the data. Depending on the data and the requirement, the keywords can be anything. If the data in the Splunk index is of a website login transaction, then the keywords can be `Login`, `failed`, `authenticated`, `error`, and so on.

- `wildcards`: If the user wants to find the information of all the users whose IP address starts with 192.168, then the `192.168.*` wildcard can be used.

- `key_value_pairs` / `fields`: Key-value pairs are fields that are either automatically extracted by Splunk or user extracted. Key-value pairs can be `server="America"`, `android_version=5.1`, and so on, depending on the data and the requirement.

- `phrases`: The `search` command can be followed by phrases to be searched in indexes. Phrases are nothing but a set of keywords, and they are to be specified in quotes (`"`) after the `search` commands, such as `login failed`, `request timeout`, and `incorrect password`.

- `operators`: Operators such as `OR` and `AND` can be used to filter the search results

- `logical_expression`: Splunk accepts the usage of logical expressions such as `<`, `>`, `<=`, `>=`, `=`, and `!=`.

- `regular_expression`: The `search` command can be specified with a regular expression to search in the data, and the events with the specified regular expression will be returned in the search results.

- `time_specifiers`: Time range can be specified in the `search` command to restrict the search to the said time range only. Only those events that fall in the given time range will be displayed in the search result. Time can be specified using parameters such as `starttime`, `endtime`, `earliest`, and `latest`. Time format can also be specified using the `timeformat` parameter.

The following are examples of a `search` operation with two different scenarios:

```
index=web_server error 404

index=web_server IP=192.168.* AND IP=10.20.* | search "login failed" OR
"incorrect password"
```

In the first example, all the events that have an error and 404 will be shown in the search result. Here, we have used the keyword (error and 404) to be searched in the index. In the second example, the query will result in all the events that have IP (192.168.* and 10.20.*). We have used the AND Boolean operator along with wildcard (*) for the IP address to filter the required result. In the later section of the second example, after pipe (|) phrases in quotes (login failed and incorrect password) are used along with the Boolean operator OR to get all the events that have either failed to log in or used an incorrect password.

The sendmail command

The sendmail command is used to send the search result over e-mail. The search results can be sent inline in the e-mail or as a PDF attachment. This command can be used in the scripts or while scheduling reports to run search queries with the specified filters and keywords. Then, the results are to be e-mailed to the specified recipient(s).

The syntax for the sendemail command is as follows:

```
sendemail to=<email_id(s)>
        from=<email_id(s)>
        cc=<email_id(s)>
        bcc=<email_id(s)>
        subject=<enter_subject_for_email>
        format=csv/ raw / table
        inline= true/false
        sendpdf=true/false
        server=<email_server>
```

The parameter description of the sendemail command is as follows:

- email_id(s): List of e-mail ID(s) can be specified for the to, from, cc, and bcc parameters.

- subject: Subject of the e-mail can be specified, for example, hourly report of login failures, daily report of errors occurred, and so on.

- format: This parameter is used to specify how the report is to be formatted for inline e-mails. It specifies whether the result is to be displayed in a CSV, table, or in raw format in the inline e-mail.

- inline: If set to true, then the results are sent inline in the e-mail.

- sendpdf: If set to true, then the results are sent as a PDF attachment in the e-mail.

- server: The SMTP server address through which the e-mail is to be sent. If the SMTP server is configured on the same host, there is no need to specify the server, as the local host is set as the default SMTP server.

Refer to the following example for a better understanding:

```
index=_internal error | head 10 |
sendemailto=test@domain.com cc=cctest@domain.com subject="Top 10 errors
of this hour" sendpdf=true inline=true format=raw
```

The preceding search query will send an e-mail to test@domain.com, which will be Cced to cctest@domain.com with the subject Top 10 errors of this hour having a PDF attachment (sendpdf=true). The PDF will contain the top 10 errors of the _internal index events in the raw (format=raw) format, and this information will also be available inline (inline=true) in the e-mail.

The localop command

Splunk is generally deployed in a distributed architecture, and it can have many indexers and search heads in a real deployment environment. Whenever a search is run on a search head, the results are fetched from all the indexers of the distributed architecture. If the user wants to run the search on only local indexers and does not require data from all the other remote indexes, then the localop command can be used.

The syntax for the localop command is as follows:

```
|localop
```

Refer to the following example for better lucidity:

```
Index=web_server error |localop | userIP
```

The preceding search query will return userIP only from the local indexer and error from the local as well as remote indexers of Index=web_server.

Subsearch

The search that is enclosed in a square bracket and whose result is passed as a parameter value to the search is called a subsearch. Basically, subsearches are used when the search requires some input that cannot be directly specified or that keeps on changing. Hence, another search query is written, and the result is passed to the original search.

Let's assume a user wants to know the location and IP address of top three users who have failed the login attempt. Now, the top three users who are failing the login will keep on changing, so subsearches are used. The subsearch will show the top three users that will be passed to the original search. This search will result in the location and IP address of those three users.

You will learn in detail how the preceding scenarios can be solved using various subsearch commands.

The append command

The `append` command of the subsearch category, as the name suggests, is used to append the result of one search with another search result. The subsearch may or may not have the same name and the same number of fields. So, the `append` command is used to append the final result of two searches (which cannot be combined in a single search) into one result.

The syntax of the `append` command is as follows:

```
Search … |append [search …]
```

The example that follows will give you a better understanding of the `append` command:

```
index=_internal | stats count by sourcetype |head 3 | append [search
index=main | stats count by sourcetype | head 3]
```

The following screenshot describes the `append` command:

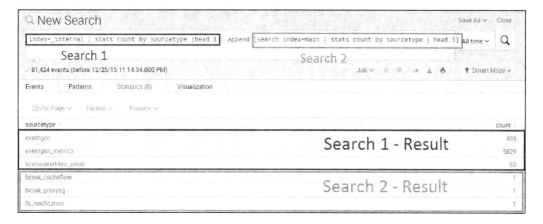

The preceding search query runs the subsearch specified under append, and the results are appended with the search result of the main search query. So, in the preceding screenshot, the first three rows are the results of the main query, and the last three rows are the results of the subsearch written in the append section of the query.

The appendcols command

This command is used to append the fields of one search result with another search result (subsearch). The resulting fields are added row wise. For example, the first row of the first search will be combined with the first row of the second search. In the scenario when the fields of the first and second search results are common, then the value will be overwritten by the result of second search.

The syntax of the appendcols command is as follows:

```
Search ... |appendcols
        [override= true/false
        | search ...]
```

The override parameter accepts the Boolean value of true or false whether to override the value of a common field with the result of a second search or not.

Refer to the following example for better lucidity:

```
index=_internal | timechart span=1d count as Count1| appendcols
   [search index=_audit | timechart span=1d count as Count2]
```

The following screenshot describes the appendcols command:

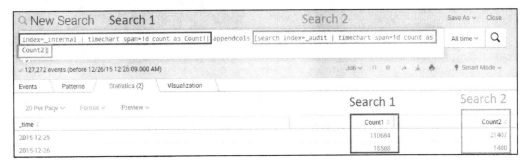

In the preceding example query, the output column `Count1` is the result of the first search query and `Count2` is the result of the second search query. The `appendcols` command can be basically used for comparative analysis of two or more search results in the same table or chart.

The appendpipe command

The `appendpipe` command is used to append the search results of the post process (subpipeline) of the current result set. In short, `appendpipe` can be used to add a summary to the current result set.

The syntax for `appendpipe` is as follows:

```
Search ... | appendpipe [search ...]
```

The following screenshot describes the `appendpipe` command:

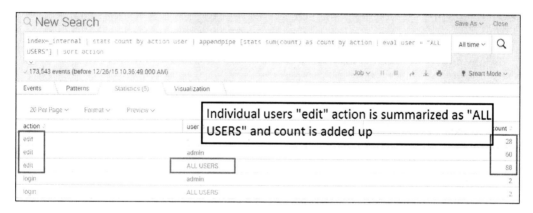

Listed as follows is an example of `appendpipe` command:

```
index=_internal | stats count by action user |
  appendpipe [stats sum(count) as count by action |
  eval user = "ALL USERS"] | sort action
```

In the preceding example, `appendpipe` creates a summary of the `edit` action whose `count` is grouped by the `user`. Thus, the third entry of the `edit` action has `ALL USERS` in the `user` filed, and the `count` is the sum of all the users. Thus, `appendpipe` can be used to create a summary of any number of fields by grouping them into one based on the specified field.

The join command

The `join` command is used to combine the results of the subsearch with the main search result. The `join` command of Splunk works similar to the `join` command used in SQL. Join in Splunk can be of mainly of two types, that is, *inner join* and *left join* (left join is also known as outer join in Splunk). There should be at least one field common for the `join` command.

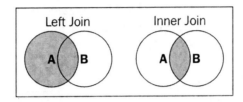

The syntax for the join command is as follows:

```
search … | join jointype [ search …]
```

The `jointype` parameter can be defined as `Left Join` (outer join) or `Inner Join`. If the join type is not defined, then the default is set to `Inner join`.

Refer the following example for a better clarity:

```
| inputlookup dmc_assets |
  stats first(serverName) as serverName, first(host) as host,
  first(machine) as machine |
  join type=outer serverName
  [   | rest splunk_server=Heart-Hackers /services/server/info
  | fields serverName, numberOfCores, physicalMemoryMB, os_name,
  cpu_arch ]
```

The following screenshot describes the `join` command:

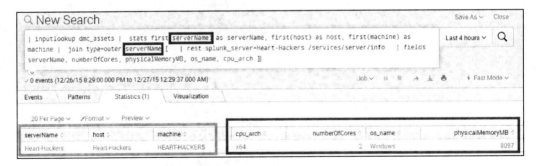

In the preceding example, the result highlighted in the left-hand box is the output of the query written before the `join` command, and the one highlighted in the right-hand box is the output of the subsearch written after the `join` command. In this example, `serverName` is the common field that is used to join the output of both the search actions, and the result is as shown in the preceding image. Information such as `cpu_arch`, `numberOfCores`, `os_names` is fetched for the `serverName` specified, and the results are matched and displayed as a single result.

Time

The time subset of commands is used to enrich the data with the ability to search based on time and make data more user friendly for analytics and visualization.

The reltime command

The `reltime` Splunk command is used to create a relative time field called `reltime`. It shows the time value in a format that humans can read, relative to current time. The time in `reltime` would appear as `2 hours ago`, `3 days ago`, `1 month ago`, and so on.

The syntax for the `reltime` command is as follows:

```
... | reltime
```

Refer to the following example for better clarity:

```
index=_internal |reltime
```

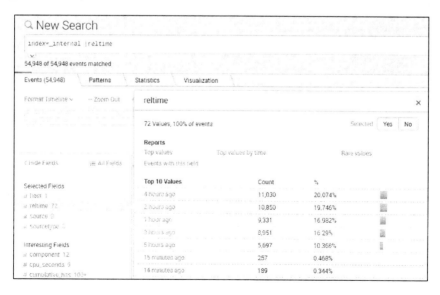

As shown in the preceding screenshot, `reltime` creates a more user friendly and human readable format output of relative time, which can be used in analytics and visualizations.

The localize command

The `localize` command is used to create a list of time ranges in which the results have occurred.

The syntax for the `localize` command is as follows:

```
localize maxpause
```

The `maxpause` parameter can be used to specify the maximum time between two consecutive events for a given time period. The default value for this parameter is 1 minute.

Mentioned as follows is an example of the `localize` command:

```
index=_internal |localize maxpause=5m
```

The preceding Splunk query will return all the events within a five minute time range.

Fields

The fields subset of commands on Splunk is used to add, extract, and modify fields and field values. These commands help users enrich the data, do mathematical and string operations on the fields, and derive insight from the data.

The eval command

The `eval` command of Splunk is very useful and powerful. It can be used to evaluate Boolean, mathematical, or string expressions. It can also be used to create custom (new) fields using existing fields or arbitrary expressions. This command can be used to create new fields, which is the result of some calculations, or use conditional operators such as `if`, `case`, `match`, and so on to apply some expression and evaluate the result.

The `eval` command can also be used to coalesce fields from different sources or indexes to create a transaction of events. The command can be used to extract information to create multiple fields from an event(s).

The syntax for the `eval` command is as follows:

```
eval fieldname = expression/Functions
```

The parameter description of the `eval` command is as follows:

- Expressions can be either arithmetic (+, -, *, /, %), Boolean (AND, OR, NOT, XOR, LIKE), comparison (<, >, <=, >=, =, ==, !=), and concatenation operator (.)
- There is a large number of functions that can be used in the `eval` expression. Some of them are abs, if, lower, min, max, pi, power, random, split, and so on.

Refer to the following examples for better clarity:

- ... | eval Expression1 = (Field1 +Field2)/Field3
- ... | eval Result = min(field1, field2)
- ... | evalComplete_Address = Address_Line1." ".Address_Line2." ".Pincode
- ... | evalAndroid_Ver_Name = case(Version == 4.4, "KITKAT", Version == 5.0, "LOLLIPOP", Version == 6.0, "MARSHMALLOW")
- index=kitkat OR index=lollipop | evalcache_errors=coalesce(dalvic_cache,art_cache)

Refer to the following list for an insight on the above examples:

- In the first example, the `eval` command is used to do a mathematical calculation where an addition of `Field1` and `Field2` is divided by `Field3` and the result is stored in `Expression1`.
- In the second example, the `eval` command will store the minimum value from `field1` and `field2` and store it in the `Result` variable.
- In the third example, a concatenation operator (.) is used to concatenate `Address_Line1`, `Address_Line2`, and `pincode` to get `Complete_Address`.
- In the fourth example, `case` condition is used to get the name of the Android version, that is, if the `Version` is 4.4, then the `Android_ver_name` field will get assigned as `KITKAT`. If the `Version` is 5.0, then `LOLLIPOP` will get assigned and so on.

- In the fifth example, `coalcese` is used along with the `eval` command to fetch information from different sources and indexes where field values are the same but field names are different. For example, for `index=kitkat`, `cache_error` is available under the `dalvic_cache` field, and for `index=Lollipop`, `cache_error` is available under `art_cache`. So, basically, depending on the index, the cache field name is changing, but the field information is the same. Hence, the `coalcese` command can be used to combine and get the result into a new field. In our example, the new field name is `cache_errors`.

The xmlkv command

This command is used when the data is in the XML format to exact the key-value pairs form the XML data. Using `xmlkv` automatically creates fields of the XML tags and makes them available for use on Splunk for analytics.

The syntax for the `xmlkv` command is as follows:

... **|xmlkv**

Refer to the following example of the `xmlkv` command:

sourcetype="xmltest" | xmlkv

The following screenshot describes the `xmlkv` command:

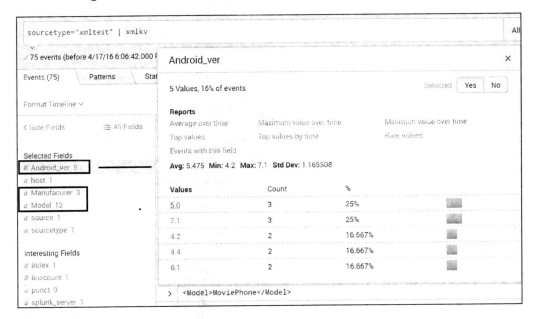

The test XML file uploaded on Splunk looks like this:

```
<phone id="phone101">
  <Manufacuter>TestPhone1</Manufacuter>
  <Model>C2123</Model>
  <Android_ver>4.2</Android_ver>
  <price>44.95</price>
</phone>
```

After running the `xmlkv` command, fields from the XML file, such as `Manufacturer`, `Model`, `Android_ver`, and `price` automatically get extracted from the file and are available as fields that can be used to create analytics and visualizations. This `xmlkv` command makes it easier to do to analysis on XML files.

The spath command

This command is similar to the `xmlkv` command, but unlike `xmlkv`, which can be used only for XML files, `spath` can be used on any structured data, such as JSON and XML files, to extract the tags from the structured data into fields. `spath` commands can be used to extract multivalued fields from JSON and XML events or to extract a subset of an attribute.

The syntax for the `spath` command is as follows:

... |**spath**

    input=field_name

    output=field_name

    path=datapath

The parameter description of the `spath` command is as follows:

- `input`: The field from which the data is to be extracted can be specified in this parameter. The default value for this parameter is `_raw`.

- `output`: The name of the field to which the data is to be extracted to. This is used where a custom name of the field is needed rather than the auto extracted field name.

- `path`: This is the path of the value that is to be extracted. Let's take an example of a path from the following sample XML file:

```
<library>
  <book category="Technical">
    <title lang="en">Splunk Basic</title>
    <author>Jack Thomas</author>
    <year>2007</year>
```

```
        <price>520.00</price>
    </book>
</library>
```

Now, the path of the tag `year` will be `library.book.year` and so on. Depending on the hierarchy, the path can be defined and specified accordingly.

Take a look at the following example:

sourcetype="_json" | spath

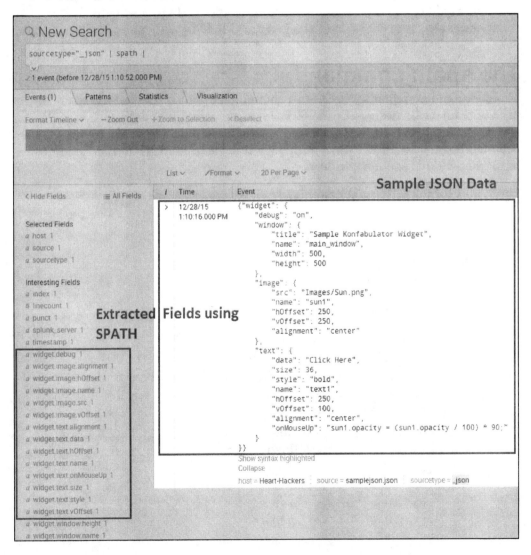

As shown in the preceding example, using `spath`, structured data tags can be extracted into fields. In the left box in the image, the path to the data can be seen like an access `alignment` field and the `path` would be `widget.image.alignment`. The `output` parameter can be used to get the value from the specified path into a fieldname of user choice.

The makemv command

This `makemv` Splunk command is used to convert a single value field into a multivalued field based on the specified delimiter. This command can be useful to extract information that is available in a single file. For example, from an e-mail ID, `xyz.abc@ domain.com`, the username and domain can be extracted using the `makemv` command.

The syntax for the `makemv` command is as follows:

```
makemv delim=Delimiter_string
    | tokenizer=Regex/tokens
      Allowempty=true/false
      setsv=true/false
```

The description of the parameters is given as follows:

- `delim`: Splits the string on every occurrence of the delimiter specified here. The default delimiter is a single space.
- `tokenizer`: A regular expression of a token that is to be matched in the string to split.
- `setsv`: If this parameter is set to `true`, then there is simultaneous existence of multivalue and single value for the same field.

An example of the `makemv` command is discussed as follows:

```
sourcetype=EmailFile | makemvdelim="@" EmailID | table EmailID
```

As shown in the preceding screenshot and example, we will convert all the single value `EmailID` fields into multivalued attributes by breaking them on every occurrence of `@`. Hence, the `EmailID` field, after applying the `makemv` command, will have two values, that is, `username` and the `domain`.

The fillnull command

The `fillnull` command of Splunk is used to replace null values in fields with specific user-defined values. Null values are those values that are present for one field but not for another field in a result set. For example, we have a table that displays the personal information of students, such as `Name`, `Address`, `Phone Number`, `PAN Number`, `SSN Number`, and so on. It may happen that some students may not have a PAN number or SSN number, so for that specific user, the corresponding filed value will be `null`. Using `fillnull`, those null fields can be filled with user-defined values.

The syntax for the `fillnull` command is as follows:

```
... | fillnull value=String
```

Here, the `value` parameter is a string that the user wants in place of null.

Take a look at the following example of the `fillnull` command:

```
index="_audit" | table action info | fillnull value="NOT AVAILABLE"
```

As shown in the example, any null field will be filled with the user-defined value. In our example, the user-defined value is NOT AVAILABLE. If the `value` parameter is not specified, then the default value, that is, `0` will be entered.

The filldown command

The `filldown` Splunk is a customized version of the `fillnull` command, where instead of filling user-defined or zero values to the null fields, the previous non-null value for the field or field set is applied. In a scenario where there is no non-null previous fields, then it will be left blank (NULL).

Refer the following command skeleton for the syntax of the `filldown` command:

```
... | filldown field-list
```

The `field-list` parameter is a list of fields to which `filldown` is applied. If the `field list` is not specified, then all the fields are applied with `filldown`.

Take a look at the following example for a better understanding:

```
index="_audit" | table action info | filldown
```

As shown in the `fillnull` example image, the fields with `null` values were filled with the user-defined string NOT AVAILABLE. On using `filldown` for the same instead of `null`, the previous non-null value, that is, granted, is assigned to that respective field.

The replace command

The `replace` command of Splunk works similar to the `fillnull` command. In the `fillnull` command, only the null fields were filled up with respective user-defined values, whereas in the `replace` command, any field value can be replaced with a user-defined string. `replace` can be used to make the output more readable and understandable to end users or so on. For example, if the user wants the 127.0.0.1 hostname to be replaced with `localhost`, or say, in my data, `android_version` is 5.0 and the user wants 5.0 `android_version` instead to read `lollipop` then the `replace` command can be used.

The syntax of the `replace` command is as follows:

```
...|replace old_string WITH new_string IN Field_list
```

The parameter description is as follows:

- `old string`: The string that is to be changed
- `new string`: Specifies the new string to which the old string is to be changed
- `Field_list`: List of fields to which this `replace` command is to be applied

Refer to the following examples for a better understanding:

- **Example 1:** ... | `replace 127.0.0.1 WITH localhost IN host`
- **Example 2:** ...| `replace 5.0 WITH lollipop IN Android_version`

In Example 1, every occurrence of `127.0.0.1` in the `host` field will be replaced by `localhost`. Similarly, in Example 2, `5.0` will be replaced with `lollipop` in the `Android_version` field.

Results

The Results set of commands is used to manage the output of the search results. This set of commands can be used to filter the events, reformat the events, group them, reorder them, and read and write on the results.

The fields command

The `fields` command is used to keep (+) or remove (-) fields from the search results. If + is used, then only the `field list` followed by + will be displayed, and if – is used, then the `field list` followed by – will be removed from the current result set.

The syntax for the `fields` command is as follows:

```
... | fields +/- field_list
```

Refer to the following example for better clarity:

```
index=_internal | top component cumulative_hits executes | fields -
percent
```

In the preceding screenshot, we have used the `top` command. The `top` command returns the count and percentage of the specified fields. So, we have used `fields - percent`, which shows all the fields, except **percent**. Similarly, the `fields` command can be used to get the desired output.

The searchtxn command

The `searchtxn` command of Splunk is a useful command to get events that match the specific text and transaction type. This command can be used to find a transaction that satisfies a certain set of conditions. Let's say the user is interested in finding out all the login failed attempts due to an incorrect password. In this case, the `searchtxn` command can be used.

The syntax for the `searchtxn` command is as follows:

```
| searchtxn transaction-name
          search_query
```

Refer to the following for parameter descriptions:

- `transaction-name`: Name of the transaction as defined in the `transactiontypes.conf` file
- `search_query`: The *search string* for which the transactions are needed

Refer to the following example for better clarity:

```
| searchtxn webmaillogin="failed"login_error="Password Incorrect"
```

The preceding query will return all the search transactions of the webmail that has login as `failed` and a login error as `Password Incorrect`.

The head / tail command

The `head` Splunk command is used to fetch the first *n* number of specified results, and the `tail` command is used to fetch the last *n* number of specified results from the result set.

The syntax for the commands is as follows:

```
... | head n
  | Expression

... | tail n
```

The parameter description for the preceding query is as follows:

- n: The number of results to be returned.
- Expression: Any `eval` expression that returns a Boolean value. The expression will list out all the results until the `Expression` returns `false`.

The example of the `head...tail` commands is mentioned with the explanation, as follows:

```
... | head 10
... | tail 10
```

In the preceding search query, the `head 10` will list out first 10 events, and the `tail 10` will return the last 10 events in the search results.

The inputcsv command

The `inputcsv` command of Splunk is a generating command and can be used to load search results directly from the specified `.csv` file located in `$SPLUNK_HOME/var/run/splunk`. The `inputcsv` command does not upload the data on Splunk; it fetches it directly from the `.csv` file and loads the result.

Following is the syntax for the `inputcsv` command:

```
|inputcsv
    dispatch=true / false
```

```
append=true / false
events=true / false
filename
```

A parameter description of the preceding query is as follows:

- dispatch: If the dispatch parameter is set to true, then Splunk looks for the .csv file in the dispatch directory, that is, $SPLUNK_HOME/var/run/splunk/dispatch/<job id>/. The default value for the dispatch parameter is false.

- append: The append parameter, if set to true, appends the data from the .csv file to the current result set. The default value for this parameter is false.

- events: If the events parameter is set to true, then the content loaded from the .csv file is available as events in Splunk where timeline, fields, and so on will be visible as if the file is uploaded on Splunk. Generally, for the CSV file to get loaded as events, a timestamp is required in the file.

- filename: The name of the CSV file. Splunk first searches for the filename. If it does not exist, it searches for the .csv filename. So, this means if the file exists but does not have a .csv extension, that file will still get loaded using the inputcsv command.

An inputcsv query looks like the one shown following:

```
| inputcsv TestCSV
```

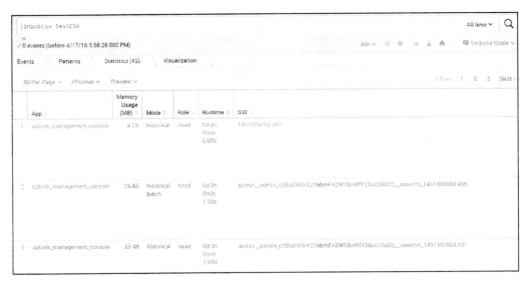

As shown in the preceding screenshot, the `TestCSV` file gets loaded into Splunk using the `inputcsv` command from `$SPLUNK_HOME/var/run/splunk` as the `dispatch` parameter is not set and by default it is `false`.

The outputcsv command

The `outputcsv` command of Splunk works exactly opposite to the `inputcsv` command. This command exports the results into a `.csv` file at `$SPLUNK_HOME/var/run/splunk`.

The syntax for the `outputcsv` command is as follows:

```
Outputcsv
        append=true / false
        create_empty=true / false
        dispatch=true / false
        singlefile=true / false
        filename
```

The parameter description for the `ouputcsv` command is as follows:

- `append`: If append is set to `true`, then the results are appended to the file if it exists or a new file is created. If there is a pre-existing file and it has headers, then headers are omitted during appending. The default value for this parameter is `false`.

- `create_empty`: In a scenario when there is no result and this parameter is set to `true`, then Splunk creates an empty file with the name specified. If append and `create_empty` are set to `false` and there is no result, then in this case, any pre-existing files will be deleted.

- `dispatch`: If set to `true`, then the output will be saved in the `dispatch` directory, that is, `$SPLUNK_HOME/var/run/splunk/dispatch/<job id>/`.

- `singlefile`: If this parameter is set to `true` and the result is in multiple files, then Splunk collapses the output in one single file.

- `filename`: Name of the file in which the result is to be stored.

Refer to the following example of the `outputcsv` command:

```
index=_internal | top component cumulative_hits | outputcsv ResultCSV
```

The preceding Splunk query will output the result of the query in to a filename, `ResultCSV`, which will be stored at `$SPLUNK_HOME/var/run/splunk`.

Summary

In this chapter, you studied Visualization using examples and gained in-depth knowledge on using the important search commands needed for data manipulation, searching, and basic analysis on the uploaded data. Now, in the next chapter, you will study with practical examples and illustrations, how to use advanced analytics commands.

5
Advanced Data Analytics

This chapter will take you through important advanced data analytics commands to create reports, detect anomalies, and correlate the data. You will also go through the commands for predicting, trending, and machine learning on Splunk. This chapter will illustrate with examples the usage of advanced analytics commands to be run on Splunk to get detailed insight on the data.

In this chapter, we will cover the following topics:

- Reports
- Geography and location
- Anomalies
- Prediction and trending
- Correlation
- Machine learning

Reports

You will now learn reporting commands that are used to format the data so that it can be visualized using various visualizations available on Splunk. Reporting commands are transforming commands that transform event data returned by searches in tables that can be used for visualizations.

The makecontinuous command

The Splunk command `makecontinuous` is used to make x-axis field continuous to plot it for visualization. This command adds empty buckets for the period where no data is available. Once the specified field is made continuous, then `charts/stats/timechart` commands can be used for graphical visualizations.

The syntax for the `makecontinuous` command is as follows:

```
... | makecontinous
    Field_name
    bin_options
```

The parameter description of the `makecontinuous` command is as follows:

- `Field_name`: The name of the field that is to be plotted on the x axis can be specified.
- `Bin_Options`: This parameter can be used to specify the options for discretization. This is a required parameter and can have values such as `bins` / `span` / `start-end`. The options can be described as follows:
  - `bins`: This parameter is used to specify the number of bins in which the data is to be discretize.
  - `span`: This parameter is used to specify the size of the bin based on time or log-based span.
  - `start-end`: This parameter is used to define the maximum and minimum size of the bins for discretization.

Refer to the following example for better clarity:

```
| inputcsv datanse.csv |eval _time=strptime (date, "%e-%b-%y") | table
_time DAX | makecontinuous span=1w DAX
```

The following screenshot describes the `makecontinuous` command:

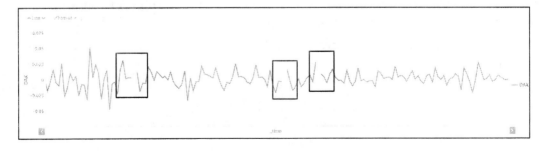

The preceding screenshot shows the output of the search result on the Splunk web console under the **Visualization** tab. The following screenshot shows the output of the same result under the **Statistics** tab:

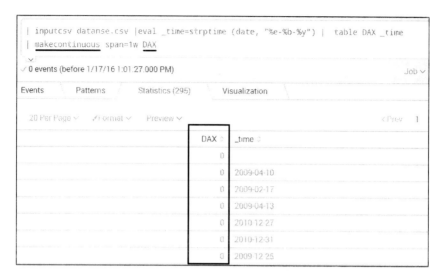

The preceding example output graph shows how there are breaks in the line chart when there is non-continuous data. So, the makecontinuous command adds empty bins for the period when no data is available, thus making the graph continuous. The second tabular image shows the time field along with the **DAX** field, which is specified to be made continuous and has values of 0. The span parameter is set to one week (1w), which is basically the size/range of the bin created to make the data continuous.

The addtotals command

The Splunk addtotals command is used to compute the total of all the numeric fields or of the specified numeric fields for all the events in the result. The total value of numeric fields can either be calculated for all the rows, for all the columns, or for both of all the events.

The syntax for the addtotals command is as follows:

```
... | addtotals
    row=true / false
```

```
col=true / false
labelfield=Field_name
label=Label_name
fieldname=Fieldnames/ Field_list
```

Refer to the following list for parameter description about the options of the `addtotals` command:

- `row`: The default value for this argument is `true`, which means that when the `addtotals` command is used, it will result in calculating the sum of all the rows or for the specified `field_list` for all the events. The result will be stored in a new field named as `Total` by default or can be specified in the `fieldname` parameter. Since the default value is `true`, this parameter is used when the total of each row is not required. In that case, this parameter will be set to `false`.

- `col`: This parameter, if set to `true`, will create a new event called the summary event at the bottom of the list of events. This parameter results in the sum of column totals in a table. The default value for this parameter is `false`.

- `labelfield`: The `Field_name` can be specified to the newly created field for the column total. This field is used when the `col` parameter is set to `true` to override the field name of the summary field with the user specified `field_name`.

- `label`: The `label_name` can be specified to name the field for row total, which, by default, has `label_name` as `total` with the user-specified fieldname.

- `fieldname`: The list of `fieldnames`/`field_list` delimited by a space for which the sum is to be calculated is specified in this parameter. If this parameter is not specified, then the total of all the numeric fields is calculated.

Take a look at the following example of the `addtotals` command:

```
|inputcsv datanse.csv | table EM EU | addtotals col=true
```

The output of the preceding query will be similar to the following screenshot:

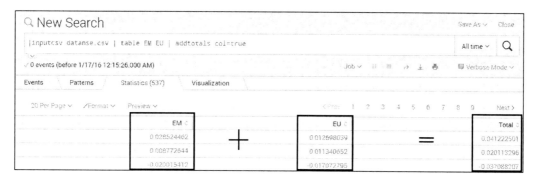

The Splunk `addtotals` command computed the arithmetic total of fields (EM and EU) and resulted in the fieldname **Total**. The parameter `col` is set to `true`, which means each column total is also calculated and resulted in the output.

The xyseries command

The Splunk `xyseries` command is used to convert the data into a format that is Splunk visualization compatible. In other words, the data will be converted into a format such that the tabular data can be visualized using various visualization formats such as line chart, bar graph, area chart, pie chart, scatter chart, and so on. This command can be very useful in formatting the data to build visualizations of multiple data series.

Refer to the following query block for the syntax:

```
xyseries
    grouped=true / false
    x_axis_fieldname
    y_axis_fieldname
    y_axis_data_fieldname
```

The description of the parameters of the preceding query is as follows:

- `grouped`: This parameter, if set to `true`, will allow multifile input, and the output will be sorted by the value of `x_axis_fieldname`
- `x_axis_fieldname`: The fieldname that is to be set as x axis in the output
- `y_axis_fieldname`: The fieldname that is to be used as a label for the data series
- `y_axis_data_fieldname`: The field or list of fields containing the data to be plotted

Refer to the following example for better clarity:

```
|inputcsvabc.csv |stats sum(Hits) AS Hits by Date UserID Transaction
  | eval temp=Date+"##"+UserID| table temp Transaction Hits |
  xyseries temp, Transaction Hits | fillnull | rex field=temp
  "(?<Date>.*)##(?<UserID>.*)" | fields - temp | table Date, UserID *
```

The output of the preceding query would look similar to the following screenshot:

Date	UserID	Hits	Transaction
1/1/2016	Test123	1	Login
1/1/2016	User512	1	Purchase
1/1/2016	User512	1	Logoff
1/1/2016	User321	2	Login
1/1/2016	Test121	3	Purchase
1/1/2016	User512	3	Login
1/1/2016	Test121	1	Wishlist
1/1/2016	User512	1	Login
1/1/2016	User321	1	Login
1/1/2016	Test123	1	Logoff

The preceding screenshot is the sample data image, which shows the data points on which we will run the xyseries command. The following screenshot shows the output of the search result on the given dataset:

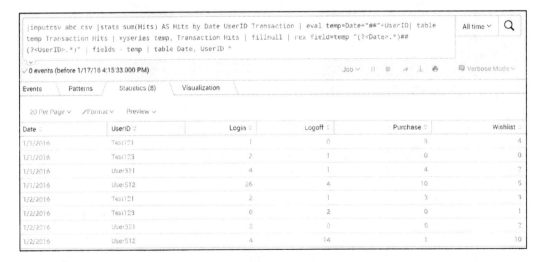

The first screenshot displays the data that is basically logging off the type of transaction and number of hits with respect to **UserID** and **Time**. In a scenario when the user wants a summary of, for example, all transactions done by each user on each date in the dataset, then the `xyseries` command can be used. In the example of `xyseries`, first, the `stats` command is used to create a statistical output by calculating the sum of hits based on `Date`, `UserID` and `Transaction`. Then, a temporary variable `temp` is created using the `eval` command to add `Date` and `UserID` into a fieldname `temp`. The `xyseries` command of Splunk is used to create a statistical output, and then, the temporary variable `temp` is expanded into its original variables, that is, `Date` and `UserID`. Hence, you get the result as required (shown in the second screenshot). Thus, the `xyseries` command can be used to plot data visualization for multiple data series.

Geography and location

Here, you will learn how we can add geographical information in the current dataset by referencing to the IP address, or if the data already has location information, then how that data can be made visualization ready on the world map.

The iplocation command

The Splunk `iplocation` command is a powerful command that extracts location information such as city, country, continent, latitude, longitude, region, zip code, time zone, and so on from the IP address. This command can be used to extract relevant geographic and location information, and those extracted fields can be used to filter and, create statistical analytics based on location information. Let's suppose we have data with IP addresses of users making transactions on the website. Using the `iplocation` command, we can find the exact location and analytics, such as the highest number of transactions done from which state or continent, or in a location an e-commerce site is more popular. Such kind of location-based insight can be derived using the `iplocation` command.

The syntax for the `iplocation` command is as follows:

```
... | iplocation
    allfields= True / False
    prefix=Prefix_String
    IPAddress_fieldname
```

The description of the parameters of the preceding query is as follows:

- **Allfields**: If this parameter is set to `true`, then the `iplocation` command will return all the fields, such as `city`, `country`, `continent`, `region`, `Zone`, `Latitude`, `Longitude` and `Zip code`. The default value is `false`, which returns only selected fields such as `city`, `country`, `region`, `latitude`, and `longitude`.

- **Prefix**: This parameter can be used to prefix a specific string (`Prefix_String`) before each of the fields generated by the `iplocation` command. For example, if `Prefix= "WebServer_"`, then the fields will be `WebServer_City`, `WebServer_Country`, and so on. This command is generally useful to avoid clashing of the same field `name` and also if the `iplocation` command is used on more than one index or sourcetype of different data sources then the `prefix` command can help us identify which generated fields belong to which data.

- **IPAddress_fieldname**: This is the field name in which IP addresses are available. This field can be an autogenerated or extracted field that contains an IP address.

Take a look at the following example:

```
index="web_server" | iplocationallfields=true prefix=VisitorIP_ device_ip
| fields + VisitorIP_* device_ip
```

The output of the preceding query would look similar to the following screenshot:

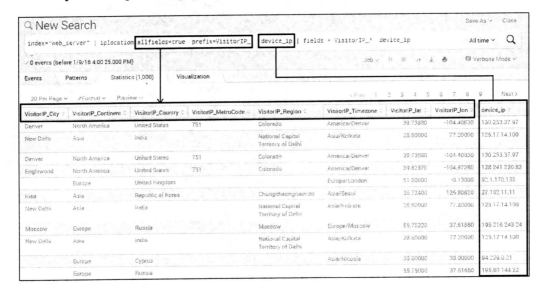

In the preceding example, the `allfields` parameter is set to `true`. Hence, all the fields are generated with the respective IP address. Also, the prefix is set to `VisitorIP_`, and hence, all the fields `city`, `country`, `continents`, and so on are prefixed with the given prefix and the field names are `VisitorIP_city`, `VisitorIP_country`, and so on. The `IPAddress_fieldname` for the preceding example is `device_ip`, which, as shown in the preceding image is the file with the IP address. Also, in the example, the `fields` command, which was explained in the previous chapter, is used to display on selected fields, that is, fields that have `VisitorIP_` as a prefix and `device_ip`. In the preceding screenshot, it can be seen that some fields are not populated for some specific IP addresses. This is because the information is fetched from a database, and it may be that not all information is available for respective IP addresses in the database.

The geostats command

The Splunk `geostats` command is used to create statistical clustering of locations that can be plotted on the geographical world map. If the data on Splunk has an IP address, we can use the `iplocation` command to get the respective location information. If the data already has location information, then using `geostats`, the location can be summarized in a way so that it can be plotted on the map. This command is helpful in creating visualization showing the required information on the map marked at its location. Let's suppose, in our web server data, we can use the `geostats` command to see the count of users doing transactions from all over the world on the map.

The syntax for the `geostats` command is as follows:

```
... | geostats
    latfield= Latitude_FieldName
    longfield= Longitude_FieldName
    outputlatfield=Output_Latitude_FieldName
    outputlongfield=Output_Longitude_FieldName
    binspanlat=Bin_Span_Latitude
    binspanlong=Bin_Span_Longitude
    Stats_Agg_Function... by-clause
```

The parameter description of the `geostats` command is as follows:

- `Latfield`: The fieldname of the field that has latitude co-ordinates from the previous search result.

- `Longfield`: The fieldname of the field that has longitude co-ordinates from the previous search result.

- `Outputlongfield`: The longitude fieldname in the `geostats` output data can be specified in this parameter.

- `Outputlatfield`: The latitude fieldname in the `geostats` output data can be specified in this parameter.

- `Binspanlat`: The size of the cluster bin in `latitude` degrees at the lowest zoom level can be specified in this parameter. The default value for this parameter is `22.5`, which returns a grid size of 8*8.

- `Binspanlong`: The size of cluster bin in `longitude` degrees at the lowest zoom level can be specified in this parameter. The default value for this parameter is `45.0`, which returns a grid size of 8*8.

- `Stats_Agg_Function`: Stats functions such as `count`, `sum`, `avg`, and so on can be used followed by `by-clause`.

Take a look at the following example:

```
index="web_server" | iplocationallfields=true prefix=VisitorIP_ device_ip
|geostatslatfield=VisitorIP_latlongfield=VisitorIP_lon count by status
```

The output of the preceding query would look similar to the following screenshot:

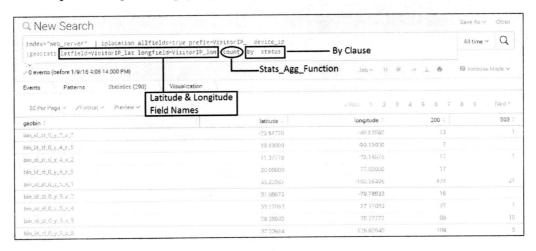

As shown in the preceding example, by running the `geostats` command, the `geobin` field with clusters of latitude and longitude are created. They output the information on the world map. Depending on the data and parameters specified, clusters are created accordingly, and hence, the relevant information that is available in the preceding screenshot as a tabular format can be available in the visualization of the world map. You will learn how to create customized world map visualizations in detail in the upcoming chapters.

Anomalies

Anomaly detection, also known as outlier detection, is a branch of data mining that deals with identification of events, items, observations, or patterns that do not comply to a set of expected events or patterns. Basically, a different (anomalous) behavior is a sign of an issue that could be arising in the given dataset. Splunk provides commands to detect anomalies in real time, and this can useful in detecting fraudulent transaction of bank credit cards, network and IT security frauds, hacking activity, and so on. Splunk has various commands that can be used to detect anomalies. There is also a Splunk app named **Prelert Anomaly Detective App for Splunk** on the app store. It can be used to mine the data for anomaly detection. The following commands can be either used to group similar events or to create a cluster of anomalous or outlier events.

The anomalies command

The `anomalies` Splunk command is used to detect the unexpectedness in the given data. This command assigns a score to each event, and depending on the threshold value, the events are then classified as anomalous or not. The event will be reported as anomalous if the unexpected score generated by the `anomalies` command under the `unexpectedness` field is greater than the threshold value. Due to this, it is very important to decide and specify the appropriate threshold value to detect anomalies in the given dataset.

According to Splunk documentations, the unexpectedness score of an event is calculated based on the similarity of that event (x) to a set of previous events (P) based on the following formula:

unexpectedness = [s (P and X) - s(P)] / [s(P) + s(X)]

The syntax for the `anomalies` command is as follows:

```
... | anomalies
    threshold=threshold_value
    normalize= True / False
    field=Field_Name
    blacklist=Blacklist_Filename
```

All the parameters for this command are optional. Running the `anomalies` command creates the `unexpectedness` field with the unexpectedness score. The parameter description of the `anomalies` command is as follows:

- `Threshold`: The `threshold_value` parameter is the upper limit of normal events. All the events having the `unexpectedness` field value greater than this threshold value will be reported as anomalous.

- `Normalize`: The default value of this parameter is `true`, which means the numeric text in the events will be normalized. In the process of normalizing, all the numeric characters from 0 to 9 are considered identical to calculate the unexpectedness value.

- `Field`: Using this parameter, the field on which the unexpectedness value is to be calculated to detect the anomaly can be specified. The default value for this parameter is `_raw`.

- `Blacklist`: The name of the file located at `$SPLUNK_HOME/var/run/splunk/` containing the list of events that should be ignored while calculating the unexpectedness score.

Take a look at the following sample query:

```
source="outlierData" | anomalies labelonly=false by Strength | table
Strength Latitude unexpectedness
```

The output of the preceding query would look similar to the following screenshot:

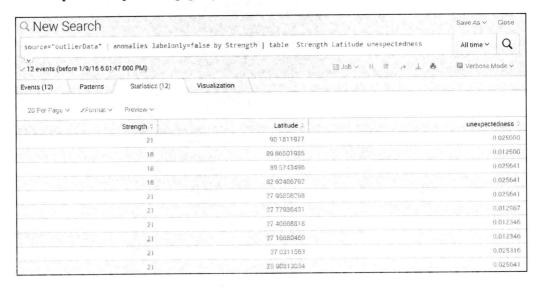

The example dataset is of mobile signal strength with respect to location. The dataset has respective signal strength (fieldname — **Strength**) reported by the mobile device at the given location (fieldname — **Latitude**). The Splunk `anomalies` command resulted in 12 anomalies in the dataset, with their respective unexpectedness value. Thus, using the `anomalies` command can help find out the anomalies in the given dataset, along with the unexpectedness value. The `threshold` parameter can be set to get the result with less or more unexpectedness value.

The anomalousvalue command

The Splunk `anomalousvalue` command, as the name suggests, is used to find the anomalous value from the given dataset. This command calculates the anomaly score for the specified field-list by calculating the frequency of occurrence or by means of standard deviation. This command can be used to find anomalous values that are less frequent or the values that are at a distance from the other values of respective fields of the dataset.

The syntax of the `anomalousvalue` command is as follows:

```
... | anomalousvalue
      action = filter / annotate / summary
      pthresh = Threshold_value
      field-list
```

The parameter description of the `anomalousvalue` command is as follows:

- `Action`: This parameter defines what action is to be taken on the result. If the value of this parameter is `filter`, which is also the default value of this parameter, it will show only the anomalous value in the result. The non-anomalous values are ignored in the result. If the value of this parameter is `summary`, then the result shows the statistical table containing fields such as `count`, `distinct count`, `mean`, `Standard deviation`, `Support`, and various statistical frequencies. If the action is set to annotate, then the result will show a new field containing the anomalous value.

- `pthresh`: This parameter is used to specify the threshold value to mark a value as an anomalous value. The default value of this parameter is `0.01`.

- `field-list`: The list of fields for which the anomalous value is to be outputted. If the field list is not specified, then all the fields of the events will be considered to calculate the anomalous value.

Refer to the following example for better clarity:

```
source="outlierData" |table Strength Latitude | anomalousvalue Strength
```

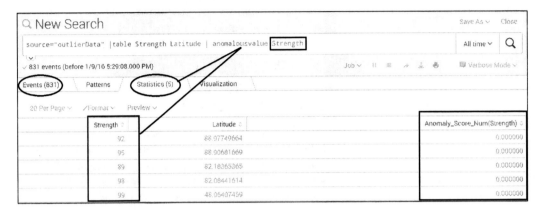

The dataset used for this example is the same as the preceding example of the `anomalies` command. The `anomalousvalue` Splunk command on the strength field, **Strength**, resulted in five events out of a total of 831 events. This means that for the respective `Latitude` values, the corresponding `Strength` value is anomalous in the result. This command also resulted in `Anomaly_score` for the `Strength` field, which depicts the anomaly score of the respective anomalous value.

The cluster command

Clustering is a process of grouping events on the basis of their similarity. The `cluster` Splunk command is used to create groups based on content of events. According to the Splunk documentation, Splunk has its own algorithm of grouping the fields into clusters. The events are broken into terms (`match=termlist`), and then the vectors between events are computed. This command creates two custom fields, one that is the size of the cluster and the other cluster has the grouped events in it.

The syntax of the `cluster` command is as follows:

```
... | cluster
        t = Threshold_value
        field = Fieldname
        match = termlist / termset / ngramset
        countfield = Count_FieldName
        labelfield = Label_FieldName
```

The description of the parameters of the preceding query is as follows.

There are no compulsory parameters for this command. All the parameters are optional:

- T: This parameter is used to specify `threshold_value` to create the clusters. The default value for this parameter is 0.8, which can range from 0.0 to 1.0. Let's say if `threshold_value` is set to 1, that means a greater number of similar events will be required to be placed in one cluster than if the value is 0.8.

- Field: This parameter can be used to specify on which field of every event the clusters are to be created. The default value for this parameter is the `_raw` field.

    - Match: The grouping to create clusters in Splunk is done in the following three ways, which can be specified in this parameter:

    - Termlist: This is the default value for a match parameter that required the exact same ordering of the terms to create a cluster.

    - Termset: An unordered list of terms will be considered to create the cluster.

    - Ngramset: Compares sets of three character substrings (trigram).

Take a look at the following example:

```
source="DataSet.csv" |cluster
```

The output of the earlier query would generate an output like the following:

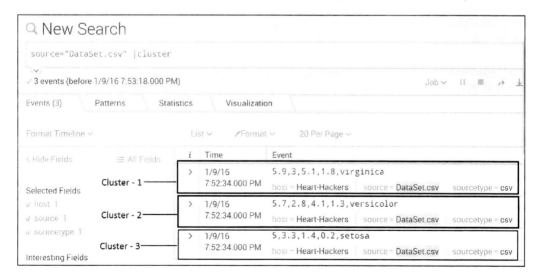

The dataset used for this example contains sepal length, sepal width, petal length, and petal width of three different species of plants. Given the values of sepal length, sepal width, petal length, and petal width their species could be determined. The `cluster` Splunk command creates three clusters, each containing each of the species in the given data. This is a very simple example for explanatory purpose, but this command can be very useful in creating clusters of events with similarities. Splunk provides the `match` parameter, which can be used for different grouping methods such as `Termlist`, `Termset`, and `ngramset`. If the algorithm is not giving accurate results of the clusters, then the threshold value can be set accordingly by proving value to the `T` parameter in this command.

The kmeans command

K-means is an algorithm of cluster analysis in data mining. The `kmeans` Splunk command is used to create clusters of events defined by its mean values. The k-means clustering can be explained with the help of an example. Let's say I have a dataset that has information about Jaguar cars, jaguar animals, and Jaguar OS. Using k-means, three clusters can be created, with each cluster having events of respective types only. Basically, k-means creates a cluster of events on the basis of their occurrence of other events. If event X occurs, then almost 90 percent of the time, event Y also occurs. Hence, k-means can be used to detect issues, frauds, network outages, and so on in real time.

Take a look at the following query syntax:

```
... | kmeans
    k = k_value
    field_list
```

The list that follows describes the parameters of the preceding query.

There are no mandatory parameters for this command. All the parameters are optional.:

- `K`: Specifies the `k_value`, which is the integer value defining the number of clusters to use in the algorithm. The default value of k is 2.
- `Field_list`: List of fields that are to be considered to compute the algorithm. By default, all the numeric fields are considered and non-numeric fields are ignored.

An example of the `kmeans` query looks like the one that follows:

```
sourcetype=kmeans | table Group Alcohol diluted_wines |kmeans k=3
```

The output would look similar to this:

The dataset used in the preceding example is data containing various ingredients of three different alcohols. The Splunk command kmeans creates three cluster (k=3) under the **CLUSTERNUM** fieldname. To verify the result, if the clusters made by kmeans match with the actual group, the **Group** field is shown in the preceding example image. Cluster 1 matches with group 1, and cluster 2 matches with group 2. The kmeans command can be useful in creating clusters as per requirement. Let's suppose we are aware that the dataset is of three different alcohol types but want to cluster it into two groups only. In this case, k=2 can be used in the command. The kmeans command also calculates the centroid of each field and displays it in the result. K-means is one of the efficient algorithms of clustering.

The outlier command

According to statistics, an outlier is an event that is at a distance from other events in the typical distribution of data points. An outlier can be caused due to issues or errors in the system from where the dataset is generated. The outlier Splunk command is not used to find out the outliers, but it *removes* the outlier events from the data. This command removes the outlying numeric values from the specified fields, and if no fields are specified, then the command is processed on all the fields.

The Splunk documentation states the filtering method used in the outlier command is **Inter-quartile range (IQR)**.that is; if the value of a field in an event is less than *(25th percentile) - param*IQR* or greater than *(75th percentile) + param*IQR*, that field is transformed or that event is removed based on the action parameter.

The syntax for the `outlier` command is as follows:

```
... | outlier
      action = remove / transform
      mark = true / false
      param = param_value
      uselower = true / false
```

The parameter description of the `outlier` command is as follows.

There are no mandatory parameters for this command. All the parameters are optional:

- `Action`: This parameter specifies the action to be performed on the outliers. If set to `remove`, then the outliers containing events are removed, whereas if set to `transform`, then it truncates the outlying values with the threshold value. The default option for this parameter is `transform`.

- `Mark`: This command prefixes the outlying value with `000` if `action` is set to `transform` and this parameter is set to `true`. If `action` is set to `remove`, then this parameter is ignored. The default value for this parameter is `false`.

- `Param`: This parameter defines the threshold value for the `outlier` command with the default value as `2.5`.

- `Userlower`: If set to `true`, then the values below the median will also be considered for the outlier calculation. The default is set to `false`, which only considers the values above the median.

Take a look at the following example:

```
source = "outlier2.csv" | outlier action=remove Strength
```

The output should look like that shown in the following screenshot:

source	_time	_raw	Strength ^	Latitude
			Outlier values are removed since action=remove	
outlier2.csv	2016-01-09 17:15:58	31,67.2930291	31	67.2930291
outlier2.csv	2016-01-09 17:15:58	31,67 20949824	31	67 20949824
outlier2.csv	2016-01-09 17:15:58	31,67.14738556	31	67.14738556
outlier2.csv	2016-01-09 17:15:58	31,66.99960019	31	66.99960019
outlier2.csv	2016-01-09 17:15:58	31,66 93177599	31	66.93177599
outlier2.csv	2016-01-09 17:15:58	31,66.84967302	31	66.84967302
outlier2.csv	2016-01-09 17:15:58	92,88 97749664		88 97749664
outlier2.csv	2016-01-09 17:15:58	95,88.90681669		88.90681669
outlier2.csv	2016-01-09 17:15:58	89,82.18365365		82.18365365

Events (831) Patterns Statistics (831) Visualization

20 Per Page ∨ ✏Format ∨ Preview ∨ ‹ Prev

As explained earlier, the `outlier` Splunk command can be used to either remove or transform the outlier values. In the preceding example, `action` is set to `remove` for the `outlier` command on the `strength` field which removes the outlying values from the result. In the preceding screenshot, the last three entries of strength are not available as those values of the strength field were `outliers`. Using this command and setting action to `transform` can transform the outlying values into the threshold limit. Thus, this command can be useful in finding out outlier values for the specified or, by default, for all the numeric fields.

The rare command

As the name suggests, the `rare` Splunk command finds the least frequent or rare values of the specified field or field list. This command works exactly the opposite of top commands, which return the most frequent values. The `rare` command returns the least frequent values.

The syntax for the `rare` command is as follows:

```
... | rare
    countfield=Count_FieldName
    limit= Limit_Value
    percentfield= Percentage_FieldName
    showcount= true / false
    showperc= true / false
    Field_List... by-clause
```

The description of the parameters of the preceding query is as follows.

Of all the preceding parameters, `Field_List` is the compulsory field. The rest are optional and can be used as per requirement:

- `Field List`: This is the only compulsory field of this command is used to specify the list of fields on which the `rare` command is to be run to calculate the rare values. The specified fields or the field list's rare values will be calculated and shown in the results. The field lists can be followed by the `by` clause to group one or more fields.

- `CountField`: This parameter defines the field name (`Count_FieldName`) where the count of rare values is written. The default value for this parameter is `count`.

- `Limit`: This parameter defines the number of results returned by this command. The default value is `10`.

- `PercentField`: The fieldname (`Percentage_FieldName`) in which the percentage values are to be stored can be specified in this parameter.

- `Showcount`: If this field is set to `false`, then the `Count` field is not shown in the results. The default value of this parameter is `true`.

- `Showperc`: If this field is set to `false`, then the `Percentage` field is not shown in the results. The default value of this parameter is `true`.

The sample query should look like this:

```
index="web_server" | rare limit=6 countfield=RareIPCount PercentField=Per
centageRareValuesdevice_ip
```

The above query will generate an output like the following screenshot:

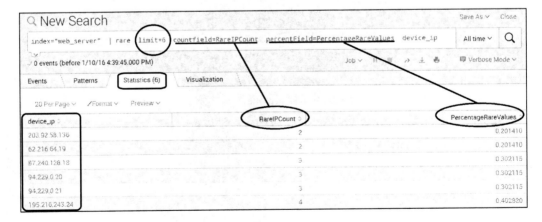

In the preceding screenshot, for the `rare` Splunk command, we have used data that contains visitor information on an Apache-based web server. Using this command on the `device_ip` field with a limit of 6 resulted in the top six rare IP addresses, along with the count (`RareIPCount`) and the percentage (`PercentageRareValues`). Thus, this command can be used to find rare values from the given dataset, along with the count and percentage of their occurrence.

Predicting and trending

The following set of commands are used to predict the future values based on the historic values and pre-existing data sets and to create trends for better visualization of the data. Using the prediction technique, an error or issue that could arise in future can be predicted and then preventive measures can be taken. The following set of commands can be used to predict possible network outage, any device/server failures, and so on.

The predict command

The Splunk `predict` command can predict the future values of time series data. Time series is a set of values in the given dataset over time intervals. Examples of time series data can be data generated by machines as per their daily usage. This can be stock values of any script over the day, week, month, year, and so on. Basically, time series data can be any data that has data points over the time interval. Let's take an example. The `Predict` command can be used to predict the network condition of an LTE network for the next week based on the data of the current month or the number of visitors the website can probably get in the next week, based on the current dataset. Thus, this command can be used to predict future performance, requirements, outages, and so on.

Take a look at the following query block for the syntax:

```
... | predict
    Fieldname (AS NewFieldName)
    Algorithm = LL / LLP / LLT / LLB / LLP5
    Future_timespan = Timespan
    Period = Period_value
    Correlate = Fieldname
```

Only the fieldname for which new values are to be predicted is the compulsory parameter. The rest all are optional parameters. The parameter description of the `predict` command is as follows:

- `Fieldname`: The name of the field for which values are to be predicted. The `AS` command followed by `NewFieldName` can be used to specify the custom name for the predicted field.

- `Algorithm`: This parameter accepts the algorithm to be used to compute the predicted value. Depending on the dataset, the respective algorithm can be used. According to the Splunk documentation, the `predict` command uses `Kalman Filter` and its variant algorithms, namely `LL`, `LLP`, `LLT`, `LLB`, and `LLP5`:

  ○ `Local Level` (`LB`): Univariate model that does not consider trends and seasonality while predicting.

  ○ `Seasonal Local Level` (`LLP`): Univariate model with seasonality where periodicity is automatically computed.

  ○ `Local Level Trend` (`LLT`): Univariate model with trends but with no seasonality.

  ○ `Bivariate Local Level` (`LLB`): Bivariate model with no trends and no seasonality.

  ○ `LLP5`: Combination of LLP and LLT.

- `Future_timespan`: This is a non-negative number (`Timespan`) that specifies the length of prediction into the future.

- `Period`: This parameter defined the seasonal period for time series dataset. The value of this parameter is required only if the `Algorithm` parameter value is set to `LLP` or `LLP5`.

- `Correlate`: Name of the field (`Fieldname`) to correlate with in the case of the LLB algorithm.

An example query for the `predict` query is shown as follows:

```
|inputcsvPrdiction.csv | eval _time=strptime(DateTime, "%d.%m.%Y
%H:%M:%S") | timechart span=10m count(Value) AS Value | predict Value as
PredictedValue algorithm=LL future_timespan=1
```

The preceding query should produce an output like the following screenshot:

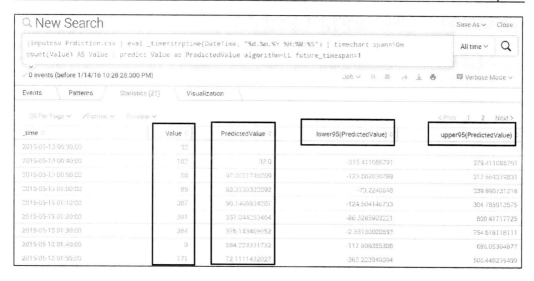

The preceding screenshot shows the tabular (statistical) output of a search result on Splunk web for the `predict` command. The following screenshot shows the same prediction in the visualization format:

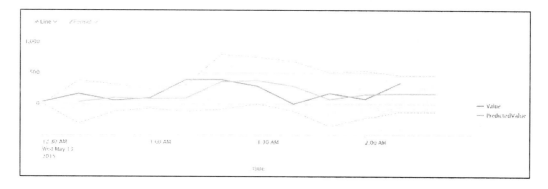

In the preceding screenshot, we used the `predict` command to predict the next 1 (`Future_timespan=1`) value of the `Value` fieldname and the `algorithm` used is Local Level (LL). We have used the `strptime` command to format the date and time (field name — `DateTime`) into Splunk understandable time (field name — `_time`) format. The predict line chart shows the prediction in a graphical format to understand and visualize the predicted result in a better format. Thus, the `predict` command can be used to predict the value of the factor specified. The `predict` command also predicts the lower and upper range of values for the predicted field. This command is very useful in predicting the demand of the product in future, given the historical data, the number of visitors, KPI values, and so on. Thus, it can be used to plan and be ready for future requirements in advance.

The trendline command

The `trendline` Splunk command is used to generate trends of the dataset for better understanding and visualization of the data. This command can be used to generate **moving averages**, which includes simple moving average, exponential moving average, and weighted moving average.

The syntax for the `trendline` command is as follows:

```
... |trendline (TrendType Period "("Fieldname")" AS NewFieldName)
       TrendType = ema / wma / sma
```

The description of the parameters of the preceding query is as follows:

- `TrendType`: The `trendline` Splunk command, at present, supports only three types of trends, that is, **Simple moving average (sma)**, exponential **moving average (ema)**, and **weighted moving average (wma)**.

  SMA and WMA are computed on a period over the sum of the most recent values. WMA concentrates more on the recent values compared to the past values.

  EMA is calculated using the following formula:

  $MA(t) = alpha * EMA(t-1) + (1 - alpha) * field(t)$

  where $alpha = 2/ (period + 1)$ and $field(t)$ is the current value of a field.

- `Period`: The period over which the trend is to be computed. The value can range from 2 to 10000.

- `Field`: The name of the field of which the trend is to be calculated is specified in this parameter. An optional AS clause can be used to specify the new field name (`NewFieldName`) where the results will be written.

Take a look at the following example query:

```
|inputcsvdatanse.csv | eval _time=strptime (date, "%e-%b-%y") |
  trendlinesma5(DAX) AS Trend_DAX
```

The output of the preceding query should look like the following:

```
|inputcsv datanse.csv | eval _time=strptime(date, "%e-%b-%y")
| trendline sma5(DAX) AS Trend_DAX
```

✓ 0 events (before 1/14/16 10:56:17.000 PM)

| Events | Patterns | Statistics (536) | Visualization |

20 Per Page ⌄   ✎ Format ⌄   Preview ⌄   ‹ Prev

	DAX ⌄	Trend_DAX ⌄	_time ⌄
	0.002193419		2009-01-05
	0.008455341		2009-01-06
	0.017833062		2009-01-07
	-0.011726277		2009-01-08
	-0.019872754	0.0077566666	2009-01-09
	-0.013525735	-0.0109004974	2009-01-12
	-0.017673622	-0.01612629	2009-01-13

The preceding screenshot shows the statistical output of the `trendline` command on the Splunk web console, whereas the following screenshot shows the same result in a visualization format:

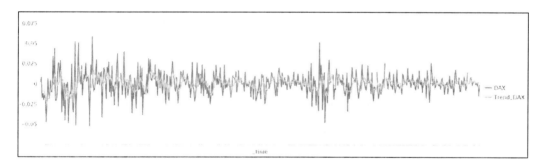

In this example, we used stock index test data. Using the `trendline` command, the moving average of the DAX field is created as `Trend_DAX`. The `trendline` command can calculate different moving averages, such as simple, exponential, and weighted. In this example, we have calculated the simple moving average (`sma`) with period value as `5`, and hence, in the example, you see `sma5(DAX)`. In the visualization, the simple moving average for DAX superimposed with original DAX values can be seen. Thus, the `trendline` command can be used to calculate and visualize different moving averages of the specified field and proper inference can be made out from the dataset.

The x11 command

The Splunk command `x11` is like the `trendline` command and is also used to create trends for the given time series data. The difference is the method that is based on the x11 algorithm to create the trend. The `x11` command can be used to get the real trends of the data by removing seasonal fluctuations in the data.

Take a look at the syntax for the `x11` command:

```
... | x11
    Add() / Mult()
    Period
    Field_name AS New_Field_name
```

The parameter description for the `x11` command is as follows:

- `Add()/Mult()`: This parameter with default value `mult()` is used to specify whether the computation is to be additive or multiplicative.
- `Period`: This parameter can be used to specify the periodicity number of the data, that is, the period of data relative to the count of data points.
- `Field_name`: The name of the field for which the seasonal trend is to be calculated using the x11 algorithm. This command can be followed by the `AS` command to specify the name of the new field, which will be shown in the result with the computed values of trends.

Take a look at the following example:

```
|inputcsvdatanse.csv | eval _time=strptime (date, "%e-%b-%y")| table
_time DAX   |x11 DAX AS Trend_X11_DAX
```

The output generated should be like the one that follows:

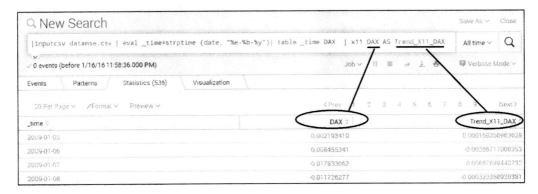

The preceding screenshot shows the output of the x11 command in a tabular (statistical) format, whereas the following screenshot shows the same result in the form of visualization:

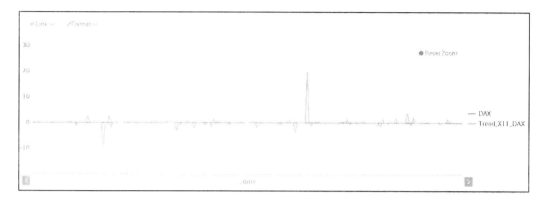

As explained earlier, the Splunk command x11 is used to compute the trends of the data by removing seasonality. The data used to showcase this example is the same as for the trendline command. The output result of both the trendline and x11 commands can be compared as both are commands to compute the trends. The visual difference in the graphs shows how the trends will look like when seasonality is removed while computing the trends.

Correlation

The following set of commands that belongs to the set of the Correlation category of Splunk is used to generate insight from the given dataset by correlating various data points from one or more data sources. In simple terms, correlation means a connection or relationship between two or more things. The set of commands includes associate, contingency, correlate, and so on.

The correlate command

The correlate Splunk command is used to **calculate** the correlation between different fields of the events. In simpler terms, it means that this command returns an output that shows what is the co-occurrence between different fields of the given dataset. Let's say I have a dataset that has information about web server failures. Then, using the correlate command, a user can find out whenever there is a failure what other field values have also occurred most of the time. So, insight can be generated to show that whenever X set of events occurs, Y also occurs, and hence, failures can be detected beforehand and action can be taken.

Syntax for the `correlate` command is as follows:

```
... | correlate
```

The example query should looks like the following one:

```
index="web_server" | correlate
```

The screenshot that follows shows the output of the preceding query:

This command of Splunk does not require any parameters. The dataset used to showcase this example is a test data, having visitor information on an Apache web server. The `correlate` Splunk command resulted in a matrix that shows the **correlation coefficient** of all the fields in the given dataset. The correlation coefficient determines the relation or dependency of the respective fields with each other.

The associate command

The `associate` Splunk command is used to **identify** the correlation between different fields of the given dataset. In general, association in data mining refers to identifying the probability of co-occurrence of items in a collection. The relationship between co-occurring items are expressed as association rules. Similarly, this command identifies the relationship between fields by calculating the change in entropy. According to the Splunk documentation, entropy in this scenario represents whether knowing the value of one field can help in predicting the value of other fields. Association can be explained by the famous bread-butter example. In a supermarket, it is observed that most of the time, when bread is purchased, butter is also purchased, and bread and butter have a strong association.

The syntax for the `associate` command looks like following:

```
... | associate
    Associate-options
    Field-list
```

The parameter description of the `associate` command is as follows:

- `Associate-options`: This parameter can be replaced by the values of `supcnt`, `supfreq`, and `improv`. The output will depend on the use of the respective parameters:

  - `supcnt`: This parameter, having the default value as `100`, is used to specify the minimum number of times the key-value pair should appear.

  - `supfreq`: This parameter specifies the minimum frequency of the key-value pair as a fraction of the total number of events. The default value of this parameter is `0.1`.

  - `improv`: This parameter is basically a threshold or limit specifier for minimum entropy improvement for the `target` key. The default limit is `0.5`.

- `Field-list`: The list of fields that is to be considered to analyze the association.

The output of this command will have various fields, namely `Reference Key`, `Value`, `Target key`, `Entropy`, and `Support`.

Refer to the following example for better clarity:

```
index=_internal sourcetype=splunkd | associate
```

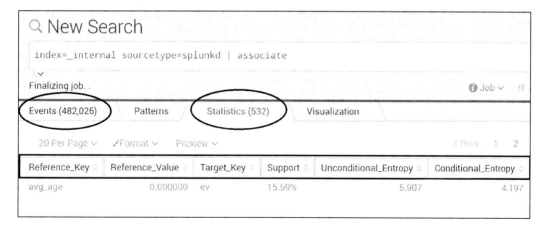

The result of the associate command is quite long horizontally. Hence, the preceding screenshot shows the first section of the result, whereas the following screenshot shows the second section of the result on the Splunk Web console:

Unconditional_Entropy	Conditional_Entropy	Entropy_Improvement	Top_Conditional_Value	Description
5.907	4.197	1.710127	2 (7.32% -> 21.27%)	When 'avg_age' has the value '0.000000', the entropy of 'ev' decreases from 5.907 to 4.197.

In the preceding example, the associate Splunk command is run on the Splunk internal index (_internal), which logs various activities of the Splunk instance, the sourcetype splunkd logs data that is required to troubleshoot Splunk. The associate command on this data resulted in values in fields such as reference_key, reference_value, target_key, Support, Entropy (Conditional and Unconditional), and Description. As shown in the example, the description parameter explains that when the avg_age has a value of 0.0, the entropy of ev decreases from 5.907 to 4.197. Similarly, the associate command can be run on any data to get the associativity of different fields and various parameters to understand the associativity between them.

The diff command

The diff Splunk command is used to compare two search results and give line-by-line difference of the same. This command is useful in comparing the data of two similar events and deriving an inference out of it. Let's say we have a failure case due to a **Denial of Service (DOS)** attack on the web server. Using the diff command, the results of the last few failure cases can be compared, and the difference between those results can be outputted in the result so that such cases can be avoided in future.

The syntax for the diff command looks as follows:

```
... | diff
    position1=Position1_no
    position2=Position2_no
    attribute=Field_Name
```

The parameter description for the `diff` command is as follows:

- `Position1`: This parameter is used to specify the `Position1_no` of the table of the input search result which is to be compared to the value of `Position2`

- `Position2`: This parameter is used to specify the `Position2_no` value of the table that will be compared to `Position1`

- `Attribute`: This parameter is used to specify the `field_name`, whose results are to be compared with the specified `position1` and `position2`.

Following is an example of the `diff` command:

```
index="web_server" | diff position1=19 position2=18
```

The preceding `diff` query should produce an output like that in the following screenshot:

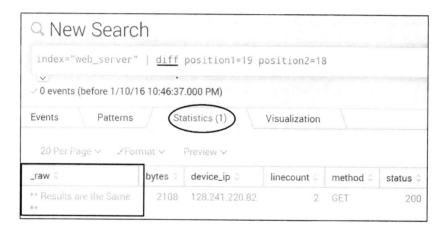

The dataset used for this example is the test visitor information of the Apache web server, which was used in earlier examples. The `diff` Splunk command is used to compare the results of the specified position (in our example, the positions are 19 and 18). The results show that there was no difference between the results of position 18 and 19 for the _raw field as no value was passed to the `attribute` parameter. Thus, this command can be used to find the difference between the results of two positions.

The contingency command

The contingency Splunk command is used to find support and confidence of the association rule and build a matrix of co-occurrence of values of the given two fields of the dataset. Basically, the contingency table is a matrix that displays the frequency distribution of the variables that can be used to record and analyze the relation between two or more categorical variables. The contingency table can be used to calculate metrics of associations such as the phi coefficient.

Refer to the following query block for the syntax:

```
... | contingency
    contingency-options - maxopts / mincover / usetotal / totalstr
    field1
    field2
```

The description of the parameters of the preceding query is as follows:

- contingency-options: The contingency option for this parameter can be any one of the following options. All of them are optional:
    - maxopts: This parameter can be used to specify maxrows and maxcols, that is, the maximum number of rows and columns to be visible in the result. If maxrows=0 or maxcols=0, then all the rows and columns will be shown in the result.
    - mincover: This parameter is used to specify the percentage of values per column (mincolcover) or row (minrowcover) to be represented in the output table.
    - usetotal: If this parameter is set to true, then it adds rows, columns, and complete totals.
    - totalstr: The fieldname of the total rows and column.
- Field1: The first field name to be analyzed
- Field2: The second field name to be analyzed

Refer to the following example for better clarity:

```
index="web_server" | contingency useragent device_ip
```

The following screenshot is the output of the preceding query:

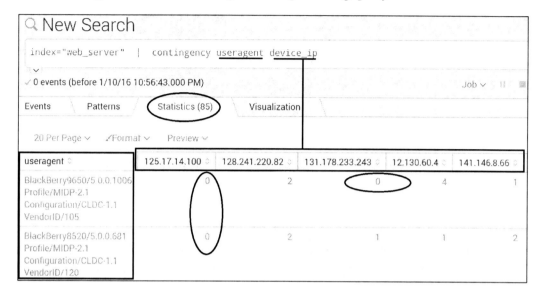

The `contingency` Splunk command is used build a matrix of co-occurrence of the values. The dataset is the same as the one used in the preceding command example. Here, in this example, the `contingency` command on fields (`useragent` and `device_ip`) resulted in the co-occurrence matrix of both the specified fields. For example, from the first row, inference can be derived that all but the first and third users (`device_ip`—`125.17.14.100` and `131.178.233.243`) have accessed the web server from `Blackberry9650`. Similarly, except the first user (`device_ip`—`125.17.14.100`), others have accessed the web server from `BlackBerry8520` and so on. Thus, using contingency, such useful hidden insights can be derived and used.

Machine learning

Machine learning is a branch of computer science that deals with pattern recognition to develop artificial intelligence. The intelligence thus studies and generates algorithms that can be used to make precise predictions on the given dataset. Machine learning can be used and implemented to analyze public interest from social media data and make pricing decisions using data-driven statistics for an e-commerce website. Thus, machine learning can be very useful to track the given data and reach to a conclusion for business decisions. Machine learning can be effectively implemented on data financial services, media, retail, pharmaceuticals, telecom, security, and so on.

You already know the Splunk commands for predicting and trending, but now, you will learn how machine learning can be effectively applied on the data using Splunk and apps from the Splunk app store.

The process of machine learning is explained in the following diagram:

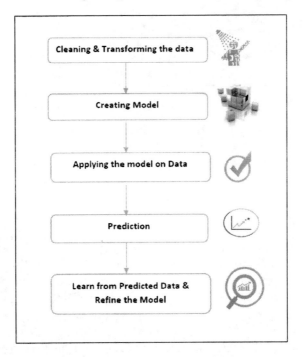

The preceding flowchart can be explained and understood well using the following example:

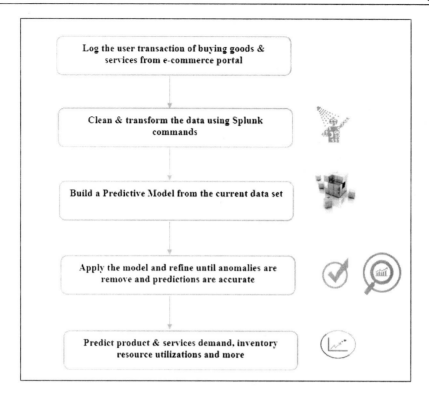

The Splunk machine learning command `fit` (modeling using training), `apply` (learning), and `Summary` (prediction)) can be used to implement machine learning. The Splunk app **ML Toolkit** needs to be installed to implement machine learning.

The Splunk ML Toolkit app provides the end user with the facility to create a model, refine the model, apply to make a prediction, and detect anomalies for better and efficient prediction. The toolkit app has various examples of machine learning implemented using numerical and categorical values.

Thus, using the Splunk app, artificial intelligence about the data can be developed and crucial business decisions can be taken beforehand by predicting the condition based on historical data.

Summary

In this chapter, you learned about various advanced Splunk commands that can be used for reporting and visualizations. You also learned to detect anomalies, correlate data, and predict and trend commands. This chapter also explained about the Machine Learning Toolkit capabilities and how they can be used in implementing **artificial intelligence (AI)** for efficient prediction, thus enabling users to make informed business decisions well in advance. Next, you will learn about various visualizations available in Splunk and where and how they can be used to make data visualization more useful.

6
Visualization

In the previous chapter, you learned various important commands that can be used in Splunk over data. These Splunk commands provide data in a statistical format. Now, in this chapter, you will learn the details of the basic visualizations that can be used in Splunk to represent the data in an easy-to-understand format. You will learn data representation in terms of visualization and along with that, we will also go through how to tweak graphics as per the required format that is more understandable.

The following topics will be covered in this chapter:

- Tables
- Single value
- Charts
- Drilldown

Prerequisites – configuration settings

The Splunk command usually opens the **Statistics** tab by default when we run Splunk search queries over the web console. The following are generic steps to be taken to view the respective visualization on the Splunk Web dashboard. When we run a search command on Splunk, the results are shown in the **Statistics** tab, as shown in the following screenshot:

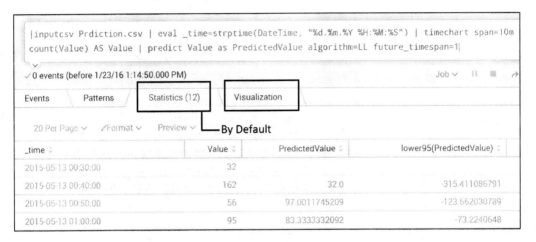

Once the output is available and a statistical command is used in the search query, when we click on the **Visualization** tab, the default visualization will be visible, as shown in the following screenshot. The top-left option, **Format**, can be used to format of the visualization:

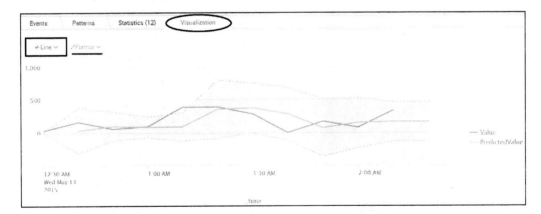

The respective visualization can be chosen from the visualization picker (marked with a rectangular box in the preceding screenshot), which is available at the top-left corner of the **Visualization** tab. The following screenshot shows the default visualization available in Splunk, and apart from the following visualization, custom and advanced visualization can also be added, which we will cover in the next chapter:

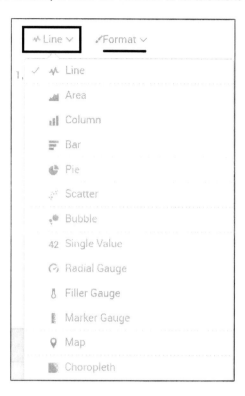

Now, since we are aware of how to choose different types of visualization, as shown in the preceding screenshot, we can start learning which visualization is used in which scenario.

The preceding visualization can be added to a dashboard panel so that we can access **XML (eXtensible Markup Language)** to customize the visualization in a more convenient and required format.

The following are the steps to add visualization as a dashboard panel:

1. Run the Splunk search query so that the result is available in the "**Statistical**" or "**Visualization**" panel on the Splunk Web console.

2. From the top-right corner, navigate to **Save As | Dashboard Panel**. A window similar to following one will pop up:

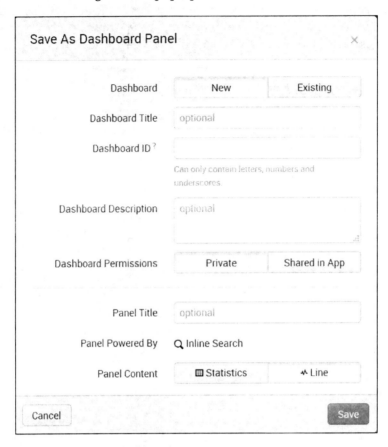

3. Fill in all the details, such as **Title**, **Description**, and **Content**, and then click on **Save.**

4. The next screen will take you to a dashboard, where the search panel with the output will already be available.

5. To customize the panel with the prebuilt options, from the top-right corner **Edit** option choose the **Edit Panels** option. Then, all the respective panels' **Searching**, **Formatting**, and **Visualization** options can be configured.

6. To customize a single panel or complete dashboard with the features that are not prebuilt in the option menu, we need to modify XML. XML can be changed by navigating to **Edit | Edit Source**:

7. In the **Source edit** screen, for each row and for each panel in the dashboard, the search query and formatting options' code will be available. In the section, a new code can be added for the customization. Once the modification is done in the code, click on **Save** to see the changes in the result.

In order to make changes and access values in XML, respective tokens need to be defined and accessed from time to time. The following is the list of comprehensive tokens that can be used in XML of the Splunk dashboard to set or access corresponding values from the visualization:

*   `$click.name$`: This token will return the field name of the leftmost column of the clicked row

*   `$click.value$`: This token will return the value of the leftmost column of the clicked row

*   `$click.name2$`: This token will return the field name of the clicked row value

*   `$click.value2$`: This token will return the value of the clicked row

*   `$row._time$`: This token will return the value `holder by _time field` of the clicked row

*   `$row.fieldname$`: This token will return the value of the respective field name of the clicked row

*   `$earliest$`: This token can be used to get the earliest time specified for the search query

*   `$latest$`: This token can be used to get the latest time specified for the search query

The following screenshot illustrates a necessary example to understand the use of the preceding tokens. The sharp-cornered boxes are values of the round-cornered boxes (tokens):

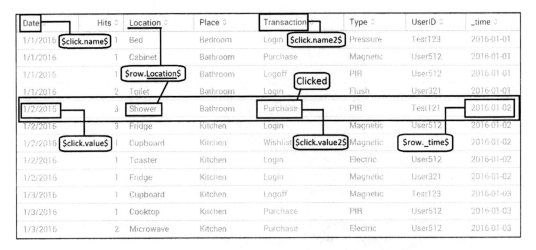

The following are the respective values of the token when the fifth row, **Purchase** (as marked in the preceding screenshot), is clicked as present in the **Transaction** field:

- `$click.name$`: **Date**
- `$click.value$`: **1/2/2016**
- `$click.name2$`: **Transaction**
- `$click.value2$`: **Purchase**
- `$row._time$`: **2016-01-02**
- `$row.Location$`: **Shower**
- `$row.Place$`: **Bathroom**
- `$row.Hits$`: **3**
- `$row.Type$`: **PIR**
- `$row.UserID$`: **Test121**

Tables

Most of the Splunk commands result in an output that is in a tabular format and displayed in the **Statistical** tab on Splunk Web. Now, you will learn about all the feature customizations and formatting that can be done on the tabular output.

Tables – Data overlay

The important point to note here is that the **Table** output is available on the **Statistical** tab and not on the **Visualization** tab. The tabular output is basically a simple table displaying the output of a search query. The tabular output can be obtained by either using statistical and charting functions, such as stats, charts, timecharts, or various other reporting and trending commands.

The following is the list of formatting and customization options available directly from the Splunk Web console in the **Format** option of the tabular output:

- **Wrap result**: Whether the result should be wrapped can be enabled or disabled from here.
- **Row numbers**: This option can enable the row number in the result.
- **Drilldown**: The tabular output can be enabled to drilldown either on a cell level or row level from this option. If drilldown is not required, it can be disabled as well.
- **Data overlay**: The heat map or data overlay can be enabled from the format option of the tabular output.

Let's see how to create a tabular output and format options with the help of the following example:

```
index=* | top sourcetype
```

The preceding search query will search all the indexes of Splunk and return the count and percentage (top) on the basis of sourcetype.

The output of the preceding search query is as follows:

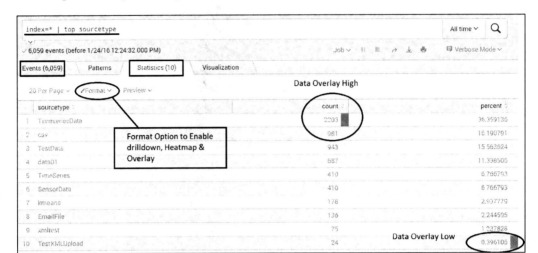

In the preceding example, we enabled row numbers, row drilldown, and low and high data overlay. Similarly, depending on the requirement necessary, formatting and customization options can be enabled and disabled.

Tables – Sparkline

Now, since you've learned how to enable various formatting and customization options, we will see how to show Sparkline in a table output. For Sparkline, we will make use of the `chart` command, as shown in the following example query:

```
index=* | chart count sparkline by sourcetype
```

The output of the preceding search query will result in the count of all `sourcetype` in all the indexes of Splunk. Sparkline along with the `chart` command is used here to enable Sparkline in the given output. The output has **Heat Map** enabled from the **Format** option, and hence the **count** column can be seen with **Heat Map** as shown in the following screenshot:

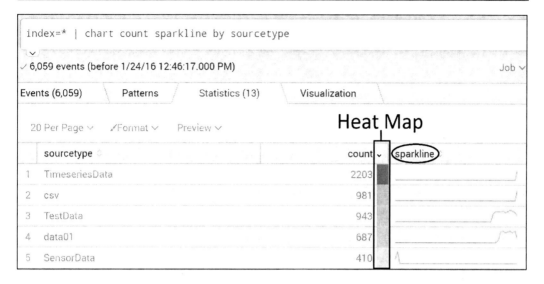

This is the basic Sparkline; we can also create customized Sparklines by modifying XML. The steps on how to access the XML code is already shown in the *Prerequisites – configuration settings* section of this chapter. Now, you will learn how to modify the code for customized visualizations.

Sparkline – Filling and changing color

In the preceding section, we looked at Sparkline. Now, we will see a variant of Sparkline wherein we can change colors and fill colors in Sparkline. Let's see how to do this with the help of an example.

The following code needs to be added in XML to change the fill in the Sparkline and to change the color of the Sparkline:

```
<format type="sparkline" field="sparkline">
  <option name="lineColor">#5379af</option>
  <option name="fillColor">#CCDDFF</option>
</format>
```

In the preceding code, `field` should be the name of the field holding the Sparkline. As shown in the preceding example's screenshot, Sparkline is available under the field name **Sparkline**. The `linecolor` and `fillcolor` option is provided with the HTML format's color code to be applied on the Sparkline.

The preceding code needs to be added to the respective panel of the dashboard, which can be identified using `<title>` or search query in case the dashboard has many panels. The code needs to be added just before the end of `</table>`, as shown in
the following screenshot:

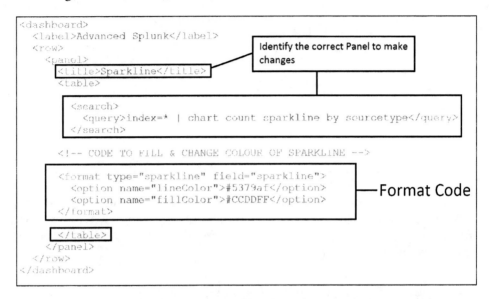

The output of the preceding change in the code is as follows. The color has been changed and Sparkline is filled with the given color. The following output can be compared to the example in the earlier section of Sparkline and the difference can be seen:

sourcetype	count	sparkline
EmailFile	136	
SensorData	410	
TestData	943	
TestMailSample	10	
TestXMLUpload	24	
TimeSeries	410	
TimeseriesData	2203	
_json	1	
csv	981	
data01	687	

Sparkline – The max value indicator

In this section, we will have a look at a Sparkline that has a maximum value indicator. This can help us easily spot the maximum value with the help of the maximum value indicator using Sparkline.

The following code will add a max value indicator to Sparkline:

```
<format type="sparkline" field="sparkline">
<option name="lineColor">#5379af</option>
<option name="fillColor">#CCDDFF</option>

<!-- Max Value Indicator -->
<option name="maxSpotColor">#A2FFA2</option>
<option name="spotRadius">3</option>

</format>
```

The output of the preceding code is as follows:

sourcetype	count	sparkline
EmailFile	136	Max Value Indicator
SensorData	410	
TestData	943	
TestMailSample	10	
TestXMLUpload	24	
TimeSeries	410	
TimeseriesData	2203	
...json	1	
csv	981	
data01	687	

Sparkline – A bar style

XML can be customized to change wave-styled Sparkline into bar-styled Sparkline using the following code:

```
<format type="sparkline" field="sparkline">
  <option name="type">bar</option>
  <option name="barColor">#5379AF</option>
</format>
```

The output of the preceding code is as follows:

sourcetype ⬦	count ⬦	sparkline ⬦
EmailFile	136	
SensorData	410	
TestData	943	
TestMailSample	10	
TestXMLUpload	24	
TimeSeries	410	
TimeseriesData	2203	
_json	1	
csv	981	
data01	687	

Along with bar-style Sparkline, a color map can be used by adding the following code:

```
<option name="colorMap">
  <option name="2000:">#5379AF</option>
  <option name=":1999">#9ac23c</option>
</option>
```

Tables – An icon set

The table element provides us with the functionality of showing icons on the basis of the range of the values of the fields. Let's take an example to better understand the use of an icon set in a tabular output. Suppose the output of a search query results in a few values, and the user is interested in categorizing those values in a range where if the value is between 0-100, then it can be tagged as good, if it is in the range of 100-200, then moderate/average, and if it is above 200, then it is severe. Then, the rangemap command can be used to categorize the values in the output in the required categories. To make the categorization more visual, icons can be added, for example, the good ones are marked with a green tick mark, the moderate ones with an orange triangle, and the severe ones with a red circle. Similarly, depending on the need and categorization, different icons can be used to visualize data in a more reader-friendly style.

Splunk provides users with the functionality of adding custom **CSS (Cascading Style Sheet)** and **JS (JavaScript)** to add such customizations in the output result. Now, we will see how we can get such customization in a table element.

The following is the search query used to explain how an icon set is added to a table element:

```
index=* | chart count by sourcetype | rangemap field=count low=0-
100 elevated=101-1000 default=severe
```

In the preceding search query, the `rangemap` command will categorize the specified value (`count`) to the `field` parameter on the basis of conditions (`low=0-100`, `elevated=101-1000`, and `default` as `severe`).

The output of the preceding search query will be as follows:

sourcetype	count	range
EmailFile	136	elevated
SensorData	410	elevated
TestData	943	elevated
TestMailSample	10	low
TestXMLUpload	24	low
TimeSeries	410	elevated
TimeseriesData	2203	severe
_json	1	low
csv	981	elevated
data01	687	elevated

Now, we will add custom CSS and JS so that instead of range values (**elevated**, **low**, and **severe**), respective icons are shown in the table.

The CSS and JS files need to be added to the static folder for the respective apps' file location, that is, `$SPLUNK_HOME\etc\apps\<app_name>\appserver\static`, where `app_name` is the name of the app in which the `panel/dashboard` is created. In our example, the panel is created in the search app's dashboard, so the path to create custom CSS and JS files in our case will be `$SPLUNK_HOME\etc\apps\search\appserver\static`.

The name of the JS and CSS files can be anything as per the user's needs. In our example, the names of the JS file is `icons.js` and the CSS file is `icons.css`. The names of the JS and CSS files need to be noted and remembered, as they are to be referenced in the XML file. The JavaScript file defines what needs to be done on which fields, and the CSS file holds formatting options such as `color`, `font`, `size`, and so on.

The code of the `icons.js` JavaScript file is as follows:

```
require ([
  'underscore',
  'jquery',
  'splunkjs/mvc',
  'splunkjs/mvc/tableview',
  'splunkjs/mvc/simplexml/ready!'
], function (_, $, mvc, TableView) {
  // Translations from rangemap results to CSS class
  var ICONS = {
    severe: 'alert-circle',
    elevated: 'alert',
    low: 'check-circle'
  };
  var RangeMapIconRenderer = TableView.BaseCellRenderer.extend({
    canRender: function(cell) {
      // Only use the cell renderer for the range field
      return cell.field === 'range';
    },
    render: function ($td, cell) {
      var icon = 'question';
      // Fetch the icon for the value
      if (ICONS.hasOwnProperty(cell.value)) {
        icon = ICONS[cell.value];
      }
      // Create the icon element and add it to the table cell
      $td.addClass('icon').html(_.template('<i class="icon-<%-
icon%> <%- range %>" title="<%- range %>"></i>', {
      icon: icon,
      range: cell.value
    }));
    }
  });
mvc.Components.get('testtable').getVisualization(function(tableVie
w) {
  // Register custom cell renderer, the table will re-render
automatically
  tableView.addCellRenderer(new RangeMapIconRenderer());
  });
});
```

In the preceding JavaScript code, the important things to be noted are the sections that are highlighted. These sections are explained in detail in the following bullets:

- In the top section, icons are defined, that is, the conditions for which icon should be shown in case of a respective category.

- In the middle section, the field name on which the value is to be replaced by icons is to be specified. In the preceding code, the field name is `range`.

- In the last section of the code, we need to set the table ID on which this visualization is to be applied. There can be many tables in a dashboard or in an app, but we may require to apply this visualization in only one table, so we need to specify the table ID. In our case, the table ID is `testtable`. This value is to be noted as it is to be used in the later section.

The code of the `icons.css` CSS file is as follows:

```
td.icon {
   text-align: center;
}
td.icon i {
   font-size: 25px;
}
td.icon .severe {
   color: red;
}
td.icon .elevated {
   color: orangered;
}
td.icon .low {
   color: #006400;
}
```

The preceding CSS file defines the color for each of the icons and alignments. Now, since the JS and CSS files are in place, the following changes are required in the XML of the dashboard holding the table in which the icons are to be displayed.

The name of the CSS and JS file is included in the `<dashboard>` tag of the XML file, and the table in which the range values are to be replaced with an icon is set as the same table ID that we have set in the preceding JS file. In our case, the table ID is `testtable`. The following screenshot shows how the CSS and JS files are included along with the table ID to map the icons in place of range values:

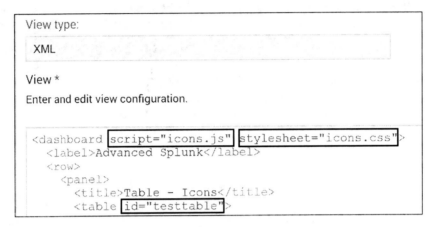

Once the preceding settings are done, click on **Save** and restart Splunk to make the changes effective. Once Splunk is restarted, the `range` field will have icons in place of values, as shown in the following screenshot:

sourcetype	count	range
EmailFile	136	⚠
SensorData	410	⚠
TestData	943	⚠
TestMailSample	10	✓
TestXMLUpload	24	✓
TimeSeries	410	⚠
TimeseriesData	2203	❗
.json	1	✓
csv	981	⚠
data01	687	⚠

Similarly, depending on the need, different levels of customization are possible in the table element output. A row/cell of the table can be highlighted on the basis of field values, data bars can be added in the table output, and so on.

Single value

The Splunk single value visualization is used to represent information or the result of the Splunk command, which is basically a single value that can be a number/statistics/single information on which an inference can be made. Like a single value, visualization can be used to represent a number of errors, number of visitors, number of fraud detected, number of failures, last error occurred, top users, number of invalid accounts, time of last failure, and so on.

Splunk 6.3 has enhanced single value visualization with various functional customizations such as adding trend indicators, Sparkline, labels, and other aesthetic customizations by adding custom CSS. You will now learn how to create single value visualization on the Splunk Web console.

The following is the list of customizations and formatting that can be done on a single value:

- **Single value**: This is the basic one that is by default with no customization and formatting. It will just display the number or text returned by the search query in the **Visualization** tab, as shown in the following screenshot:

- **Single value (label)**: Using the **Format** option in the **Visualization** tab, there are three types of labels that can be applied to describe a single value. As in the following figure, **Before Label (Today Avg of)**, **After Label (Visitor)**, and **Under Label (Avg No. Visitors)** are applied to describe that the single value is depicting the average number of visitors. Similarly, the respective label can be used to describe a single value in order to make it understandable to the readers:

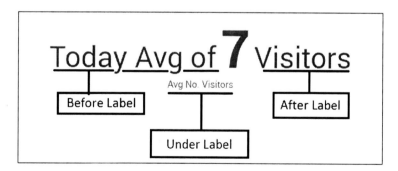

- **Single value (Sparkline and Trend indicator)**: If the Splunk `search` command has a `timechart` command, then Sparkline and Trend can be enabled from the **Format** option. Sparkline and Trend can be formatted using the **Color** option and conditional coloring can also be done on the basis of the value using the **Format** option. The below image shows the single value with Sparkline and Trend indication:

For example, the visitor information data from a test web server is used to showcase how a single value can be used. The following search query on Splunk will return the average number of visitors visiting the web server, and since the `timechart` command is used, trend and Sparkline can also be enabled. Now, this information can be displayed using a single value; you just need to choose it from the list of visualizations, as shown at the start of the chapter.

Our search query is as follows:

```
||inputcsv webserver.csv | eval _time=strptime (date, "%e-%b-%y")
|timechart avg(Visitors) span=7d
```

This query will produce the following output:

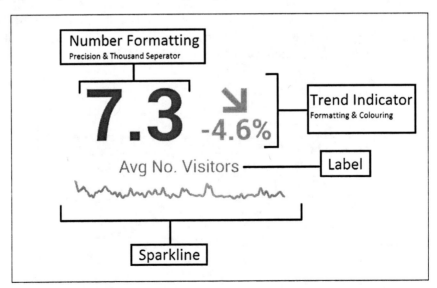

So, single value visualization can be used to depict required information along with trend and Sparkline. Splunk 6.3 gives all the formatting and customization right from the Splunk web console **Format** option itself. Conditional coloring, that is, the color of the value will change depending on the range in which the value lies or on the basis of the trend. The precision and thousand separators can be enabled and configured from the **Format** option.

Charts

Splunk's inbuilt visualization has many types of inbuilt charts such as an area chart, a line chart, bar chart, column chart, pie chart, scatter chart, bubble chart, and so on. Inbuilt visualization can be used depending on the commands used and the type of data. Depending on the data and commands, Splunk shows the recommended type of charts, but users can choose the chart type according to their requirement and suitability to depict information.

Charts – Coloring

The general formatting options for charts are defining a legend and its positioning, custom title for *x* and *y* axis, defining the interval, min values, and max values for the charts which are present in the **Format** option. The chart's **Format** option doesn't provide users with the option to change the color of the charts and their background.

We will now see how to use custom CSS and JS and how colors of charts and their background can be customized.

Our search query is as follows:

```
index=* | chart count by sourcetype
```

The chart type used for the result of the preceding search query is a pie chart, and the output is as follows:

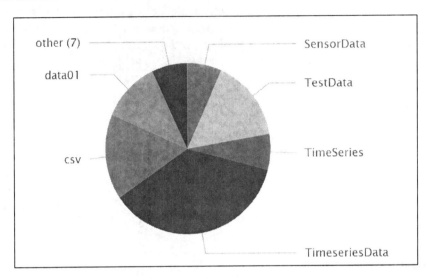

Now, the XML file of the dashboard can be added with the following markup options to make the necessary changes:

- To change the background color of the chart, the following markup option is to be added with the required color in the HTML format:

  ```
  <option name="charting.backgroundColor">#D9EFF1</option>
  ```

- To change the foreground color, use the following line of code:

  ```
  <option name="charting.foregroundColor">#9A5E2C</option>
  ```

- To change the font color (axis labels, legends), use the following line of code:

  ```
  <option name="charting.fontColor">#9A2C2C</option>
  ```

- To change the color to be used in the chart, the following syntax can be used to specify the series of colors:

  ```
  <option name="charting.seriesColors">
  [0xF1F815,0xC2D1E0,0xF4F797,0xFEE000,
  0xFECF00,0xC69D2D,0xED8107,0xED6A07,0xF25805,0xFF9360]</opt
  ion>
  ```

The following will be the output after adding the preceding code. The important point to note here is that the preceding formatting is applicable for all types of charts in the visualization section:

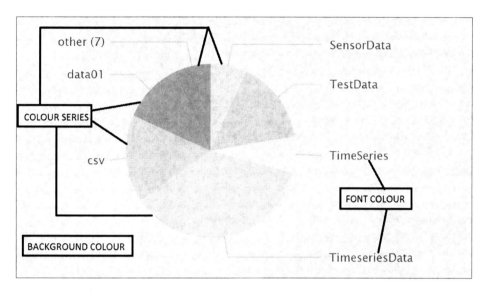

Chart overlay

Splunk provides an inbuilt functionality to define a field that can be used as an overlay on charts. Chart overlays can be used to show bounds/limits in data using a line chart in a bar chart. Using chart overlays, dual axis charts can be made in Splunk. Let's understand this through an example. Our search query is as follows:

```
|inputcsv webserver.csv | eval _time=strptime (date, "%e-%b-%y") |
table _time Visitors LoginFailure LoginSuccess
```

The output of the preceding search query will be a simple table having fields as `time`, `Visitors`, `LoginFailure`, and `LoginSuccess` with their respective values.

The following are the steps to enable chart overlay from the **Visualizations** tab of the Splunk Web console:

1. On the top-right corner of the panel that has respective visualization in which overlay is to be added, click on the **Format** option (the icon with a paint brush).

2. Navigate to the **Chart Overlay** section of the **Option** menu.

3. In the **Overlay** field, specify the field name that is required to be used as a line (overlay) in the chart, and then, the view on the **Axis** option can be set on.

Now, in the following output, the **Visitors** field is used as chart overlay from the **Format** options. Here, the website's visitor data is used and the respective bars show **LoginFailure** and **LoginSuccess**, and the line chart over it shows the number of visitors. So, in the same chart, on the basis of the number of visitors, the number of login failures and success can be found out:

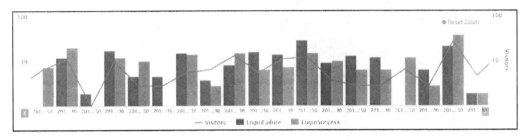

Bubble charts

According to Wikipedia, a bubble chart is a type of chart that is used to display three dimensions of data in one single chart. In the Splunk **Visualization** list, a bubble chart is not available, but using D3 extension, it can be implemented in the Splunk dashboard.

Bubble chart visualization allows us to plot the magnitude of specified fields as the size of the bubble along with categorizing the fields using different colors for each field.

Let's understand how to implement a bubble chart in the Splunk dashboard with the help of an example.

Our Splunk query is as follows:

```
|inputcsv bubble | stats count by UserID Transaction
```

The output of the preceding search query in a statistical format will be as follows:

UserID ⌄		Transaction ⌄		count ⌄
Test121		Login		3
Test121	Categorization	Logoff		1
Test121		Purchase		7
Test121		Wishlist		7
Test123		Login		2
Test123		Logoff		3
Test123		Wishlist		1
User321		Login	Size of Bubble ─◯ 5	
User321		Logoff		1
User321	Colour of Bubble	Purchase		6
User321		Wishlist		4
User512		Login		7
User512		Logoff		6

The bubble chart of the preceding statistical output is as follows. Looking at the following visualization, it can be clearly said that a user (**user321**) purchased six products, added four products in the wish list, logged in five times, and then logged off. Similarly, the bubble chart can be used to make visualizations to derive such insight from the data:

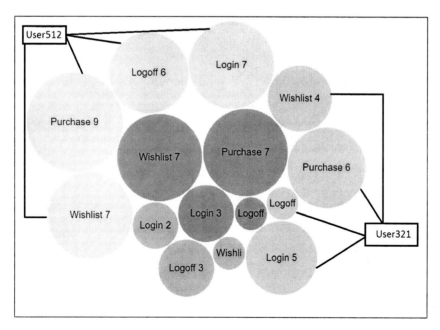

The following are the customizations and scripts to be added to convert the preceding tabular statistical output in bubble chart visualization. We will be using a D3 extension to implement a bubble chart in the Splunk dashboard:

1. First, download **Splunk App Custom Visualizations** from the Splunk App store, which has the important JS and CSS files required to implement bubble chart visualization.

2. Then, copy the `bubblechart` directory from the downloaded app's components folder to the respective app's static directory in which the bubble chart is to be implemented.

   For instance, in our example, all files from the `$SPLUNK_HOME\etc\apps\custom_vizs\appserver\static\components\bubblechart` directory are copied to the `bubblechart` directory of the search app located at `$SPLUNK_HOME\etc\apps\search\appserver\static\components\`.

Now, once the preceding D3 JS and CSS files are in place and Splunk is restarted, we can implement the bubble chart in the respective dashboard,

- Creating an HTML element in a simple XML dashboard and

- Referencing dashboard to use `autodiscover.js`:

  ```
  <dashboard script="autodiscover.js">
  ```

The following is the code that implements bubble chart visualization in the dashboard, and here, we have marked the important things that need to be changed as per the requirements:

```
<html>
    <h2>Bubble Chart - Advanced Splunk</h2>
    <div id="bubbleChart"
        class="splunk-manager"
        data-require="splunkjs/mvc/searchmanager"
        data-options='{
            "search": "|inputcsv bubble | stats count by UserID Transaction",
            "status_buckets": 0,
            "cancelOnUnload": true,
            "auto_cancel": 90,
            "preview": true
        }'>
    </div>
    <div id="bubbleChart"
        class="splunk-view"
        data-require="app/search/components/bubblechart/bubblechart"
        data-options='{
            "managerid": "bubbleChart",
            "nameField": "Transaction",
            "categoryField": "UserID",
            "valueField": "count",
            "height": 450
        }'>
    </div>
</html>
```

Path of JS, CSS & JSON file for Bubble Chart

The important points to be modified in the preceding HTML content of the simple XML are as follows:

- The `div id` and `managerid` values should be referenced correctly to make sure that the search and fields are properly mapped. This is very important, and in case of discrepancies in this ID, the result will not be loaded on the dashboard.

- The search query should be replaced according to the required result in the bubble chart.

- The `data-require` parameter should be properly referenced to the path containing `bubblechart.js`, `bubblechart.css`, and `bower.json`.

- `nameField`, `categoryField`, and `valueField` should be properly referenced with the field names of the output of the search query that we've already specified.

Drilldown

Splunk visualization provides a feature to drill down events by clicking on a cell or row. This feature can be enabled from the **Format** option, and either cell drilldown, row drilldown, or none can be selected from the menu options. The drilldown features help users to navigate to the events and have a detailed analysis and inference of the findings that are derived from the events. Instead of looking at the entire large dataset, the drilldown feature takes the user to the filtered set of events for better insight.

Apart from the cell and row drilldown using custom settings, various other customizations can be brought in the Splunk drilldown feature and more user-interactive dashboards can be built. Now, you will learn how custom drilldowns can be implemented in Splunk visualization. Custom drilldowns include dynamic drilldown, contextual drilldown, URL field value drilldown, and single value drilldown.

Dynamic drilldown

The dynamic drilldown feature in Splunk visualization can be used to control the content filter and the drilldown destination by passing the required information via a click. The dynamic drilldown feature can be implemented to pass an x-axis or y-axis clicked token to a form or destination page and a row or column value/name to populate a form or destination page.

Let's see how to implement the dynamic drilldown feature.

The x-axis or y-axis value as a token to a form

The following is our search query for the line chart visualization:

```
index=* | chart count by sourcetype
```

The output of the preceding search query for the line chart visualization is as follows:

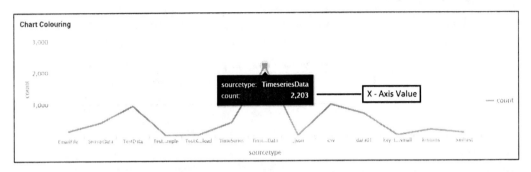

In the preceding figure, if drilldown is enabled, clicking on any point on the line chart will run a search command, showing the events relevant to the clicked data. Now, we will customize that instead of running the search query to show events, and the value that we've clicked on should be sent to a form:

```
<drilldown>
    <link>/app/search/test_form?form.textvalue=$click.value2$</link>
</drilldown>
```

Adding the preceding code in the XML file of the dashboard will navigate you to the test_form dashboard of the search app and will pass the clicked value to the field value that has the textvalue token of the test_form dashboard.

In the preceding example, when we clicked on the y-axis of the line chart, as shown in the preceding figure, it passed the **2203** value to the textvalue input of the test_form dashboard.

Similarly, if the visualization is a bar chart instead of a line chart, the same code can be used to pass the x-axis value to the form.

Dynamic drilldown to pass a respective row's specific column value

The heading sounds confusing, but this can be explained with the help of the following screenshot. Taking reference of the following example figure, when you click on **TestData**, it will pass **943** as the value to the field of the navigating form or search query as a token value. Similarly, for any row that we've clicked on, a corresponding value of the **count** field is passed:

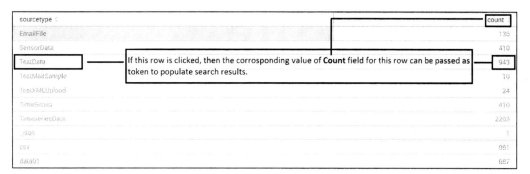

The following code can be added in the respective panel of the dashboard in which this customization is required:

```
<drilldown>
   <link>/app/search/test_form?form.textvalue=$row.count$</link>
</drilldown>
```

In the preceding code, the corresponding value of the **count** field (`$row.count$`) will be passed to the `textvalue` input token of the `test_form` dashboard. If the value of any other field is to be passed, then in the preceding code instead of `$row.count$`, the count can be replaced in the field name of the file whose value is to be passed or used in a search query on drilldown.

Dynamic drilldown to pass a fieldname of a clicked value

The following code will facilitate the use of the fieldname as a value that can be passed as a parameter or can be used as a search query to filter results based on the fieldname of the clicked row or column:

```
<drilldown>
    <link>/app/search/test_form?form.textvalue=$click.name2$</link>
</drilldown>
```

The preceding code can be modified with the following dynamic `textvalue` to get desired results as explained in the following list:

- `click.name2` can be used to pass the fieldname of the clicked row or column
- `click.value2` can be used to pass the clicked value of the row or column
- `row.fieldname` can be used to pass the value of the corresponding field name of the clicked row or column

Contextual drilldown

Now, you will learn how to create an in-page contextual drilldown, that is, drilldown to access contextual information without leaving the page. In this section, you will learn how to pass the required value from a table/chart to another search query whose result will be populated on the same page below the current search result.

Let's first understand with an example what is contextual drilldown, the search query for which is as follows:

```
index=* |chart count by sourcetype
```

The output of the preceding search query will return a count of all **sourcetype** in all the indexes of Splunk. Now, suppose the user wants a scenario where clicking on a **Sourcetype** option shows the events of that respective sourcetype in the same page. This can be done using contextual drilldown. In the following screenshot, the top panel is the output of the preceding search query and the following panel is the result of clicking on **EmailFile** and the following search query:

```
index=* sourcetype=$sourcetype$
```

The preceding code generates the following output:

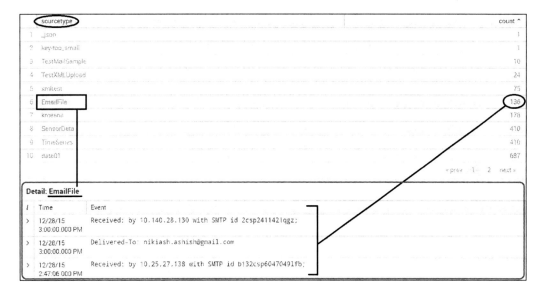

In the preceding example, the clicked value of the sourcetype field is passed as a value to the second search query, which runs on the second panel of the preceding screenshot. Let's see how we can customize a panel to implement contextual drilldown.

The following code needs to be added to the respective panel of the dashboard where contextual drilldown is to be implemented.

First, enable drilldown in the respective panel by adding the following code. The following code enables row drilldown. Then, it can be added in the XML file (the source code of the corresponding panel anywhere after the </search> tag or before the </table> tag):

```
<option name="drilldown">row</option>
```

The following code will get the value in the sourcetype token from the click event:

```
<drilldown>
  <set token="sourcetype">$row.sourcetype$</set>
</drilldown>
```

If the dashboard has any input field and the clicked event value is to be updated in the input field, then the following code can be added using the `form` keyword along with the ID of the input field. If the ID of the input field is `sourcetype`, then the token will be `form.sourcetype`. The following is the example code:

```
<drilldown>
  <set token="form.sourcetype">$row.sourcetype$</set>
</drilldown>
```

Now, the following source code is to be added for the second panel, which is not visible until we click on an event in the first panel:

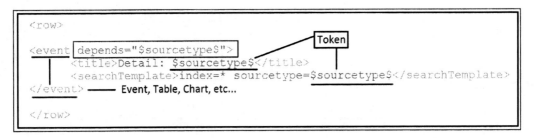

The following are important sections and their use in the preceding code snippet:

- `<event>`: The `<event>` tag describes that the result of search query will be shown in the event format. This can be replaced with a table, chart, or any other type of visualization.

- `depends`: This parameter should be provided with the value of the token. The `depends` parameter describes that the search query will run only when the token is available. If the token value is not available, then the panel will not be visible, since the token value will not be available and the search query will not result in any output.

- `title`: This is optional, but can be used to specify any static or dynamic title. In our example code, we used `$sourcetype$` as a title to have the value of the clicked `sourcetype` dynamically on every click.

- `<searchTemplate>`: This parameter is used to specify the search query whose result will be shown in the output of the second panel when we click on a respective event.

Thus, using the preceding set of code in XML, contextual drilldown can be implemented.

The URL field value drilldown

In this drilldown customization feature of Splunk Visualization, the field value having a URL can be used as a drilldown link. We will now see how to take a URL field value and configure drilldown to redirect users to that site.

Let's understand how to implement the URL field value drilldown using an example. Our search query is as follows:

```
sourcetype=urldrilldown | table _time user referer link
```

The output of the search query is as follows:

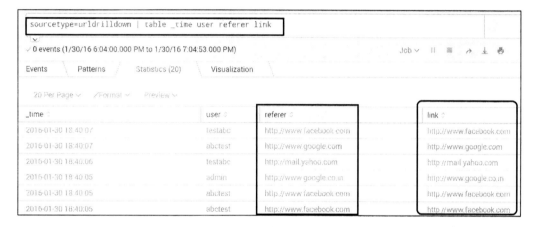

Now, we will customize the **link** field so that the drilldown on any link navigates to the respective URL that was clicked.

Create a new JavaScript file with the `url_field.js` name at `$SPLUNK_HOME\etc\apps\<app_name>\appserver\static`. The content of the JS file is as follows:

```
require([
    'underscore',
    'jquery',
    'splunkjs/mvc',
    'splunkjs/mvc/tableview',
    'splunkjs/mvc/simplexml/ready!'
], function(_, $, mvc, TableView) {
    var CustomLinkRenderer = TableView.BaseCellRenderer.extend({
        canRender: function(cell) {
            return cell.field === 'link';
        },
        render: function($td, cell) {
            var link = cell.value;
            var a = $('<a>').attr("href", cell.value).text("Click to Navigate URL");
            $td.addClass('table-link').empty().append(a);

            a.click(function(e) {
                e.preventDefault();
                window.location = $(e.currentTarget).attr('href');
                // or for popup:
                // window.open($(e.currentTarget).attr('href'));
            });
        }
    });

    // Get the table view by id
    mvc.Components.get('link').getVisualization(function(tableView){
        // Register custom cell renderer, the table will re-render automatically
        tableView.addCellRenderer(new CustomLinkRenderer());
    });
});
```

Annotations in the figure:
- Fieldname containing the URL for URL Drilldown (pointing to `'link'`)
- Text to be displayed in the visualization against the URL (pointing to `.text("Click to Navigate URL")`)

In the preceding JS file, for field name (`link` in our example) and the text (`click to Navigate URL`), which the user wants to be visible on, visualization needs to be modified and the rest of the code can be used as it is.

In the dashboard XML file, add a reference to the JS file, as follows:

```
<dashboard script="url_field.js ">
```

Also, add `id` to the table for a reference using the following code:

```
<table id="link">
```

The output after the preceding customization will be as follows; clicking on any value of the **link** field will navigate you to the search with the actual URL link:

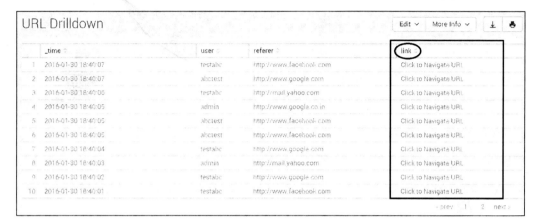

Single value drilldown

There is no option by default for drilldown in single value visualization. You will now learn how to modify the XML of the panel holding a single value to link the other pages or run a search query to show events filtering the single value.

We will see how to add links for drilldown to the single value result, before the label, after the label, and under the label using XML customization.

The following code needs to be added in the XML panel that holds the single value:

```
<option name="drilldown">all</option>
```

The preceding code enables drilldown when we click on a single value result from the dashboard. Clicking on a single value navigates to the search screen with the search query used to derive the single value. This drilldown can be useful when comprehensive information or events are needed. Let's understand this with the help of an example. If the search query results in a number of errors, then drilldown customization can list down those errors.

The following code will be required to create a drilldown for Before Label, Under Label, and After Label:

- For **Before Label**, we need the following code:

```
<option name="linkFields">beforelabel</option>
```

- For **After Label**, we need this code:

```
<option name="linkFields">afterlabel</option>
```

- For **Under Label**, we need the following code:

```
<option name="linkFields">underlabel</option>
```

The following code can be used to see the result:

```
<option name="linkFields">result</option>
```

The following code will be required to specify any search query for `linkFields` (`beforelabel`, `afterlabel`, and `underlabel`). The search query can be specified as per the requirement and visualization/insights required:

```
<option name="linkSearch"> index=* | chart count by sourcetype
</option>
```

Summary

In this chapter, we thoroughly covered basic visualization along with examples and the code that is used to implement the respective visualization. Since you've learned the the basic visualization, such as a table, chart, single value, and various drilldown customizations, let's now proceed to the next chapter to learn advanced visualization so that we are able to showcase data in a better format.

7
Advanced Visualization

You already learned how to create and customize basic visualizations in the previous chapter. Now, in this chapter, we will go through advanced visualizations that can be implemented in Splunk. You will learn how to implement advanced visualizations such as Sunburst, custom decoration, calendar heatmap, and force directed graphs. Many of these visualizations were introduced in the latest version of Splunk 6.3. These advanced visualizations can even be used by a non-technical audience to generate useful insight and derive business decisions.

In this chapter, we will cover the following topics:

- Sunburst sequence
- Geospatial visualization
- Punchcard visualization
- Calendar heatmap
- Sankey diagram
- Parallel coordinates
- Force directed graph
- Custom chart overlay
- Custom decorations

Sunburst sequence

Splunk supports various advanced visualizations, and now, you will learn how sunburst visualization can be implemented in Splunk dashboards and what type of data can be best visualized in a sunburst sequence.

What is a sunburst sequence?

A sunburst sequence chart is sometimes also known as a ring chart. A multilevel pie chart is a chart that can be used to display a hierarchical type of data and its overall distribution in a circular pie chart like visualization. It is a multi-circle chart in which each ring represents a level of hierarchy with the innermost circle as the top level of hierarchy. A sunburst chart having multiple levels depicts how inner and outer rings are related, and a sunburst sequence without hierarchical data looks like a doughnut chart. The sunburst sequence chart is one of the most effective visualizations to show how one ring is distributed/broken into its contributing constituents.

Example

Let's see how we can implement a sunburst sequence in the Splunk dashboard. The data used in this example has a manufacturer (mobile device manufacturer), OS (mobile device OS), and an OS version, as shown in the following screenshot:

Manufacturer ⌄	OS ⌄	Version ⌄
YotaPhone	Android	4.4
YotaPhone	Android	5
Samsung	Android	4.4
Samsung	Android	5.1
Samsung	Windows	7
Samsung	Windows	7.8
Nokia	Windows	7
Nokia	Windows	7.8
Nokia	Windows	8
Nokia	Windows	8.1
Nokia	Windows	10
Motorola	Android	4.2
Motorola	Android	4.4
Motorola	Android	5
Motorola	Android	5.1
Motorola	Android	6
Microsoft	Windows	8
Microsoft	Windows	8.1

Basically, the data has a list of mobile OSes, their manufacturers, and their respective OS versions. Now, we will create a sunburst sequence on this data. The sunburst sequence will look like the following diagram:

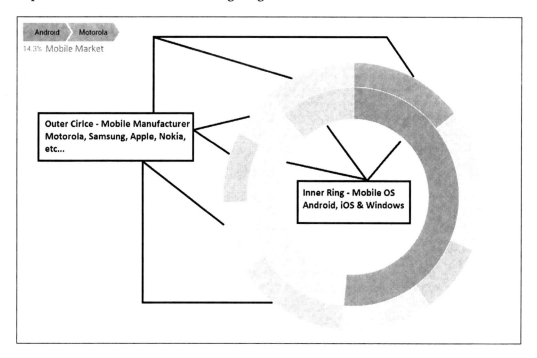

The innermost circle of the sunburst sequence shows the distribution of total mobile OSes, and the next circle (outer circle) shows mobile manufacturers for respective mobile OSes. As shown in the preceding screenshot, the innermost circle is Android. When you hover the mouse over the outer circle, you can see that out of the total mobile market, 14.3 percent is taken over by Motorola. Similarly, hovering respectively on the inner and outer circles will show the market segment on the basis of mobile OSes (inner circle) and on the basis of manufacturers (outer circle).

Some of the insights that can be derived from the above sunburst sequence are as follows:

- 51.4 percent, 11.4 percent, and 37.1 percent of the total mobile market is by Android, iOS, and Windows OS, respectively
- Out of the total Android OS phones, Samsung constitutes only 5.71 percent

So, sunburst can be used for various kinds of data to get such useful insights. Let's now learn how to create sunburst sequence visualization on the Splunk dashboard.

Implementation

We require two fields to create asunburst sequence: `steps` and `count`. Practically, field names can be anything as per the defined user, but the content format should be as required. The `steps` field should have various fields of data separated by "-" (without quotes). In our example, the search query to create the `steps` and `count` fields is as follows:

```
|inputcsv phonedata.csv |stats dc(Version) as count by Manufacturer, OS|
eval steps=OS+"-"+Manufacturer |table steps count | outputcsv MobileData.
csv
```

The preceding search query creates a `steps` field, which has the OS and manufacturer separated by - and a distinct count on the basis of the version. The output of the preceding search query will appear as shown in the following screenshot.

In the `steps` field, the first value will be the inner circle, then the next value after - will be the second circle, and so on. Depending on the number of – available, the respective number of circular rings depicting the data will be available in the Sunburst chart:

steps	count
Android-Acer	3
iOS-Apple	4
Android-Asus	3
Windows-HTC	3
Android-LG	3
Windows-Microsoft	3
Android-Motorola	5
Windows-Nokia	5
Android-Samsung	2
Windows-Samsung	2
Android-YotaPhone	2

The preceding search query outputs the result into a `MobileData.csv` CSV file, which we will use in the search query of the Sunburst sequence. It is not necessary to output the result into the CSV file and then use it in sunburst. This search query can be used in the Sunburst itself, resulting in the same output:

1. First, download the **sequences-sunburst** or **Custom Visualizations** Splunk app from the Splunk app store, which requires important JS and CSS files for Sunburst. There is a slight variation in the JS and CSS files for either of the apps, but the steps and procedure remain the same. We are using the **sequences-sunburst** app as a reference in the following example.

 Sequences-sunburst on the Splunk app store is shown to be compatible with Splunk 6.0 and 6.1 only, whereas it works perfectly fine until version 6.3.3. If there is some compatibility issue, then it is suggested that you use the **Custom Visualizations** app.

2. Then, copy the `components` directory from the downloaded app's `static` folder to the respective app's `static` directory in which the sunburst sequence is to be implemented.

   For instance, in our example, all `files` from the `$SPLUNK_HOME\etc\apps\ sequences-sunburst\appserver\static\sequences_sunburst` directory are copied to the `components` directory of the search app located at `$SPLUNK_ HOME\etc\apps\search\appserver\static`.

   The dashboard in which sunburst is to be added is modified to include `autodiscover.js`, which you have also done in various visualizations learned in previous chapter:

   ```
   <dashboard script="autodiscover.js">
   ```

3. The following code needs to be added in a panel of the dashboard where Sunburst is required. For understanding and readability purposes, I have replaced `andquot;` from the `data-options` tag:

```
<panel>
  <html>
    <div id="sunburst-search"
         class="splunk-manager splunk-searchmanager"
         data-require="splunkjs/mvc/searchmanager"
         data-options="{"app": "search",
                        "search":"|inputcsv MobileData.csv | table steps count", }"
    />
         In data-options tag any quotes (") in between { & } is to be replaced by &quot;
    <div id="sunburst"
         class="splunk-view"
         data-require="app/search/components/sunburst/sunburst"
         data-options="{"managerid": "sunburst-search",
                        "pathField": "steps",
                        "count": "count",
                        "height": 500   }"
    />
  </html>
</panel>
```

4. In the code inside the screenshot, `div id` and `managerid` should be the same. The `data-require` field in the section should be given a proper path of the `components` folder discussed previously.

5. The search query with the proper fieldname should be provided in the `pathField` and `count` parameters of the code in the preceding screenshot.

6. Once all the changes are done, the dashboard can be saved, and sunburst visualization will be visible.

Thus, now, we know how we can implement sunburst sequence visualization on your data on Splunk to generate insights from the data.

Geospatial visualization

The Splunk visualization list has two types of visualizations to show geographical data on maps. **Maps visualization** can be used from the visualization list to show data on the geographical world map. In its version 6.3, Splunk introduced powerful **choropleth visualization** to show more metrics and much more customized data mapping on maps to get insight from the data belonging to the geospatial domain. Choropleth visualization can be used to spot the pattern to sense the complete insight on the data.

Splunk used standard definition to describe the boundaries of colored polygons on choropleth maps visualization. Splunk 6.3 has included countries' maps updated with the latest boundaries and information and 50 states of the United States by default. That doesn't mean that the visualization will be limited to only these two boundaries, but it supports widely used the KMZ format of polygon definition of maps' boundaries and data.

Splunk's choropleth visualization supports one of the greatest features: **point in polygon** lookup. It allows us to map any longitude/latitude combination to any of the polygons in the visualization. This feature, along with choropleth visualization, can also be used in other charts such as bar chart, line chart, and many more.

Example

Let's now learn what all kind of insights and customization can be made on choropleth visualization and how to implement it in the Splunk dashboard.

The geom Splunk command is used to add a geom fieldname to each event defining geographical data for polygon geometry in the JSON format, which can be used to create choropleth map visualizations.

Syntax

The syntax for chloropleth visualization is as follows:

```
... | geom
        Featurecollection
        FeatureIdField=Field_name
```

The description for the parameters discussed earlier is as follows:

- Featurecollection: Splunk supports two feature collections out of the box: geo_countries and geo_us_states. If any other geographical lookups are required for the given data, then KMZ files for the respective locations can be installed and used.

- FeatureIdField: This parameter can be specified with the field_name of the field containing the geographical parameter to be used to generate choropleth map visualization.

Search query

The following search query will use the geo_countries feature collection with featureIdField as country to create the geom field for all the events of data containing the JSON format polygon geometry of the countries listed in the country field:

```
| inputlookup geo_attr_countries | geom geo_countries
featureIdField=country
```

The output of the preceding search query will look like the following screenshot:

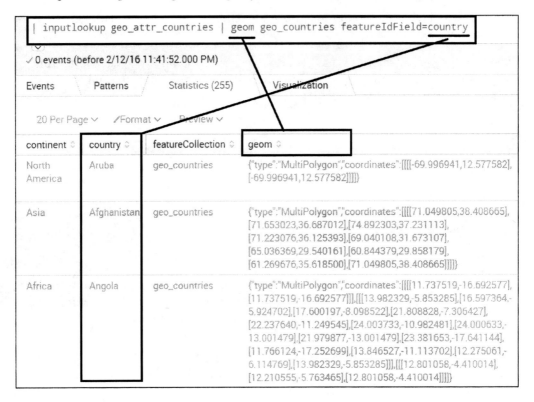

Implementation

The choropleth visualization of the preceding search query will be as follows, showing the **countries of the world** on the map. It uses various color combinations and the legends describing the colors corresponding to the geographical location:

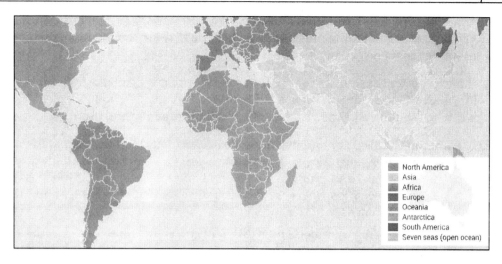

As you have already learned, Splunk 6.3 comes inbuilt with geographical information of the United States (`geo_us_states`). The following search query will plot the data specific to the geographic location of the United States. Similarly, other location KMZ file can be installed, and depending on the requirement, required locations visualization can be made available:

```
| inputlookup states_pop_density.csv | geom geo_us_states
featureIdField=state
```

The visualization of the preceding search query will look similar to the one shown in the following image, with the states plotted on the United States (US) map. The following screenshot displays 50 states of the United States (US) in the choropleth visualization:

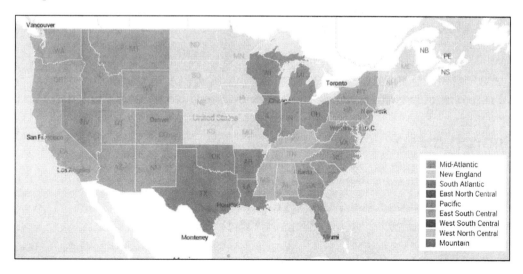

The formatting option on the Splunk dashboard can be used to further customize the choropleth visualization for features such as drilldown, color combination, minimum and maximum zoom level, and so on.

One of the important customizations in terms of color that is available in Splunk is **Color Modes**. Depending on the scenario and requirement, the following color modes can be used to make the visualization more informative and useful:

- **Sequential**: One color and its different shades are used in the map to display the information. This type of color mode is used to show information such as sale of product and traffic to a web portal. Basically, this color mode is beneficial in scenarios where the data is in distribution of variables and can be defined in ranges.

- **Categorical**: This color mode uses different colors for different categories. All the places whose data belongs to the same category will be in the same color. An example of this kind of color mode in visualization can be used by banks/financial institutions to show the transactions across different locations as safe (green), moderate (orange), and unsafe (red) color.

- **Divergent**: This color mode uses two colors and their different shades, converging to a white neutral point. This kind of color mode can be used to show how much a variable is below or above the neutral point.

Punchcard visualization

Punchcard visualization is another advanced visualization. It can be used to show insight from the data, and using those insights, informed business decisions can be made. Punchcard charts are used to visualize data by hour/day/week at the same time. A punchcard chart can be used to analyze the power consumption of a location over the week, sales on an e-commerce portal by hour of the day, and so on.

Example

Let's see how punchcard visualization can be implemented on the Splunk dashboard.

Search query

Here is the search query to be run to get the output that will be required for punchcard visualization:

```
| inputcsv punchcard.csv | eval _time=strptime (Date, "%m/%e/%Y") | eval
day=strftime (_time, "%a") | stats count by day, Transaction
```

The output of the preceding search query in the statistical form will be displayed as shown in the following screenshot:

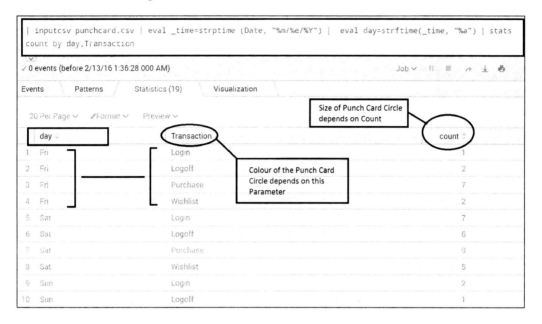

The preceding tabular data, when shown in punchcard visualization, will appear as shown in the following diagram. The size of the circles is proportional to the count (occurrence) of the respective transaction over the distribution of days of the week. The different colors of the circles correspond to different transactions as listed on the right-hand side of the punchcard card visualization in the following diagram:

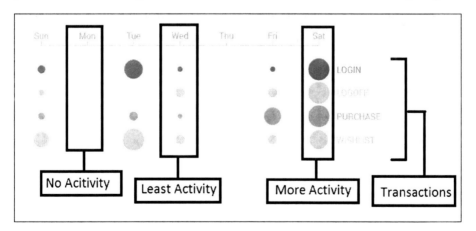

In the preceding punchcard visualization diagram, hovering the mouse on a circle will display the count value for each of the events of the hovered transaction. This functionality is coded in the `punchcard.js` file and can be customized per user requirement.

Implementation

Here are the steps to be taken in the Splunk dashboard to create a punchcard visualization similar to the previous diagram:

1. To implement punchcard visualization, JS and CSS files will be required, and they can be obtained by downloading the *Splunk 6.X dashboard examples* Splunk app from the Splunk app store.

2. Then, copy the `punchcard` directory from the downloaded app's `static` folder to the respective app's `static` directory, where punchcard visualization is to be implemented. Explained in the following are some scenarios:

   ○ For instance, in our example, all files from the `$SPLUNK_HOME\etc\apps\ simple_xml_examples\appserver\static\components\punchcard` directory are copied to the `punchcard` directory of the search app located at `$SPLUNK_HOME\etc\apps\search\appserver\static\components`.

   ○ The JS and CSS files from the preceding directory can be used as they are without any modification. If the user wants any customization with respect to color aesthetics (CSS) and functionality (JS), they can be modified.

3. The dashboard in which the punchcard visualization is to be shown is modified to include `autodiscover.js`, similar to what we have done in *Sunburst sequence* section in the previous section of this chapter. The dashboard script should look like the following:

   ```
   <dashboard script="autodiscover.js">
   ```

4. The preceding search query that we used to create statistical output needs to be defined in the XML code of the dashboard with ID as follows:

```
<search id="search_query">                    Search Query
    <query>
    | inputcsv punchcard.csv | eval _time=strptime (Date, "%m/%e/%Y")
    | eval day=strftime ( _time, "%a") | stats count by day, Transaction
    </query>
</search>
```

5. The following HTML code needs to be added in the `<panel>` section of the XML code of the dashboard to get the punchcard visualization. The `id` used in the preceding search query should be the same in the `managerid` section of the following code:

```html
<html>
    <div id="punchcard"
        class="splunk-view"
        data-require="app/search/components/punchcard/punchcard"
        data-options='{
            "managerid": "search_query",
            "range_values": ["Sun", "Mon", "Tue", "Wed", "Thu", "Fri", "Sat"]
        }'>
    </div>
</html>
```

Path of JS & CSS of Punchcard Visualization

Search Id

Range Values (example - days of week, months of year, time of day, etc.)

6. Modify the respective fields highlighted in the preceding screenshot with the required information and click on **Save**. Punchcard visualization is ready to be visible on the dashboard of Splunk.

Calendar heatmap visualization

Calendar heatmap visualization is derived from traditional heat map visualization where the data is plotted on **Calendar**. Calendar heatmap can be plotted in a way such that, month can be used as a column, days as a row and data points being a data with different colors or shades of color. Calendar heatmap can be a good visualization to display time series data varying across time. According to Google's definition of calendar heatmap visualization, it is used to show activity/transaction over a long period of time, say months or years. It can be useful to display activity trends over time.

Example

Let's now learn what information can be derived from Calendar heatmap visualization, and then, we will look at the implementation of this visualization on the Splunk dashboard.

The data used for this visualization is the test data from the web server. It has the time and count of any failed transaction. The statistical data used to create calendar heatmap is described in the subsections that follow.

Search query

The search query for calendar heatmap visualization is as follows:

```
|inputcsv Calender.csv | table _time Failed_Transaction
```

The output of the preceding search query is shown in the following screenshot:

_time ⇕	Failed_Transaction ⇕
2016-02-13 10:42:00	2
2016-02-13 10:43:00	5
2016-02-13 10:44:00	4
2016-02-13 10:45:00	6
2016-02-13 10:46:00	2
2016-02-13 10:47:00	5
2016-02-13 10:48:00	6
2016-02-13 10:49:00	7
2016-02-13 10:50:00	3
2016-02-13 10:51:00	6
2016-02-13 10:52:00	8

Count of Failed Transaction over time

Now, we will plot this data on calendar heatmap visualization to derive useful insight from the data by just looking at it. The calendar heatmap for the preceding data is shown as follows:

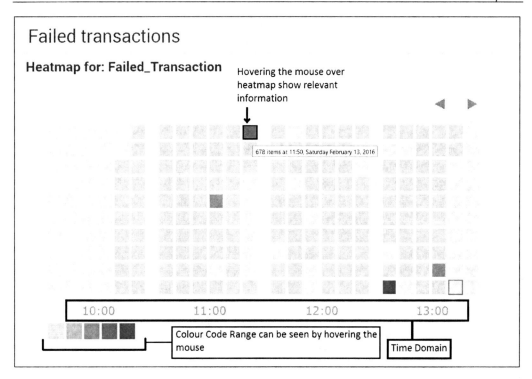

In the preceding calendar heatmap visualization, the failed transactions are plotted over every hour range, and different shades of green color are used to plot the data on the calendar map. The ranges and color legend is available in the lower-left corner of the visualization. On hovering the mouse on the legend, you can see the range of the selected color.

On hovering the mouse pointer over any of the boxes of the calendar heatmap, you can see the number of failed transactions (678 as in the preceding screenshot) and the exact time. Similarly, in the preceding visualization, different shades are seen. The darker shades depict a greater number of failed transactions. So, by looking at this visualization, defined business actions can be taken to avoid unnecessary issues. This kind of visualization will be beneficial to plot the information of 1 month or year and take corrective business decisions.

Implementation

Now, let's learn how we can create a calendar heatmap visualization on the Splunk dashboard. The following steps are required for calendar visualization implementation:

1. Similar to geospatial and punchcard visualization, the `CalenderHeatMap` directory from the downloaded app's `static` folder is copied to the respective app's `static` directory where calendar heatmap visualization is to be implemented. The JS (`calendarheatmap.js`) and CSS (`calendarheatmap.css`) files from the directory can be used without any modifications, unless any customization is required in the visualization.

2. The dashboard in which calendar heatmap visualization is to be shown is modified to include `autodiscover.js`:

   ```
   <dashboard script="autodiscover.js">
   ```

3. The following is the sample code that needs to be added in the panel section of the XML source of the dashboard where this visualization is required. The important parameters that need to be changed as per the data and specific user requirement are marked in the following screenshot:

4. In the preceding code, the search query, path of the JS and CSS files (`data-require`), search ID, manager ID, and time domain need to be customized per user needs. The preceding code will result in the calendar heatmap chart as shown in the **Example** section of **Calendar heatmap**.

The Sankey diagram

The Sankey diagram is a special type of visualization that is used to display flow among systems; many-to-many mapping between groups or set of groups; or to visualize energy, material, or cost transfers between processes. In the Sankey diagram, the width of the arrow is directly proportional to the quantity of the flow. Things that are being connected are called **nodes** and connections are called **links**. The Sankey diagram visualization is quite widely used to derive quick insights from the dataset. Google uses the Sankey diagram visualization to show the flow of traffic from one page to other pages of a website.

The Sankey diagram can be useful to show information such as:

- Flow of money (money earned and spent)
- Flow of energy from source to destination
- Product manufacturing and sale lifecycle

Example

Let's now learn what information and insights can be generated from the Sankey diagram visualization over the data, and then, we will see how we can implement Sankey diagram in the Splunk dashboard.

To create a Sankey diagram, it is required to have fields with fieldnames `from`, `to`, and `count`. The following screenshot is a snapshot of test data that is used for the Sankey diagram:

from	to	count
Home ──────→	Offer ──	16
Home	Order-list	17
Home	Deal-of-Day	24
Home	Checkout	5
Home	Cart	6
Offer	Deal-of-Day	8
Offer	Home	1
Offer	Order-list	4

This describes total 16 users visited offers page from Home Page

When the preceding data is plotted on the Sankey diagram visualization, it looks like the following screenshot. You can see (with the highlighted markings) that a moderate number of people navigated from the **Home** page to the **Offers** page of the e-commerce portal and then moved to the **Payment** page. Similarly, it can be seen that quite a large number of people navigated from the **Home** page to the **Order** list and so on. So, looking at the following Sankey diagram, various inferences can be derived and then an informed decision can be made:

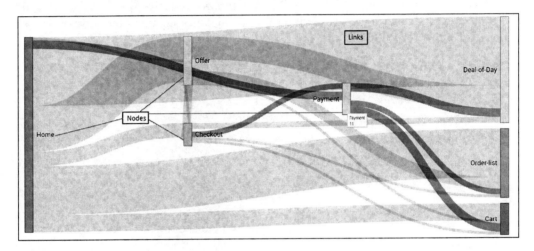

Implementation

Now, let's see how to implement the Sankey diagram visualization on our dataset on the Splunk dashboard.

Follow the given steps to implement the Sankey diagram.

1. We will use the JS (`sankey.js`) and CSS (`sakey.css`) files from the `Sankey` directory of the app's `static` folder. It is similar to what is already described in the `implementation` section of previous visualizations. There is no need to modify the JS and CSS files until and unless any specific look or functional customization is needed other than what is already provided by default.

2. Similar to the previous visualization, `autodiscover.js` is added in the XML of the dashboard:

   ```
   <dashboard script="autodiscover.js">
   ```

3. The following code when added in the dashboard with the respective changes as shown in the screenshot will result in a Sankey diagram, as shown in the example section previously. The search query needs to be replaced with the query that should result in an output having `from`, `to`, and `count` fields necessary to draw the Sankey diagram. The `data-require` parameter should have a proper path of the `Sankey` folder containing the JS and CSS files:

```
<panel>
    <search id="sankey_diagram">          Search Query resulting
                                          from, to & count fields

        <query>|inputcsv Sankey.csv | table from to count</query>

    </search>
    <html>                                Relative Path of JS & CSS
        <div id="sankey"                  file of Sankey Diagram
             class="splunk-view"

             data-require="app/search/components/sankey/sankey"

             data-options='{
                         "managerid": "sankey_diagram"
                    }'>
        </div>
    </html>
</panel>
```

4. The Sankey diagram created after following the previous steps allows us to move the nodes to make the visualization clear and understandable in the case of many nodes and links. On hovering the mouse, relevant information becomes visible, and links connected via the respective nodes get highlighted to make it clearer.

5. Thus, the Sankey diagram visualization can be used in various scenarios to plot data into a visualization describing the path or intermediate steps between the system in the same way we saw in our example, the user behavior on e-commerce shopping portal.

Parallel coordinates

Parallel coordinates visualization is a very powerful tool to understand a multidimensional, multivariate numerical dataset. This visualization works best for datasets with a moderate number of dimensions with around a few thousand records. The parallel coordinates visualization is related to time series visualization. Rather, it is applied on data whose axes do not correspond to points in time.

Parallel coordinates visualization is a very versatile and useful technique to find structures in the given dataset. It can be used to quickly find patterns and the strength of correlation in a mid-sized dataset.

Example

Let's now see what data can be plotted with parallel coordinates visualization and the insights derived from it. Then, we will look at implementing it on the Splunk dashboard.

Search query

The following search query is used for parallel coordinates visualization:

```
index=_internal sourcetype=splunkd component=Metrics group=pipeline
| dedup 2 name, processor | table name processor cpu_seconds executes
cummulative_hits
```

The preceding search query uses the `internal` index where Splunk logs its activity by default, and the result of the search query is as follows:

name ⌃	processor ⌃	cpu_seconds ⌃	executes ⌃
typing	sendout	0.000000	102
typing	regexreplacement	0.000000	102
typing	readerin	0.000000	102
typing	previewout	0.000000	102
typing	annotator	0.000000	102
parsing	utf8	0.000000	21
parsing	sendout	0.000000	102
parsing	readerin	0.000000	21
parsing	linebreaker	0.000000	21

The preceding statistical output can be termed as an informative type of output, as no inference seems to be taken directly by looking at the output. Also, the preceding output is just a subset of the complete result. To derive inference, let's now plot this on the parallel coordinates visualization to understand the data better and in an informative way.

Let's see how the parallel coordinates visualization for the preceding dataset looks. The following image shows four fields (`name`, `processor`, `cpu_seconds`, and `executes`) and their interrelation with each other using different colors/shade lines. Thus, by looking at the following chart, a quick inference can be made that most/all of the processors are taking less (the same) CPU_SECONDS to execute. Also, we can derive inferences such as `indexerpipe` is having the highest number of executes (*150+*) and so on.

Such a kind of inference, and that too very quickly, would have been very difficult if there had been a large number of records to be analyzed in a statistical tabular output. Thus, parallel coordinates can be handy and useful to derive inference and take quick corrective decisions.

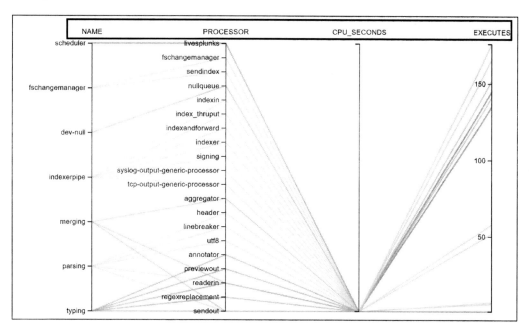

Implementation

Now, since we have seen the dataset and the uses of parallel coordinates, let's see how we can implement parallel coordinates on the Splunk dashboard with users' own dataset.

The following are the steps to be taken for implementation of the parallel coordinates visualization:

1. The parallel coordinates visualization also uses D3 extension similar to what we have already seen in other visualizations such as the Sankey diagram, punchcard visualization, calendar heatmap, and so on. Similarly, we will use the JS (parallelcoords.js) file from the parallelcoords directory of the app's static folder. The JS file needs to be copied to respective apps directly, similar to what we have already done in previous D3 visualizations.

2. We can modify the XML of the dashboard to include autodiscover.js as follows:

    ```
    <dashboard script="autodiscover.js">
    ```

3. The following code is to be added in the XML source of the dashboard to make parallel coordinates available on the dashboard. The search query and the relative path needs to be modified per the requirement to make the visualization work in the user dashboard. Since the dashboard may have more than one visualization, the search id and managerid should be properly mapped:

```
<row>
    <html>
        <h2>Metrics: Pipeline</h2>
        <div id="custom_search"                              Search Query
            class="splunk-manager"
            data-require="splunkjs/mvc/searchmanager"
            data-options='{
                "search": "index=_internal sourcetype=splunkd component=Metrics
                group=pipeline | dedup 2 name,processor
                | table name processor cpu_seconds executes cummulative_hits"
            }'>
        </div>                                          Relative Path of JS File
        <div id="custom"
            class="splunk-view"
            data-require="app/search/components/parallelcoords/parallelcoords"
            data-options='{
                "managerid": "custom_search"
            }'>
        </div>
    </html>
</row>
```

The force directed graph

The force directed graph is a visualization in which the nodes of a graph are positioned in two or three dimensions by assigning the forces among the set of edges and set of nodes based on their relative positions. There are various types of algorithms available to implement force directed graphs.

As per Wiki, force directed graph has the following advantages due to which it is widely used for visualization of various types of datasets:

- **Good quality results**: For a mid-sized dataset, the force directed graph yields very good results based on criteria such as uniform edge length, vertex distribution, and symmetry

- **Flexibility**: Force directed graph gets easily adapted and extended to fulfil aesthetic requirements

- **Simplicity**: It is very simple to implement, and important inference and insights can be derived quickly for relatively larger datasets

Example

Now, since we are acquainted with the force directed graph, let's see an example of the force directed graph. Then, later on, we can implement it on the Splunk dashboard.

The dataset is the same one that we used in the case of the Sankey diagram, which has information about user navigation from one page of the e-commerce portal to the other, along with the count of occurrence.

The subset of the dataset in a tabular format looks like the following screenshot:

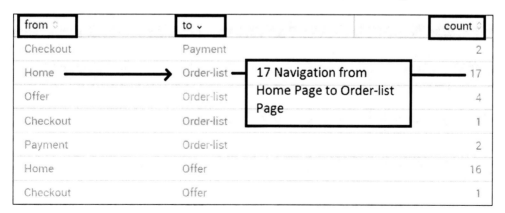

The preceding tabular output when mapped to the force directed graph will look like the following diagram:

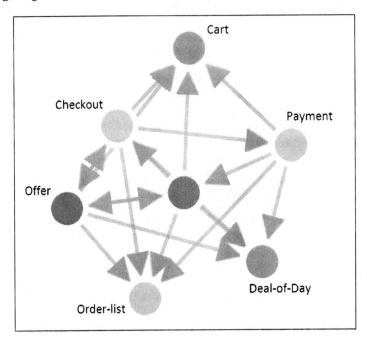

The preceding force directed graph helps a user derive the following inferences:

- The **Cart** page has only inward navigation, that is, users from other pages are navigating to the **Cart** page, but there is no outward navigation from the **Cart** page. Looking at it, the probable issues can be checked as to why users are not navigating from the **Cart** page and tackle it accordingly.

- Users are navigating to the **Order-list** page from the **Offer, Checkout, Payment**, and **Home** pages, which means that either user is trying to check the status of the order already placed or it may also happen that user is not able to locate the order in the order list. Similarly, such kinds of hidden insights can be quickly derived by just looking at the visualization of the force directed graph. This can be used on relatively large datasets, and hence, it is very useful.

Implementation

Now, let's have a look at how we can implement the force directed graph on the Splunk dashboard.

The following are the steps to be taken in the Splunk dashboard to create a force directed visualization similar to the previous example:

1. The force directed graph visualization uses a D3 extension similar to some of the visualizations already explained. Similarly, we will use the JS file (`forcedirected.js`) from the `forcedirected` directory of the app's `static` folder. The JS file needs to be copied to respective apps directly, similar to what we have already done in previous D3 visualizations.

2. We can modify the XML of the dashboard to include `autodiscover.js` as follows:

   ```
   <dashboard script="autodiscover.js">
   ```

3. The following HTML code needs to be added in the panel of the XML dashboard where the visualization is required. Then, click on **Save** to get the visualization on the dashboard panel:

```
<row>
  <panel>
    <search id="FDirectedGraph">                    Search Query
      <query>
        | inputcsv Sankey.csv |table from to count
      </query>
    </search>

                                          Relative Path of JS File for
                                          Force Directed Graph
    <html>
      <div id="custom"
           class="splunk-view"
           data-require="app/search/components/forcedirected/forcedirected"
           data-options='{
                 "managerid": "FDirectedGraph"
           }'
           style="height: 500px;">
      </div>

    </html>
  </panel>
</row>
```

As in all the D3 extension supported visualizations, the search query and the relative path need to be modified as per the requirement to get the correct visualization on the Splunk dashboard. The previous code snippet results in the force directed graph visualization, which is explained in the preceding *Example* subsection.

Custom chart overlay

You have already learned what chart overlay is and how to create it in a previous chapter (*Chapter 6, Visualization*). Now, we will see how to create custom chart overlay using a D3 extension. Basically, it is an advanced and more customized visualization option of chart overlay.

Example

Let's look at the tabular dataset that we will use to create custom chart overlay. Later, you will learn how to implement it in the Splunk dashboard.

The following screenshot is the subset of the total dataset that we will use to visualize custom chart overlay:

_time	Visitors	LoginFailure	LoginSuccess
2009-01-05	36	5	38
2009-01-06	25	8	32
2009-01-07	29	30	26
2009-01-08	62	3	85
2009-01-09	10	22	10
2009-01-12	29	23	42
2009-01-13	15	2	0
2009-01-14	41	34	36
2009-01-15	1	1	17
2009-01-16	22	8	32

The preceding dataset that has login failure, login success, and number of visitors along with time from a web server will look like the following screenshot when implemented for D3 custom chart overlay. Hovering the mouse over the chart shows the required relevant information. It also shows that behaviors can be customized from the JavaScript code of custom chart overlay:

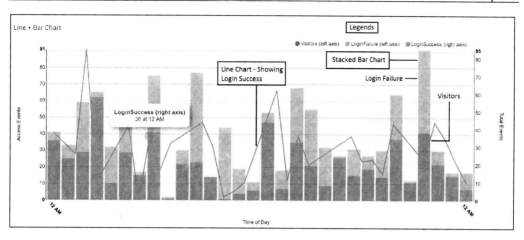

Implementation

The following are the steps to be taken in the Splunk dashboard to create a custom chart overlay visualization using D3 extension similar to one show in the preceding graph:

1. To implement custom chart overlay, a JS (`Custom_Chart.js`, `d3chartview.js`) and CSS (`custom_chart.css`) file will be required, and they can be obtained from the Splunk app, *Splunk 6.X dashboard examples*, which we already used in our previous visualizations.

2. The required JS and CSS files are located at `$SPLUNK_HOME\etc\apps\simple_xml_examples\appserver\static\`.

3. The JS and CSS files from the preceding directory can be used without any modification. In the case of any customization, the respective JS file needs to be modified.

4. The dashboard in which the chart overlay visualization is to be implemented is modified as follows:

```
<dashboard script="custom_chart.js, autodiscover.js"
  stylesheet="custom_chart.css">
```

5. The following code needs to be added in the XML of the dashboard to implement custom chart overlay in Splunk:

```
<row>
    <html>
        <h2>Line + Bar Chart</h2>
        <div id="D3chart-overlay"
            class="splunk-manager"
            data-require="splunkjs/mvc/searchmanager"
            data-options='{
                "search": "|inputcsv webserver.csv | table _time Visitors
                LoginFailure LoginSuccess "
            }'>
        </div>
        <div id="chart2"
            class="splunk-view"
            data-require="splunkjs/mvc/d3chart/d3chartview"
            data-options='{
                "managerid": "D3chart-overlay",
                "type": "linePlusBarChart"
            }'>
        </div>
    </html>
</row>
```

Search Query

Type of Chart

6. The respective search query needs to be replaced with the required query, and the type of chart can also be defined in the type parameter in the preceding code.

7. Click on **Save**, and the required custom chart overlay visualization will be available in the panel of the Splunk dashboard.

Custom decorations

You have learned most of the advanced visualizations that we can implement on the Splunk dashboard along with examples. Now, in this section of the chapter, we will look at how custom decoration can be done on Splunk single value visualization to make it aesthetically pleasing and more informative in terms of using signs/symbols, and color combinations.

Example

Let's look at a few examples of custom decorations that can be implemented on single value visualization, which you have already learned in the previous chapter.

The preceding image shows the default Splunk icons that can be used in a single value to depict specific information. These icons can be made dynamic, and depending on the specified condition, the relevant icons will be shown. This example shows decorations using tokens from search results, HTML panels, and some custom CSS. The icons are displayed using the **Splunk Icon** font.

Let me explain how the preceding customized decorations can be useful. If the single value is used to display information such as **KPIs (Key Performance Indicators)** of a specific field, then depending on the value of the KPI, the respective icon should be displayed.

For example, if the KPI value is between 0-100, that means it is performing well, and the single value should show a green tick. If the value is between 100-200, that means it is performing fine (neither good nor bad). Then, it should show an orange circle with an exclamation mark in the single value visualization. If the range is above 500, then red-cross icons should be visible.

The following image shows the custom decoration along with the single value:

What is the use of such custom decorations?

The most important use of this custom decoration is that it is very informative. The user who is looking at the single value visualization need not remember the threshold of good, bad, or worst range of KPI values. The range of threshold is already coded, so depending on the value, the respective decoration is shown along with the single value.

So, just by looking at the icon, informative or corrective actions can be taken instantly. Thus, custom decoration can be very useful to show relevant important information using custom icons.

Implementation

Now, since we are aware what custom decoration is and how it can be useful along with single value visualization, let's see how we can implement such custom decorations.

Let's first have a look at the CSS (`custom_decorations.css`) that needs to be used to implement this visualization on the Splunk dashboard. Similar to all the above D3 visualizations, this CSS file is also available in the `static` folder of the `app` directory, and it can be used from there.

The following steps need to be taken to implement custom decorations:

1. The XML should include the CSS (`custom_decorations.css`) by modifying it as follows:

   ```
   <dashboard stylesheet="custom_decorations.css">
   ```

2. The following code snippet will result in a custom decoration along with a single value:

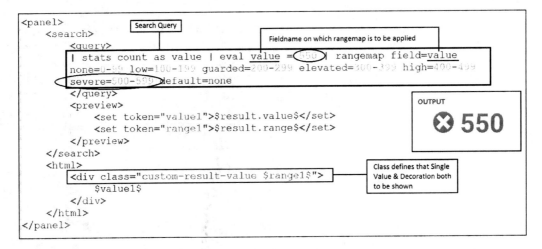

3. In the preceding code snippet, the search query has `rangemap` whose `field` parameter is used to specify `fieldname` (value) on which `rangemap` is to be checked. The value is `500` in the example, which belongs to the severe range (500-599). Hence, the output will be a red cross.

4. In the preceding snippet, the class is `custom-result-value`. Hence, the output has both the custom decoration and the value, that is, `500`, as shown in the preceding screenshot.

5. The class can be set as follows when only custom decoration is required. The value is not required to be displayed in the visualization:

```
<div class="custom-result-value icon-only $range1$"> </div>
```

6. On using the preceding class, the output will be as follows:

7. The definition of all the value used in `rangemap` (`none`, `low`, `guarded`, `elevated`, `high`, `severe`, `default`) are defined in the CSS file, and it can be customized as per need. The CSS uses the *Splunk Icons* font family to display custom decorations.

Similarly, by modifying the CSS and the previous code snippet, required custom decorations can be implemented on the Splunk dashboard.

Summary

In this chapter, you studied the uses and implementation of various advanced types of visualizations, along with examples. Now, we are aware of basic as well as advanced visualizations.

In the next chapter, you will learn about **Dashboard customization** to enable the making of advanced and customized dashboards on Splunk.

8
Dashboard Customization

We have already learned how to create analytics and visualization over the data on Splunk; now, in this chapter, we will learn to create fully customized, dynamic, and user-interactive dashboards. Splunk provides various customizations by default via Splunk Web console, whereas there are various customizations which can be brought into dashboards via some coding tweaks and using external plugins. In this chapter, we will go through various dashboard customization techniques, which can be implemented to make the most of the data on Splunk. We will learn to make more user-interactive, user-friendly, and user-customizable dashboards in this chapter with examples.

The following are the topics which will be covered in this chapter and explained with the help of examples and code snippets:

- Dashboard controls
- Multi-search management
- Tokens
- Null search swapper
- Switcher

Dashboard controls

In this section, we will learn about various control options related to display, input, and panel of the Splunk dashboard. We will learn the use of various dashboard controls, with examples, and then we will also learn how to implement the respective controls on Splunk.

HTML dashboard

We are already aware how to create dashboards on Splunk. The Splunk dashboards are by default in XML format, but Splunk supports the feature to convert the Simple XML dashboard to an HTML dashboard. The features that are not available under Simple XML can be implemented by converting the dashboard to HTML, which is based on the SplunkJS component of Splunk Web framework.

The following are the steps to be followed to convert any simple XML dashboard to an HTML dashboard:

1. On any XML dashboard which is to be converted or exported into an HTML dashboard, click on the **Edit** button.
2. From the **Edit** menu, choose the **Convert to HTML** option.
3. While converting to HTML, two options are available: either to create a new dashboard, which will be the HTML format of the current dashboard with a specified name and description, or to replace the current dashboard with an HTML version.
4. Choose the appropriate option and click on **Convert dashboard**.

The new HTML dashboard is ready to be used on converting a simple XML dashboard into HTML; each of the visualization's layout, definition, and related search queries get separated as follows:

- The layout of Splunk dashboard is converted into Splunk's style, which indicates placement and formatting of items on the page, very similar to Bootstrap's grid system.
- The definition of visualizations or statistical tables is converted into equivalent JavaScript in the HTML dashboard. The converted code for each visualization includes its properties and an auto-generated ID which can later be used to reference the elements of visualization.
- Any search query on an XML dashboard, whether specified for any visualization or for form input, is extracted to be represented in JavaScript. The code for each search includes its properties and an auto-generated ID.

The converted HTML dashboard can be used to implement a custom look and feel by using customized CSS and also custom functionality by using JavaScript. The following are a few high-level customizations, which can be done very efficiently in the HTML dashboard of Splunk:

- Change the layout by creating a highly customized layout of the dashboard panels.

- Implementing customization on pre-existing visualizations on the panels of the dashboard by using custom JavaScript.
- Adding custom behavior on the dashboard panels and visualizations.

Thus, HTML controls and features can be used on the Splunk dashboard by converting the Simple XML dashboard into HTML. Converting the dashboard into HTML helps to remove the limitations of XML and hence customize the dashboard as per requirements.

Display controls

Splunk provides customization options whereby the header, footer, and edit functionality of the dashboard can be set as per the need. We will learn how we can enable/disable various components of the dashboard as per the user requirement. The following is a sample dashboard with all of its components:

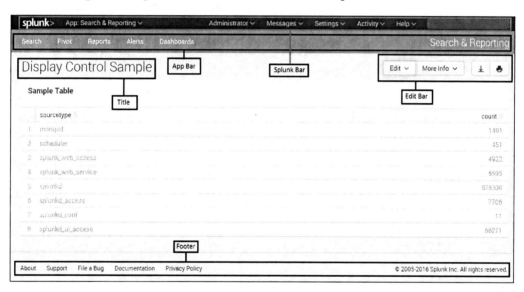

The following are the components of a sample dashboard created in Splunk:

- **Splunk bar**: This bar is useful for navigating applications, **Settings** and **Activity** options, **Messages** and **Notification**, along with Splunk administration settings.
- **App bar**: This bar provides a navigation menu to reach **Search**, **Pivot**, **Reports**, **Alerts**, and the dashboard of the selected app in the **Splunk Bar**
- **Title bar**: The title bar is used to display the name and a short description of Splunk dashboard.

- **Edit bar**: This bar is useful for editing various components of the Splunk dashboard, like title, description, XML source code, permissions, PDF delivery, and various other editing options.

- **Footer**: The footer of Splunk dashboard provides navigation link to **Support**, **Documentation**, and various Internet links of the Splunk portal.

When industry- and business-standard dashboards are created in Splunk, it may or may not be necessary that all the above components are available for aesthetics, security, and user perspective. Let's say the edit bar can be used to edit the search queries of the dashboard but it may not be required by the user to edit the queries. Thus, for security, the prospective edit bar should not be available for the user. Similarly, it may not be required for the user to be able to navigate to the different apps of Splunk or to access the **Settings** menu of the Splunk; then, Splunk bar should not be disabled, and so on.

So to consider this kind of requirement, Splunk provides options to control the various components of the Splunk dashboard as per the user's requirements and needs. All the above components can be enabled or disabled by simple tweaks in the XML source code of the Splunk dashboard.

Example and implementation

Let us see how we can customize various display components of the Splunk dashboard via XML source code modification.

The following are the parameters/attributes which can be used to customize respective components of the Splunk dashboard in XML source code:

- **Splunk bar**: To disable/hide the Splunk bar from the Splunk dashboard, use `hideSplunkBar = "true"`

- **App bar**: To disable/hide the App bar, use `hideAppBar = "true"`

- **Title bar**: The `hideTitle = "true"` parameter needs to be set to hide the title and description bar from the Splunk dashboard

- **Edit bar**: `hideEdit = "true"` is used to remove the edit bar from the Splunk dashboard

- **Footer**: To disable the footer, we need to use `hideFooter = "true"` in the XML source code of the Splunk dashboard

- We can also use `hideChrome = "true"` to hide the Splunk Bar, App Bar, and Footer, instead of disabling each one of them individually

Syntax

The following is the syntax for using the above parameters in XML source code:

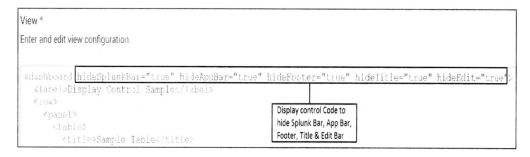

The preceding parameters/attributes can also be used in the form element of the dashboard as the following syntax:

```
<form hideSplunkBar="true" hideAppBar="true" hideFooter="true"
  hideTitle="true" hideEdit="true">
```

The preceding source code will hide Splunk Bar, App Bar, Footer, Title, and Edit Bar of the Splunk dashboard. The following screenshot shows the result of the preceding modification, namely the dashboard without any display components.

Looking at the following output image, it will be difficult to even judge that the result is a Splunk dashboard. This display component is useful when the user is not interested in having Splunk branding on the dashboard; also, this feature proves to be very useful when integrating such dashboards in any third-party applications:

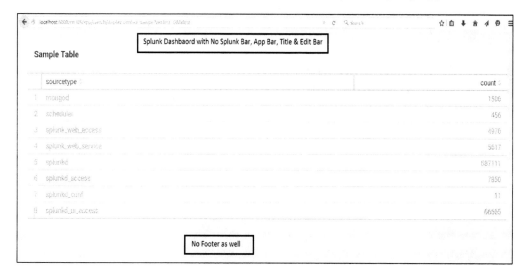

Splunk also provides features to use and modify display control components via the `http get` param. This feature can be used to show a dashboard inside a dashboard, and thus, hiding the display components gives the look and feel of a panel rather than a dashboard inside a dashboard.

The `iframe` feature is used to show the panels of a dashboard inside another dashboard by passing the URL of the other dashboard and passing the respective display components as a parameter in the URL. The following code snippet is an example of a dashboard inside a dashboard in the HTML tag of the XML source code:

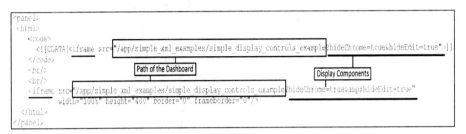

Using the preceding source code and specifying the path of the dashboard in the `src` parameter, along with displaying component parameters, can also be used to display a dashboard inside a dashboard in Splunk, as per requirements.

Form input controls

In this section of the chapter, we will learn about form input controls, which can be used to customize the behavior of form inputs on the dashboard panel. Input controls can be very useful in a scenario where there is more than one input control to control the behavior as per requirements.

Example and implementation

Let us understand the use of form input controls, along with the steps and code snippets to implement them on any Splunk dashboard.

The following are the form input controls that can be implemented on the Splunk dashboard:

- **Autorun**: This advanced form control customization can be configured to auto-populate the input fields whenever the page loads. For example, in the dashboard, there is a dropdown form input; if autorun is enabled, then on the page load itself, the values of the dropdown will be populated. The XML code to enable autorun for the form input field on the Splunk dashboard is as follows:

```
<fieldset autorun="True">
```

- **Submit button**: The Splunk dashboard can have a **Submit** button, which when clicked, will update panels with the updated value of the form input controls on the screen. For example, let us suppose that we have more than one input control, so a user selects the required value in all the input controls and then clicks on **Submit** to get the panels with output as per the value selected from all the input controls of the dashboard. The XML code snippet to enable/disable the **Submit** button on the dashboard is as follows:

    - **Enable**: `<fieldset submitButton="True">`
    - **Disable**: `<fieldset submitButton="False">`

- **Search on change**: This control helps to update the visualizations in the panel of the dashboard as soon as they are changed. There is no need to enable the **Submit** button in this case, as whenever the input control value is changed automatically, all the panels associated with the form input will get updated. For example, let us say we have a dropdown showing a list of error types and below that we have a visualization showing the details of all error types. Now, if the user selects any one specific error from the dropdown, the panel will get updated with the information associated with the selected error type in the dropdown if **Search on Change** is enabled. The XML source code to enable **Search on Change** is as follows:

```
<input searchWhenChanged="True">
```

The following is a sample code snippet with all the previously-explained form input controls implemented. We can see from the following image that autorun is enabled and **Search on Change** is also enabled, and hence the **Submit** button is set to `false`.

If **Search on Change**, is enabled, then the **Submit** button should be set to `false`, or else it will conflict in processing and could result in the component not properly working:

```
<fieldset autoRun="True" submitButton="False">              From Input Controls
    <input type="dropdown" token="username" searchWhenChanged="True">
    <default>*</default>
    <choice value="*">All</choice>
    <populatingSearch fieldForValue="sourcetype" fieldForLabel="sourcetype">
      <![CDATA[index=_internal | stats count by sourcetype]]>
    </populatingSearch>
    </input>
</fieldset>                        Search query to populate the dropdown with sourcetype
```

Panel controls

Splunk is the Google of log data and Splunk is used for log monitoring, security analytics, and so on. In many or most log monitoring scenarios, Splunk keeps on getting live data, streaming data every second. Splunk supports real-time data analytics and visualizations, so now we will learn about the refresh controls of the Splunk dashboard. Splunk provides options for enabling and disabling of auto-refresh and manual refresh on panels on the Splunk dashboard.

Splunk provides the following controls in the context of refreshing panels in the dashboard:

- Enable/disable refresh time
- Enable/disable manual refresh link
- Enable auto-refresh

Example and implementation

Let us understand, with the help of examples and implementation, the uses and differences among all the preceding refresh control options available in Splunk.

Enabling/disabling refresh time

Any visualization or statistical output on any panel of the Splunk dashboard by default has refresh time enabled, namely the panel was last refreshed or the output shown on the panel is older by how much time is shown by default. The following snapshot shows a non-customized single value dashboard panel with **Refresh time** and a **Manual Refresh** option:

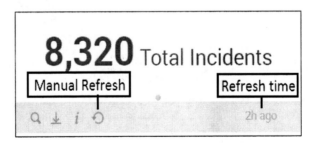

The default refresh time can be disabled by modifying the XML source code of the panel, and once that is disabled, the last refresh time will not be available, as shown in the following image. The default (refresh time enabled) and the following (disabled) image can be compared to see the difference. The placeholder where the last refresh time was available in the preceding image is now empty:

The following code snippet shows an example of a single value in which the refresh time of the panel is disabled:

```
<single>
  <title>Disable refresh time</title>
  <searchString>index= internal | stats count</searchString>
  <option name="refresh.time.visible">false</option>
</single>
```
Code to disable Refresh time from the panel

Disabling the manual refresh link

The manual refresh link is by default enabled and can be seen in the preceding example images. The manual refresh link can be disabled from the XML source code and the output will appear as in the following image after disabling the **Manual Refresh** button. As seen in the following screenshot, the refresh link is not visible, hence manual refresh is disabled:

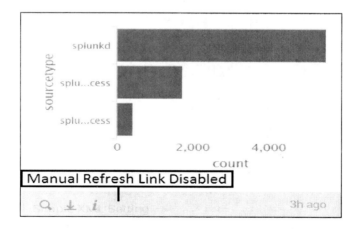

Now let us have a look at the code snippet for the preceding bar chart example to disable the manual refresh link:

```
<chart>
  <title>Disable manual refresh link</title>
  <searchString>index=_internal | top limit=3 sourcetype</searchString>
  <option name="refresh.link.visible">false</option>
</chart>
```

Enabling auto refresh

We have seen how to enable/disable the manual refresh link and refresh time visibility on the panel of the Splunk dashboard. Now we will see how we can create a panel which auto refreshes itself after every specified interval of time. The following code snippet refreshes the dashboard panel every specified interval (30 seconds). The interval can be user-defined as per requirements to get real-time analytics on the dashboard:

```
<single>
  <title>Enable auto refresh of 30s</title>
  <searchString>index=_internal | stats count</searchString>
  <option name="refresh.auto.interval">30</option>
</single>
```
Interval of Refresh

Thus, refresh controls can be used to customize the dashboard with restricting manual searches, enabling auto refresh at given intervals, as required.

Multi-search management

Multi-search management is used to manage multiple background searches to populate the results of various panels of the dashboard. Multiple searches run in the background, and the result of the search query is used to run post-process searches, which utilize the result of the background search to evaluate their own result.

Let me explain what multi-search management is so that you may understand it better. Suppose in the dashboard there are six panels and each panel takes 10 seconds for processing the search results. So for six panels, the time will be 60 seconds. Now, if we have a background search which gets all the data required by all six panels in 20 seconds, then using post-process searches instead of running a search on the whole data, the result of the background search is used and the time is reduced to almost three to four seconds per panel instead of 10 seconds per panel.

Thus, multi-search management can be used in a dashboard which has many panels to increase the speed and efficiency of the dashboard.

Example

Let me explain the uses and advantages of multi-search management in Splunk. In the following dashboard we have a background search that will result in a statistical table with a count of all the types of errors which occurred on a web server. Now as shown in the following image, the single values display the count of various types of errors. The result of the background search, which has stats of all types of errors, is run only once, and then the post-process search filters the required data for the respective search panel and displays it.

In a situation where multi-search management is not used for cases like the following, then for each panel there is a search executed on the target data, resulting in latency:

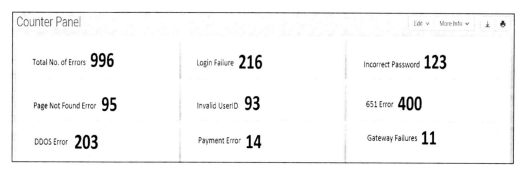

In a real-world scenario, it took close to 40-45 seconds to get the results populated in all the panels of the preceding example when multi-search management was used, whereas in case of a simple dashboard with multi-search the time was around two and a half to three minutes and thus, multi-search management proves to be efficient in real time than not using it.

To summarize, the following are the advantages of using multi-search management:

- Performance optimization by executing a single search with multiple visualizations on the same dashboard leverages
- Populating the inputs from a single global search and post-process within each input
- Performing token-based searches within a post-process so that the need to execute an expensive global search every time a new input is selected is avoided

Implementation

Now, since we are aware of the advantages of multi-search management, let us see how we can implement this on the Splunk dashboard.

The following are the key points to be remembered when implementing multi-search management:

- Background/global search can be initiated from anywhere on the page or even from the panel
- Background/global search whose result is to be later used to run a post-process search must include an ID as follows (it is not at all necessary to use the same ID `global_search` for multi-search management, as the ID can be anything the user defined):

  ```
  <search id="global_search">
  ```

- Make the post-process search aware that it needs to process the result of the background search by using the `base` parameter in the search, as follows:

  ```
  <search base="global_search">
  ```

- To use a saved search within a dashboard will require the use of the parameter `ref`, as follows:

  ```
  <search ref="mySavedSearch">
  ```

- The syntax for time will change from `earliestTime` and `latestTime` to `earliest` and `latest`, respectively

Now let's see some code snippets, which we can use to implement multisearch management by modifying the XML source code of the dashboard:

1. We will first see the creation of a global search and assign an ID. The following image shows a global search with the ID as `globalSearch`:

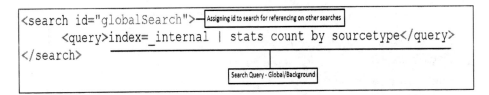

2. Use a global/background search in various other visualizations on the page. The following image shows how to use global searches in visualizations:

```
<chart>
   <search base="globalSearch" />
</chart>      Creating Chart & Table using the
              Global/Background Search
<table>
   <search base="globalSearch" />
</table>
```

3. Use the global/background search result as input to run another search (post-process search). The following search will run on the a result of search with `id` as `globalSearch` and compute its result:

```
<chart>
   <search base="globalSearch">
      <query>search sourcetype=splunkd</query>
   </search>
</chart>      Post - Process Search (Computed on Result of search
              with id=globalSearch)
```

4. If a saved search is to be made global, then the following line needs to be added to assign an ID to a saved search:

```
<search id="globalSearch" ref="mySavedSearch"/>
```

5. The following is the syntax to assign a time range when using multi-search management:

```
<search id="globalSearch" ref="mySavedSearch">
      <earliest>$time.earliest$</earliest>
      <latest>$time.latest$</latest>
</search>      Time range Syntax
         Dynamically accessing time from time picker
```

This is the way we can use multi-search in our dashboard for optimizing page performance and using Splunk efficiently.

Tokens

Tokens are nothing but variables, as in programming languages, which can be used to run dynamic queries taken from input fields or clicked events. Token name works as a reference to the information which captures value that is used to manage dashboard behavior. The delimiter used for the token is having syntax as `$token_name$`.

The following are a few ways token values can be captured:

- Tokens can be used to capture values from an input field
- Define the token to specify actions, based on conditions based on the value of the token
- Tokens can be defined in a search string, using values based on previously defined tokens
- Splunk Enterprise pre-defined default tokens

The tokens can be used in various locations and use cases on the Splunk dashboard, as described here:

- **Search events**: The result of a search based on the token value can be changed using search metadata tokens
- **Form inputs**: Depending upon the selection of the input value, the results in the visualization change
- **Drilldown tokens**: Depending upon the value/field clicked on the visualization, the respective tokens are passed and the result is obtained by the drilldown of visualizations
- **Conditional display**: Tokens are set and unset conditions for displaying the panels/content on the dashboard

Eval tokens

Tokens can be used to implement various functionalities on the Splunk dashboard. Tokens can be used as a single value visualization title, as a different functionality in case the search result is empty, or they hide/show panels on the basis of search result values.

We will learn in detail about using tokens to hide/show panels on the basis of a search result value in the next topic (*Null search swapper*) of this chapter.

The following are the tokens within the `search` event handler to access specific job properties. These features have been newly introduced in Splunk 6.3 to access search results:

- `$job.earliestTime$`: Initial job start time
- `$job.latestTime$`: Latest time recorded for the search job
- `$job.resultCount$`: Number of results a search job returned
- `$job.runDuration$`: Time, in seconds, for the search to complete
- `$job.messages$`: List of error and/or debug messages generated by the search job

The tokens can be used to add custom logic to a dashboard with an `eval` token. The dashboard's `eval` expression can be used to define a condition to match. Let us see an example of how an `eval` token can be used to implement a customized and dynamic dashboard.

Syntax of the eval token

- The `eval expression` in the `<condition>` tag:

```
<condition match="[eval expression]">
. . . [conditional actions] . . .
</condition>
```

- Token's value based on the result of the expression:

```
<eval token="token_name"> [eval expression] </eval>
```

Example

Let us go through an example of using eval tokens and understand their use. The following image shows a visualization, at the top of which is a result of the search query. The bottom section shows a time, which is nothing but the result of the time required for execution of the search query of the visualization:

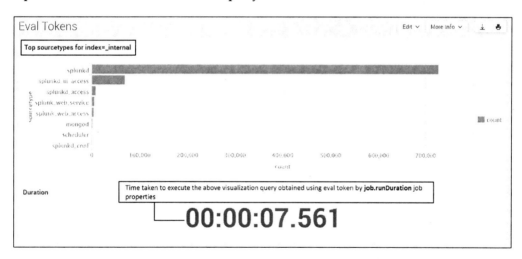

The time duration in the preceding search query is calculated on every run of the search query of the bar chart visualization. It is obtained by using `job.runDuration`, which is available as one of the `default` tokens from the Splunk Enterprise job properties of the `<progress>` tag. Similarly, an `eval` token can be used in various scenarios to display the required result even on a conditional basis on the Splunk dashboard.

Implementation

An `eval` token is very easy to implement. Let us see what needs to be modified in the XML code to implement an `eval` token on the Splunk dashboard. The following diagram shows the source code snippet, which implements the use of the `eval` token in the dashboard:

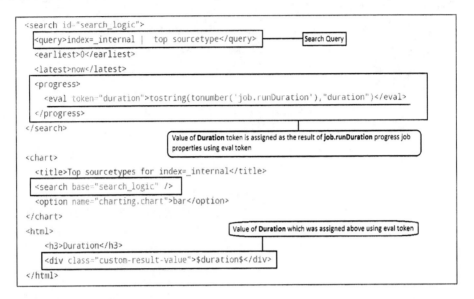

In the preceding image, the first segment is the `search` query, which results in the visualization in the explained example. The `<progress>` tag is used to get various job properties of the search event handler. In this section, the eval token named `Duration` is used to get the value in the `Duration` token of the search run duration. The `eval` token duration also has functions to convert the result into strings and numbers.

In the later section of the preceding code, a single value visualization is used to pass the result of the `duration` variable whose result was assigned by the `eval` token once the search is completed. Thus, the `eval` token can be used to customize the token as per need and helps to make a user-interactive and customized dashboard on Splunk.

Custom tokens

We have already learned in detail about tokens and eval tokens; now let us learn about custom tokens in which we will use JavaScript to set tokens in panel titles, HTML content of a panel, and also for drilldown scenarios. The custom tokens can be used to enrich the dashboard with important information relating to applications, users, and so on.

Example

Let us understand the use of custom tokens with the help of an example, and then later, we will look into implementing them on the Splunk dashboard. The following screenshot of the Splunk dashboard shows the value of custom tokens, like the username, app name, and view name. In this example, we have set custom tokens even for the drilldown on the result of the search query. Similarly, depending upon the requirement, any number of custom tokens can be defined and used:

Implementation

Now since we are aware of the use of custom tokens, let us see how to create, define, and use custom tokens on the Splunk dashboard.

The following code is the code snippet to get the app name and view name by using the `utils` library provided by Splunk Enterprise. In this snippet, we have set the values of the app name and view name obtained by the `utils` library to `app` and `view` tokens, which we will be using in the panel to display the required information. The following code snippet can be named as required; let's say we name it `app_token.js`:

```
require(['splunkjs/mvc','splunkjs/mvc/utils','splunkjs/mvc/simplexml/ready!'], function(mvc, utils){

    var unsubmittedTokens = mvc.Components.getInstance('default');
    var submittedTokens = mvc.Components.getInstance('submitted');

    // Set the token $app$ to the name of the current app
    unsubmittedTokens.set('app', utils.getCurrentApp());
    // Set the token $view$ to the name of the current view
    unsubmittedTokens.set('view', utils.getPageInfo().page);

    // Submit the new tokens
    submittedTokens.set(unsubmittedTokens.toJSON());

});
```

Using Utils Library to get App Name & View Name into custom tokkens app & view respectively

Similar to the way we got the app name and View Name, we will now get `username` from the `SplunkConfig` API to access various Splunk parameters, as follows. The following code snippet is saved as `user_token.js`:

```
require([
    'splunkjs/mvc',
    'splunk.config',
    'splunkjs/mvc/simplexml/ready!'
], function(mvc, SplunkConfig) {

    var unsubmittedTokens = mvc.Components.getInstance('default');
    var submittedTokens = mvc.Components.getInstance('submitted');

    // Set the token $currentUser$ to the name of the currently logged in user
    var username = SplunkConfig['USERNAME'];
    unsubmittedTokens.set('currentUser', username);
    submittedTokens.set('currentUser', username);

});
```

Fetching USERNAME and assigning it to a token username

The preceding two JavaScript files, `app_token.js` and `user_token.js`, in which we have defined a custom token, need to be saved in the `static` folder of respective app directory. In our example, we have saved the files in the `static` folder of the app directory, that is: `$SPLUNK_HOME\etc\apps\search\appserver\static`.

Now the custom tokens are set and can be used in the XML source code of the dashboard, like any other tokens. The important point here will be to include the `app_token.js` and `user_token.js` in the dashboard panel by specifying it in the XML, code as follows:

```
<dashboard script="app_token.js, user_token.js">
```

The following is the code snippet to get/use the custom tokens on the Splunk dashboard panels. Thus, we can use custom tokens to get the required information on the dashboard, using JavaScript:

```
<html>
    <h1>Hello, $currentUser$!</h1>
</html>
<table>
    <title>Drilldown from $view$ in $app$</title>
```

Apart from custom tokens, Splunk provides functionality to set multiple tokens within form inputs to derive multiple searches for better, user-interactive, and informative dashboards. The following are the use cases of multitoken setters:

- It can be used to set tokens for both label and value, which can be used throughout the dashboard and its panels

- It can be used to create an empty/null option that includes a unique token transformation

- It can be used to unset other tokens from the page on selection of a given form input

- A time range picker input can be created to set unique earliest and latest token values

- It can set multiple tokens based on search results and specified conditions

Null search swapper

We have already learned tokens and the use of eval tokens; now we will learn to use conditional tokens to set and unset the search query of a panel depending upon the result of the conditional tokens. Conditional tokens work similarly to an `if` loop used in programming languages. In a null search swapper, we will set tokens from the search manager to control behaviors on the page. Each search result outputs metadata around the search, the job, the server, and even the results. This feature helps users to access and set tokens from that metadata to be used throughout the page.

The null search swapper can be used to hide visualization if the result of a search query is null/empty. This kind of customization can be very useful when building highly dynamic dashboards for enterprises. For instance, the null search swapper can be used to hide a specific panel if the search result outputs nothing. So, since now the output is available instead of occupying space in the dashboard, showing no results to display, that panel will be hidden:

A conditional operation includes functions like the following:

- Modifying the search to run on the basis of a search query
- Hiding or displaying the panel or content of the panel on the basis of a condition
- Selecting a view to open based on a token value

The following are the tokens which can be used with a conditional operation with form inputs. The elements containing the attributes `depends` and `rejects` use the `<set>` and `<unset>` elements to set the token values that these attributes consume:

- `<change>`: A container element for the conditions that you define
- `<condition>`: Sets the condition based on the value of the input selection
- `<link>`: A link can be specified to a destination based on a given condition
- `<set>`: Sets the value for the given conditional token
- `<unset>`: Unsets a token which was previously set

Example

Let's understand what the use of the null search swapper is by using an example, and then we will go through the implementation part of the null search swapper.

In our example, we have two radio options asking the user to choose either one. The following are the options of the two radio buttons in the example used, along with the description:

- Sourcetype=splunkd: This search will run a search query (index=_ internal sourcetype=splunkd) and the result will be plotted in a bar chart

- Sourcetype=null: This search will run a search query (index=_internal sourcetype=null) and there will be no result returned; hence, the chart panel will be hidden

The following is the sample output of the null search swapper example when the first radio option is chosen:

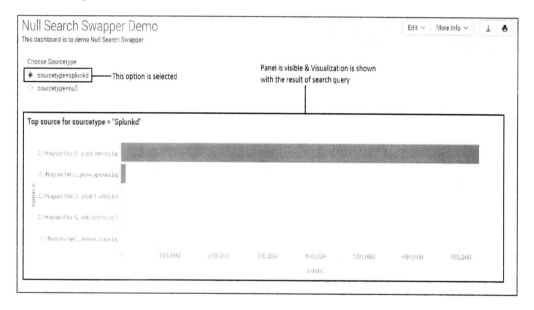

The output of the null search swapper example dashboard when the second radio option (`sourcetype=null`) is selected. Since the result of the search query is null/ no events, the panel will be hidden, with a message specified in the XML code. The following image is the example output image:

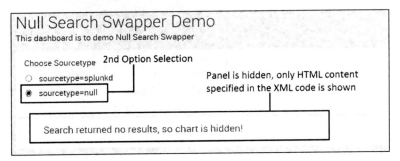

Implementation

Since we have seen, with the help of an example, the use of the null search swapper in the Splunk dashboard, let us have a look at the implementation part of it. The following are the changes required in the XML source code of the dashboard to implement the null search swapper on Splunk.

This section of code is for the radio button menu. The important point to note here is the token (`radio_option`), which we will be using in the later section for condition evaluation. The following code snippet describes which search query will run on the respective selection of a radio button:

```
<input type="radio" token="radio_option">
    <label>Choose Sourcetype</label>
    <choice value="index=_internal sourcetype=splunkd">sourcetype=splunkd</choice>
    <choice value="index=_internal sourcetype=null">sourcetype=null</choice>
    <initialValue>index=null</initialValue>
</input>
```

Code for Radio button Option

The following code snippet uses a conditional tag to match the specific condition (the count of the search result). If the value of the search result is equal to zero, then the token (`show_html`) is set and otherwise, it is unset. The following code is written in the `<progress>` tag, as the code `job.resultCount` is used to set/unset the token:

```
<search id="search_query">
  <query>$radio_option$ | top source</query>

  <!-- Progress event has access to job properties only -->
  <progress>
    <condition match="'job.resultCount' == 0">
      <set token="show_html">Search Match</set>
    </condition>
    <condition>
      <unset token="show_html"/>
    </condition>
  </progress>
</search>
```

Condition to Set & Unset depending upon the output of search result

Once the conditional tag is assigned with a value and the respective code is defined as shown, the preceding defined token is used to render a visualization action on the dashboard. In the following code snippet, as already explained, **rejects and depends** tokens are used to **unset and set**, respectively. If the condition matches an HTML paragraph specified is shown on the dashboard and if it doesn't match, then the result with the bar chart visualization will be visible:

```
<chart rejects="$show_html$">
  <title>Top source for sourcetype = "Splunkd"</title>
  <search base="search_query" />
  <option name="charting.chart">bar</option>
  <option name="charting.legend.placement">none</option>
</chart>
<html depends="$show_html$">
  <p style="color:blue;margin-left:30px;font-size:14px">Search returned no results, so chart is hidden!</p>
</html>
```

Condition 1 - When First Radio Button is selected

Condition 2 - When 2nd radio button is selected

Thus, null search swapper can be used to hide panels when the result of a search query is null, that is, the result of the search query returns nothing. The null search swapper code snippet can be modified as per need, and different conditions can be specified in the <condition> tag to get the desired result on the dashboard.

Switcher

The Splunk dashboard provides options to link various visualizations or statistical output in a panel to be switched without navigating from the **Dashboard** page. Technically speaking, links are used to perform a few sets of activities, like show/hide panel, switch visualizations, and so on, without navigating to another dashboard or screen on Splunk.

Link switcher

Data can be visualized in many forms, like tabular statistical output, or charts, graphs, and many more. From each different visualization of the same data, different kinds of insights can be derived. We have already learned in previous chapters about different types of visualization and the respective insights available from each of these visualizations. We will now use the link switcher, which is nothing but a link to toggle the content of the dashboard. The link switcher can be used to change the visualization type on the result of the same search query, or run different searches on each link, as required.

Example and implementation

Let us understand the use of the link switcher in the dashboard along with the implementation part of the link switcher on the Splunk dashboard. In our example, there are three links (**Table**, **Chart**, and **Map**), which the user can click and choose to get the selected visualization on the dashboard.

The link on the visualization dashboard looks as in the following image. In the following example image, the **Table** link is selected and hence, it looks highlighted:

The following source code is need to create a link along with the condition definition of each of the links. Let's say, for instance, when the condition value is set with **Table** by clicking on the **Table** link, then **Chart** and **Map** are hidden by the unset parameter in the <condition> tag. Similarly, for other links, respective visualization are unset and the selected visualization is set:

```
<fieldset submitButton="false">
    <input type="link" token="link_token">
        <label>Click on the view</label>
        <choice value="table">Table</choice>           Link Choices with
        <choice value="chart">Chart</choice>           respective tokens
        <choice value="map">Map</choice>               (value)
        <default>Table</default>
        <change>
            <condition value="table">
                <set token="showTable">true</set>
                <unset token="showChart"></unset>
                <unset token="showMap"></unset>
            </condition>
            <condition value="chart">
                <set token="showChart">true</set>
Conditional     <unset token="showTable"></unset>
set & unset      <unset token="showMap"></unset>
for each     </condition>
choices of       <condition value="map">
Links            <set token="showMap">true</set>
                <unset token="showChart"></unset>
                <unset token="showTable"></unset>
            </condition>
        </change>
    </input>
</fieldset>
```

Now since we have defined the conditions for the respective links, let us have a look at the source code snippet, which will be shown as a visualization on clicking respective links. Let me explain one part of the following snippet with an example. When the **Table** link is clicked, the showTable token is set and showChart and showMap are unset, as shown in the preceding code snippet image. So by setting the showTable token, the following search query gets executed and the resulting visualization is shown in the panel of the dashboard. Since the <table> tag is used, the resulting output is a statistical table; likewise, for chart <chart> and map <map> tags are used:

In the following code snippet, showTable and showChart have the same search query, and to make efficient use of it, we can use multi search management here.

```
<panel>
    <table depends="$showTable$">
        <title>Table</title>          When Table link is clicked, $showTable$ token is set and this search
        <search>                      query is executed
            <query>index=_internal | stats count by sourcetype</query>
        </search>
    </table>

    <chart depends="$showChart$">
        <title>Chart</title>          When Chart Link is selected then this search query visualization is
        <search>                      shown
            <query>index=_internal | stats count by sourcetype</query>
        </search>
    </chart>

    <map depends="$showMap$">
        <title>Map</title>            When Map Link is selected this token is set (showMap) and the
        <search>                      below query result is shown on the screen
            <query>| inputlookup geomaps_data.csv | iplocation device_ip
            | geostats latfield=lat longfield=lon count by method</query>
        </search>
    </map>
</panel>
```

The output of the preceding code snippet will be as follows, which shows the links and the selected links visualization. In the output image, as we can see, the **Chart** link is selected and hence, the visualization in the visible panel is showing the **Chart** output of the preceding code snippet search query. So, if the **Map** link is selected in the dashboard, then the chart visualization will be hidden and the map visualization will be visible in the same panel of the dashboard, and so on for the other links as well:

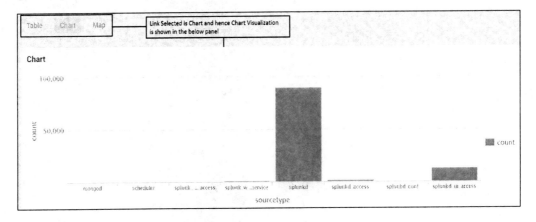

Button switcher

We have already learned about the link switcher, in which the dashboard panels are switched to different visualizations by clicking on different links on the dashboard. Now we will look into the button switcher, which is similar to the link switcher, but in this case the value of the token is set/unset by clicking on buttons. The output of the example will be the same as that of the link switcher, but the background processing and implementation logic differs. The link switcher and button switcher look analogous in terms of functionality on the dashboard, but functionality-wise, the uses of the link switcher and button switcher are different.

In the case of the link switcher, the visualization is changed in the same panel of the dashboard, whereas in the button switcher, we will add another panel, keeping the pre-existing panel also in the dashboard. For example, let's say we have a panel which shows the visualization of the data, and if the user is interested in having a look at statistical tabular output along with the visualization, a button switcher can be added.

Example and implementation

Let us understand what the button switcher actually is and how it differs from the link switcher with the help of an example. We will also have a look at the implementation of the button switcher on Splunk dashboard, along with an example.

The following panel of the Splunk dashboard has a button, which we will use as a switcher:

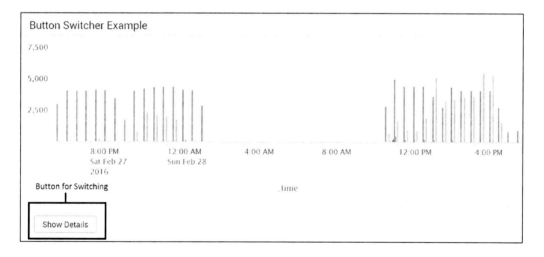

When the button (**Show Details**) is clicked, the current panel resizes itself in half, accommodating another panel with a defined visualization. The output, when clicked, shows details which look as shown here:

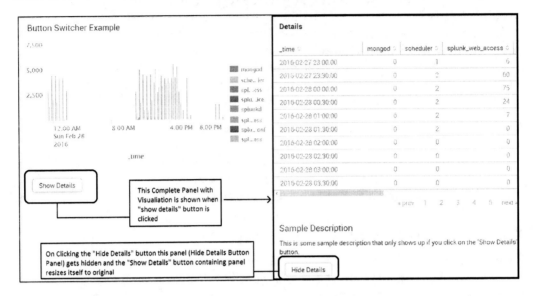

As seen from the preceding image, on clicking **Show Details**, the panel resizes itself and a new panel with a visualization and a **Hide Details** button is available. On clicking the **Hide Details** button, the panel hides itself and restores the **Show Details** panel to its original size. Thus, the button switcher can be used to create such customized dashboards where the information that is optional is kept hidden, and can be viewed by clicking a button.

Now, to summarize the difference between the link switcher and button switcher, The link switcher shows different visualizations in the same panel, whereas in the button switcher, a new panel with visualization is accommodated by resizing the current panel and thus can be useful to hold many panels in a single visualization efficiently.

The data attributes on clickable HTML elements (such as links or buttons) allow users to set or unset tokens for the dashboard. The following are the available data attributes, along with the syntax:

- The `data-set-token`, along with the `data-value` token, is used to assign/set a particular value:

```
<a href="#" data-set-token="test_token" data-value="The new value of token ">Button Switcher 1</a>
```

- To unset the value of the token, the `data-unset-token` is used:

```
<a href="#" data-unset-token="test_token "> Button Switcher 2</a>
```

- Set or unset multiple tokens `data-token-json` by using a JSON object. Assigning a token value to null unsets the token:

```
<a href="#" data-token-json= '{"token1": "value 1",
"token2": "value 2", "token3": null}'> Button Switcher 3</a>
```

Let us now have a look at the XML code to use the button switcher on the dashboard. The following image is the search query, which runs on the panel of the dashboard. The important point to note down here is the search ID (`Search_Query`), which we will be using in the later section.

```
<search id="Search_Query">
    <query>index=_internal | timechart count by sourcetype</query>
</search>
```

Now we will see the code snippet to create a button which also sets `data-set-token="show_details"`, which we will use to show the new panel with visualization:

```
<panel>
    <title>Button Switcher Demo</title>
    <chart>
        <search base="Search_Query"/>
    </chart>
    <html>
        <button class="btn" data-set-token="show details"
        data-value="show">Show Details</button>
    </html>
</panel>
```

Text to be visible on Button

The following image shows the code snippet, which depends on the show_details token. This panel will only be visible whenever the show_details token is set, and that will be done by clicking the **Show Details** button, as explained in the preceding code snippet:

```
<panel depends="$show_details$">
    <table>
        <title>Details Panel</title>
        <search base="Search_Query"/>
    </table>
    <html>
        <h2>Description</h2>
        <p>This is some sample description </p>
        <button class="btn" data-unset-token="show_details">
        Hide Details</button>
    </html>
</panel>         Button Text
```

The preceding code snippet runs when the show_details token is set with the search query defined in the Search_Query token, and results in a statistical table. The code snippet also has an HTML code to create a button (**Hide Details**), which unsets the token show_details and thus, the panel gets hidden on a click of this button.

Thus, the button switcher can be used to customize the dashboard to show a panel with a click, and then the panel can be hidden on another button click when required. This kind of customization helps in building industry-quality dashboards.

Summary

In this chapter we have learned various dashboard customization techniques to make the dashboard feature-rich, easy to use, informative, and highly interactive. The techniques learned in this chapter should be used when creating quality dashboards to make the most out of Splunk dashboard.

In the next chapter we will learn advanced dashboard customization techniques to make more interactive, highly dynamic, and feature-rich dashboards as per user requirements.

9
Advanced Dashboard Customization

You learned various dashboard customization techniques in the previous chapter. Now, you will learn some of the advanced dashboard customization techniques that will help you develop highly dynamic, customizable, and useful dashboards over data on Splunk. The dynamic and customized dashboard delivers valuable analytics and visualization.

We will cover the following topics along with examples and implementation procedures in this chapter:

- Layout customization
- Image overlay
- Custom alert action
- Custom look and feel

Layout customization

The Splunk dashboard has the option of dragging and dropping panels from controls. Splunk automatically resizes the panel equally as per the number of panels in a row. Now, you will learn to customize the dashboard panel's width and group more than one visualization in a single panel.

Panel width

Let's first understand the need for customizing panel width explicitly when Splunk automatically resizes the panel by itself with the help of an example.

Example

In the following figure, there are three panels in a single row. **Panel 1** has **Statistical Table**, **Panel 2** has **Line Chart**, and **Panel 3** has **Single Value**. Splunk's smart dashboard capability automatically resizes each panel of equal sizes in a row. In the following example, it can be seen that **Panel 3** has very less information to display, whereas **Panel 2** requires more space to display information properly and efficiently:

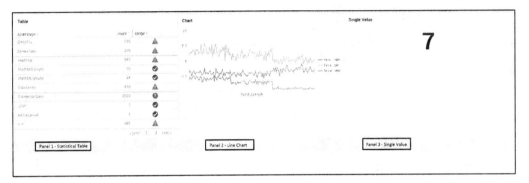

Hence, in order to make the dashboard display the required information efficiently, such as the panel that has more information is given more space and the panel that requires less space is given lesser space, automatic panel resizing can be modified and user-configured width can be applied on the panel.

Implementation

Let's see how to implement custom panel width on a Splunk dashboard.

The following is the code snippet (JavaScript) on which the panel size can be manually specified as per our need:

```
require(['jquery', 'splunkjs/mvc/simplexml/ready!'], function($) {
    // Grab the DOM for the first dashboard row
    var firstRow = $('.dashboard-row').first();

    var panelCells = $(firstRow).children('.dashboard-cell');
    // Adjust the cells' width
    $(panelCells[0]).css('width', '20%');
    $(panelCells[1]).css('width', '60%');        —Customized Panel Width
    $(panelCells[2]).css('width', '20%');
});
```

The preceding code snippet customizes the first row of the dashboard. The first panel's (denoted by panelCells[0]) width is set to **20%**, the second panel's is set to **60%**, and so on. The preceding code is saved as width_layout.js and is stored at $SPLUNK_HOME$\etc\apps\App_name\appserver\static.

The dashboard in which the preceding customization is to be obtained is directed to use the width_layout.js file in the XML code, as follows:

```
<dashboard script="width_layout.js" >
```

The result of the preceding code snippet is shown in the following screenshot. Using this code, highly customized dashboards can be made as per the required panel width:

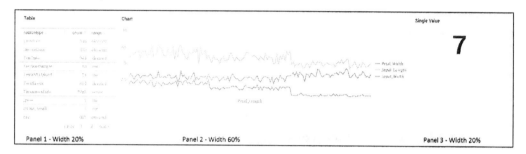

Grouping

A Splunk dashboard can be customized to group visualizations of similar types in a single panel of the dashboard either in the same row or column. Grouping similar visualization in a single panel makes the dashboard cleaner, readable, and understandable.

Let's understand the use of grouping with the help of an example.

Say, the dashboard has four single value visualizations (total number of errors, errors of type A, errors of type B, and errors of type C) and three charts. Now, instead of having each visualization as an individual panel, if we group the single-value visualization into a single panel, then it will be easier for the reader to understand the dashboard and derive insights from it. Similarly, in case of charts, if they are grouped, lesser space will be required. Thus, the dashboard will be cleaner and more useful with grouped visualization.

Example

Let's understand with the help of examples what is grouping of visualizations in a Splunk dashboard.

Single-value grouping

In the following single value visualization, the left panel has three grouped single value visualization, whereas on the right, three individual single value visualizations are shown. Both grouped and nongrouped visualizations are shown together to compare the advantages of grouped visualizations.

When there are many panels and different kinds of visualization on a dashboard, grouping similar or functionally similar visualizations together facilitates better readability. Moving/relocating them as a group auto adjusts itself either horizontally or vertically depending on the available space.

Also, from the following visualization examples, it can be clearly seen that grouping visualization also helps in saving space, which can be taken by other visualizations of the dashboard. Thus, grouping visualization makes it easy to fit it in the dashboard, more readable, and compact.

The following figure is an example of single value grouping:

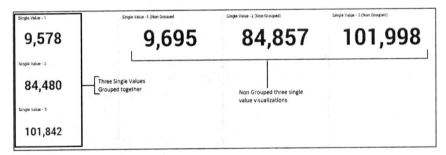

Visualization grouping

The following figure is an example of multiple visualization grouping compared to the same visualization when nongrouped. This figure clearly describes that when the visualizations are grouped, they adjust themselves in order to save space, whereas when they are left ungrouped, a lot of space is wasted:

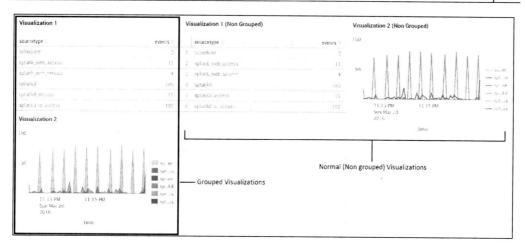

Implementation

Grouping of visualization is very simple and straightforward. Let's see how we can create a dashboard with grouped visualizations. The dashboard XML code needs to be modified to group the respective visualization.

The following code shows a sample of two nongrouped visualizations of the Splunk dashboard:

```
<row>
    <panel>                                  Visualization 1 (1st Panel)
        <table>
            <title>Table</title>
            <search>
                <query>index=* | chart count by sourcetype </query>
            </search>
        </table>
    </panel>

    <panel>                                  Visualization 2 (2nd Panel)
        <chart>
            <title>Chart</title>
            <search>
                <query>index=* | chart count by sourcetype</query>
            </search>
        </chart>
    </panel>
</row>
```

The preceding code has two visualizations in the same row, which are as follows:

- **Visualization 1**: This is the XML code for a table, as shown in the first panel
- **Visualization 2**: This is a chart shown in the second panel of the dashboard

The following are the inferences (important points) derived from the following code snippet:

- The visualizations described between `<row>` and `</row>` will be available in the same row of the Splunk dashboard.
- Both the visualizations (`<table>` and `<chart>`) are described between the `<panel>` and `</panel>` tags

Now, let's see what is the change in the preceding XML source code of the dashboard required to group the visualization:

```
<row>

    <panel>

        <table>                              Visualization 1
          <title>Table</title>
          <search>
            <query>index=* | chart count by sourcetype </query>
          </search>
        </table>

        <chart>                              Visualization 2
          <title>Chart</title>
          <search>
            <query>index=* | chart count by sourcetype</query>
          </search>
        </chart>

    </panel>

</row>
```

So, to group any number of visualizations' single value, charts, and statistical tables, they need to be kept between the `<panel>` and `</panel>` tag. As seen from the preceding grouped visualization code snippet, both the visualizations are defined under one single `<panel>` tag. Similarly, any number of visualizations can be grouped based on the similarity of the information they deliver or on the basis of similarity of the visualization type.

Panel toggle

Splunk dashboards can have any number of panels. The more the number of panels, the more scrolling is required to view. Hence, Splunk's panel toggle feature can be used to minimize the panel for which the information is not required. Similarly, the dashboard can have any number of panel toggles implemented to access the respective panels, whenever required.

Example

Let's understand what a panel toggle is and how it can be helpful in making a customized and dynamic dashboard with the help of this example:

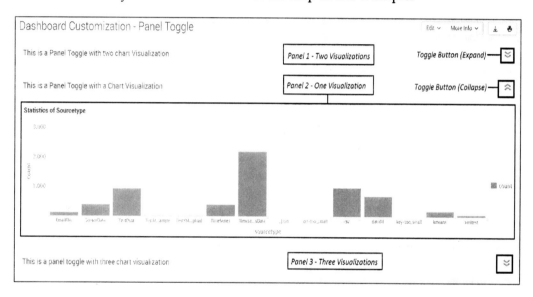

In the preceding dashboard, there are three panel toggles. Two panels (**Panel 1** and **Panel 3**) are in the collapsed mode, whereas **Panel 2** is in the expanded mode. Here, the three panels have the number of visualizations as follows:

- **Panel 1** has two visualizations
- **Panel 2** has one visualization
- **Panel 3** has three visualizations

So, a total of six visualizations can be accessible on the dashboard without scrolling, just by toggling whichever visualization is needed as per requirement. The panel toggle feature can be helpful when some of the analytics and visualization is not required all the time, so it can be hidden and it can be accessed whenever needed by the toggle expand button.

Implementation

Let's see how we can implement a panel toggle on a Splunk dashboard. To implement a panel toggle, we will inject the HTML code in the XML code.

The panel toggle can be implemented using CSS and JS. CSS is required here to define the position of the button and its aesthetics on the dashboard panel, and JS is required to implement the collapse and expand functionality in the panel.

The CSS and JS file need to be stored in a folder (`PanelToggle`) at `$SPLUNK_HOME\etc\app\App_name\appserver\static`.

The following figure shows the code snippet of the `paneltoggle.css` file:

```
.collapse {
  background-image: url(collapse.png);
  background-repeat: no-repeat;
  float: right;
  padding-right: 20px;
  cursor: pointer;
  display: inline;
  background-size: 90% 100% ;
}
```
CSS for Collapse Button on Panel

```
.expand {
  background-image: url(expand.png);
  background-repeat: no-repeat;
  float: right;
  padding-right: 20px;
  cursor: pointer;
  margin: 0px;
  display: inline;
  background-size: 90% 100% ;
}
```
CSS for Expand Button on Panel

In the preceding code snippet, there are references of the collapse button (`collapse.png`) and the expand button (`expand.png`). The respective buttons' images should be made available as required in the same folder.

Now, since the CSS file is ready, we will look at JavaScript for the expand and collapse script. The following code snippet is for the same. Let's suppose that the JS file's name is `paneltoggle.js`.

The following code snippet of JS is for expanding the panel functionality:

```
events: {
    'click .expand': function(e) {          Function with code to expand
        var img = $(e.currentTarget);       the Panel on click on the button
        var items = img.data('item');
        _(items).each(function(id) {
            var component = mvc.Components.get(id);
            if (component) {
                component.$el.slideToggle(1000);
                component.$el.resize();
            }                                Depending upon whether expanded or collapsed,
        });                                  corrosponding image is shown
        img.attr("class", img.attr("class") == "expand" ? "collapse": "expand");
    },
```

In the preceding code `expand` event is used to expand the panel, and similarly, `'click .collapse' : function()`, which is identical to the preceding code, needs to be defined to collapse the expanded panel in the `paneltoggle.js` file.

The following figure shows the `render` function that handles the functionality of collapsing and expanding the panel on the dashboard and formatting elements as well:

```
render: function() {
    this.$('.btn-pill').remove();
    if (this.settings.has('items')) {
        var hide = this.settings.get('hide') || "no";       Sets the values of
        var items = this.settings.get('items'), $el = this.$el;  various parameters by
        var first_panel = mvc.Components.get(items[0]);      getting realtime values
        var h = $('<h2></h2>');                              from dashboard & panel
        var title = this.settings.get("title") || "";
        var img = $('<div>   </div>');
        img.attr('class', "collapse");
        img.attr('alt', '#' + items[0]).data('item', items);
        img.appendTo($el);
        h.text(title);
        h.appendTo($el);
        if (hide == "yes") {
            img.attr('class', "expand");
            _(items).each(function(id) {                     Handling the Hidden
                var component = mvc.Components.get(id);      condtion of panel and
                if (component) {                             making the expand icon
                    component.$el.hide();                    visible on the dashboard
                }
            });
        }
    }
    return this;
}
```

We now have JS to handle the expanding and collapsing of the panel and CSS to show the corresponding buttons on the panel. Now, we will see what changes are required to be implemented on the dashboard on which the panel toggle functionality is to be implemented:

1. First of all, the dashboard should be pointed to use the `autodiscover.js` script using the following code:

```
<dashboard script="autodiscover.js">
```

2. The following is a sample code snippet that has two visualizations with toggle support. The code within the `<HTML>` & `</HTML>` tag is used to toggle the panel obtained from the `paneltoggle.js` file. There are two simple charts that will appear when the panel is expanded. These visualizations are mapped with an ID (`panel1` and `panel2`). The HTML code also has a `title` parameter that can be used to describe the visualizations held in the panel. The `data-require` parameter should be given the correct relative path of the folder, where the CSS and JS files are located inside the `app` folder:

```
<row>
  <panel>
    <html>
      <div id="toggle" class="splunk-view"
      data-require="app/search/PanelToggle/paneltoggle"    ── The path of JS & CSS file - In search app's
      data-options="{                                          appserver/static/PanelToggle directory
      "items": ["panel1", "panel2"],
      "title": "This is a Panel Toggle with two chart Visualization",
      "hide": "yes"
      }"/>
    </html>

    <chart id="panel1">
      <title>Statistics of Sourctypes on Splunk</title>
      <searchString>index=* | stats count by sourcetype</searchString>    ──Visualization 1
    </chart>

    <chart id="panel2">
      <title>Timechart of Sourcetype on Splunk</title>
      <searchString>index=* | timechart count by sourcetype</searchString>   ──Visualization 2
    </chart>

  </panel>
</row>
```

Similarly, taking reference of the preceding code, any number of visualizations can be hidden in a panel and can be expanded with the panel toggle feature.

Note that the complete code snippet with a sample implementation can be obtained by downloading the `custom_simplexml_extensions` app from the Splunk app store.

Image overlay

Splunk provides a very interesting functionality for overlaying single values over images. This feature can help to build dynamic dashboards explaining the workflow process with real numbers and show some easy-to-understand visualization with icons and images on the dashboard. Image overlay is very easy to implement and sometimes can be very useful in building impressive dashboards with icons and images.

Example

Let's understand what image overlay is and how it can help in creating a useful dashboard with the help of an example. The following screenshot shows an example of image overlay dashboard visualization:

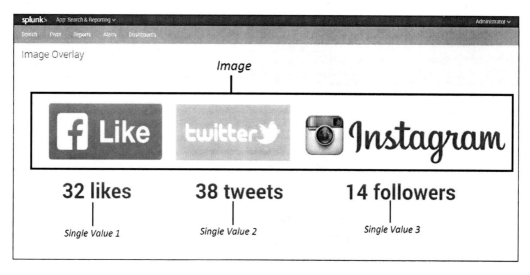

In the preceding customization, there is an image and three single value visualizations to show analytical results from the data on Splunk. The preceding dashboard can be useful to find the number of interactions available in the underlying data with respect to the corresponding social networks.

What is the use of image overlay?

As show in the preceding example image, single value visualizations are enriched with corresponding icon/images to make the dashboard more informative and useful. The information (likes, tweets, and followers) can be monitored in real time as they are search query results. It makes the dashboard fancier and informative by adding image visualization.

Where can image overlay be used?

Image overlay can be used along with single values in many places. Let's enlist a few places where image overlay could be used on Splunk:

- It can be used in security dashboards such as credit card fraud detection dashboards. The corresponding threat/attack images along with single values can be used. So, whenever any threat is detected, the single value corresponding to the detected threat will be updated.

- This customization can be used to display images along with single value analytics of the number of transactions done via different payment instruments. Images of Visa, credit cards, wallets, and cash on delivery can be added along with a single value. So, looking at the dashboard panel, we can easily visualize the analytics of the payment method used on the portal. The following is an example usage of image overlay:

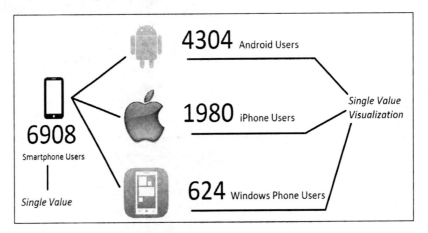

- Image overlay can also be used to show the workflow with corresponding values for each workflow step.

Now, since you have understood the use of image overlay on the Splunk dashboard along with the use case, let's see how to implement image overlay on the Splunk dashboard.

Implementation

Image overlay can be implemented on the Splunk dashboard using custom CSS and JS, as we did in the previously explained customizations. The following are the steps to implement image overlay on the Splunk dashboard:

1. First we would require an image template that is to be shown in image overlay visualization. A sample of an image template is shown in the following image. Let's say the following template image shown is named `social.png`:

2. Place the template image (`social.png`) in `$SPLUNK_HOME$\etc\apps\App_name\appserver\static`.

3. Create a CSS file (say, `social_image.css`) in the preceding folder, and put the following code snippet to embed the image (`social.png`) in the required panel of the dashboard:

```
#image_overlay_panel .image{
    background: transparent 50% 50% no-repeat url('/static/app/search/social.png');
    position:absolute;
    top: 0px;
    left: 0px;                          Path of Template Image (social.png)
    width: inherit;
    height: inherit;
}
```

4. The `image` style is loaded in CSS, and now we will see the code snippet that defines the location where the single value visualization will be displayed on the image overlay:

```
#image_overlay_panel #facebook_likes {
    position: absolute;
    top: 320px;              Position where Single Value of
    left: 80px;              Facebook will be displayed on
                             Dashboard Panel
}
#image_overlay_panel #twitter_tweets {
    position: absolute;
    top: 320px;
    left: 400px;
}
#image_overlay_panel #insta_followers {
    position: absolute;
    top: 320px;
    left: 758px;
}
```

In the preceding code snippet, the position (left and top) for each single value visualization is very important. This position can be determined in any image editing tool, such as MS Paint, by hovering the mouse to find relative pixel values. Also, depending on the number of single value visualizations, the corresponding number of CSS elements needs to be defined. As in our example, there are three single values, and hence, three elements are shown in the preceding code snippet.

5. Now that the pre-setup for image overlay is ready, we will see what customization is required in the XML code of the dashboard where the image overlay is to be implemented.

   First, modify the XML code to include the corresponding CSS file, as follows:

   ```
   <dashboard stylesheet="social_image.css">
   ```

   Then, let's see the code snippet to display the single value visualization below the Facebook icon of the image overlay. Similarly, for other single values, corresponding code snippets need to be defined in the XML code of the dashboard:

   ```
   <search id="facebook likes">
       <query>|inputcsv webserver.csv
                   |eval _time=strptime (date, "%e-%b-%y")
                   |timechart avg(Visitors) as visitor span=7d
                   | eval count = round(visitor,0) . " likes"</query>
       <preview>
           <set token="facebook likes">$result.count$</set>
       </preview>
   </search>
   ```

   Search Query which returns count of facebook likes

   The id parameter defined in the <search> tag and set in the token should match the corresponding CSS ID. In the <query> tag, the search query resulting in the output required to be displayed in the single value should be defined. Also, the variable whose value is to be displayed on the panel should be mentioned, as in our example, count is mentioned as $result. count$. The value of the variable defined in set token will be displayed below the image as a single value.

These are the steps to implement the image overlay functionality on the Splunk dashboard as per the requirement.

Note that any change in the JS and CSS file's image may not be reflected immediately and may require a restart in Splunk to reflect the changes on the Splunk dashboard.

Custom look and feel

In this section, you will learn how to use custom CSS and JS to customize the look and feel of Splunk dashboards. In the previous topics and chapter, we used CSS and JS to customize the functionality of the dashboard. In this section, we will modify the look and feel (aesthetics) of the Splunk dashboard.

The Splunk dashboard has its predefined stylesheets, which are automatically applied on any new dashboards created in Splunk. You will now learn how to override the default stylesheet behavior with your own custom CSS file.

Example and implementation

The following steps are required to use custom CSS file on any dashboard XML page:

1. Create a CSS file (say, `layout.css`) at `$SPLUNK_HOME$\etc\apps\app_name\appserver\static`.

2. Go to the Splunk **Web Console** | **Dashboard** | **Edit Source** (for which the custom layout is to be applied).

3. Direct the dashboard to use custom CSS file by modifying the XML code as follows:

   ```
   <dashboard stylesheet="layout.css">
   ```

   If the dashboard has a `form` tag, then modify it as follows:

   ```
   <form stylesheet="layout.css">
   ```

4. Now, whenever the dashboard is loaded apart from the default style, it will also load the style as defined in the custom (`layout.css`) stylesheet.

5. Since `layout.css` does not have a definition of any custom modification, the dashboard loads as it is. Now, we will see how to customize different elements of the dashboard using this custom stylesheet:

   ◦ Changing the color of the panel background: Add the following code in `layout.css` and replace the color as per your requirement, and there, you have the panel color background of your choice:

     ```
     .dashboard-panel,.dashboard-cell {
       background: #D52121 !important;
     }
     ```

The preceding code snippet will change the dashboard panel background to red (D52121). The !important value is required to override Splunk's default style with the one we specified. The following screenshot shows a panel that has no results to display and is customized by the preceding CSS code:

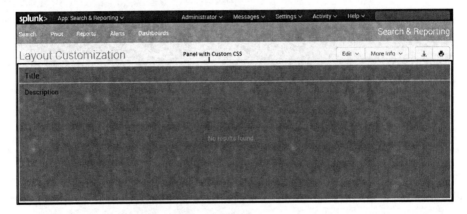

- ○ Change the color of **Title**, **Header**, and **Description** of the panel, as follows:

```
.dashboard-row {
  color: #4D0303;
}
.panel-head h3,.dashboard-header h2, p.description {
  color: #745B5B;
}
```

Depending on what element of the dashboard is to be customized, the respective CSS element is modified in this custom CSS.

The important issue that arises here is how to know which stylesheet is applied and to which segment of the dashboard so as to be able to modify any segment of the dashboard. Let's understand this with the help of an example figure:

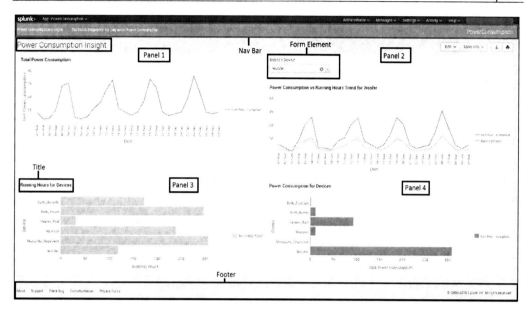

The preceding example figure is a sample dashboard highlighting the different elements of it. All the elements seen on the dashboard can be formatted as per our requirement, that is, color, font, size, and so on.

So, to change any specific element as required, how can we identify what CSS needs to be added in the preceding custom layout.css file? The browser's debugging functionality is generally accessible by pressing the *F12* button.

Let me explain how to identify the corresponding CSS file and modify it as per the requirement. The debugging console is available by pressing the *F12* button in most of the browsers, such as Mozilla Firefox, Google Chrome, and Internet Explorer.

Suppose we are interested in changing the aesthetics of the title of the dashboard. When the dashboard is open in the browser, press *F12*, and the debugging console similar to the one in the following screenshot will appear.

Note that the following example figure is explained using the Mozilla Firefox browser. The debugging console looks pretty much the same for other browsers as well:

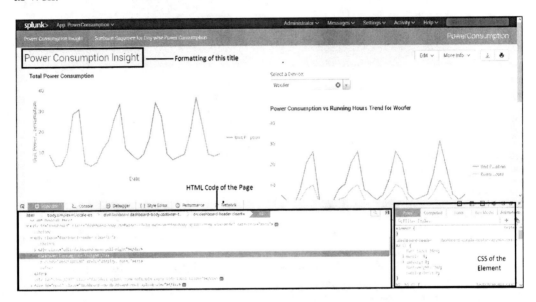

The lower part of the browser, which shows the HTML code and CSS, is part of the browser's debugging console. We are interested in changing the aesthetics of the title, as highlighted in the preceding figure. The following are the steps to implement it:

1. Right-click on the part of the element that is to be modified, and click on **Inspect Element**. In our example, the element on which we right-click is **Title**, as highlighted in the preceding figure.

2. The HTML and CSS code of the inspected element will be available in the debugging console.

3. The respective styles already applied on the element will be visible, and the CSS element tag used to modify the properties can be found in the CSS segment of the debugging console. The following figure shows the CSS debugging console:

```
.dashboard-header      dashboard-simple-bootstrap.min.css:9
h2 ⚙ {
    font-size: 24px;
  ▶ margin: 0;
  ▶ padding: 0;
    font-weight: 200;
    padding-left: 0;
}
```

So, `.dashboard-header h2` is the style applied on the title of the dashboard, and we can modify it by overriding the preceding default properties in our custom CSS file as follows:

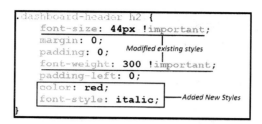

The preceding example figures show that `font-size` and `font-weight` are modified and two new styles, `color` and `font-style`, have been added to customize the title as per our requirement.

Note that the existing styles that are modified have `!important`, whereas the ones that are newly added are missing this postfix. The reason is that in CSS, `!important` is used to override wherever added. So, this postfix is added to only those that have a pre-existing style, and new styles need not have this postfix.

In many cases, the modified custom CSS code is not applied on the dashboard until the Splunk server is restarted and browser cache is cleared.

4. The result of the preceding custom modification in `layout.css` will be similar to the one shown in the following figure. The `color` value is changed to `red` from the default `black` color. The size is increased from `24px` to `44px`. The `font weight` value is increased to `300` and the `font-style` value is set to `italic`. The following is the output of these changes:

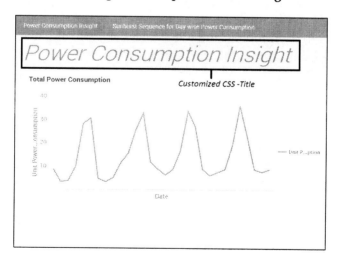

Similarly, depending on the requirement, any of the elements of the Splunk dashboard can be modified as per the requirement using custom CSS.

The custom alert action

The Splunk dashboard can be configured to implement custom alerting actions. Splunk can be integrated with other enterprise applications to automate the workflow and thus increase efficiency.

What is alerting?

Splunk is a big data tool with lots of data streaming in every second from numerous different sources, and there can be multiple dashboards and use case scenarios implemented on Splunk. It would be difficult to keep monitoring all the dashboards for any issue when it arises in real time. Hence, whenever any specific condition is met, an alert can be sent in the form of an e-mail, SMS, or chat notification informing the admin that the defined condition has been found on the data.

Thus, the feature of alerting in Splunk helps to avoid monitoring of the dashboard live and 24 x 7 for issues and thus reduces manpower. Since the process is automated, there will not be a single instance when the specific issue is caused and not reported. Thus, the alerting feature increases the efficiency of data monitoring in real time.

Alerting

The alerting feature can be useful in various business domains, such as security, compliance, fraud, IT operations, IOT, M2M, business analytics, and so on. The alerting system can be integrated with the issue tracking and ticketing system, messaging, e-mails and chatting applications, running custom scripts to switch on/ off devices, managing and monitoring IOT devices, and so on. Thus, the alerting feature of Splunk, when integrated with the enterprise application's real-time alerting and workflow, helps us obtain automation.

The following are some of the alert action examples that can be easily integrated with Splunk:

- **Issue/incident tracking/ticketing**: Most widely used incident ticketing systems such as Jira and ServiceNow can be directly integrated with Splunk to automate the creation of tickets from Splunk itself.

- **Security, compliance, and fraud**: Security and networking devices, such as firewalls and gateways, can be informed to take the necessary action. The fraud and compliance team can be informed to take the necessary action in case of any fraud detected by Splunk.

- **Alert notification**: Whenever any specified condition is met in Splunk, various alert notifications can be sent either via e-mails, SMSes, or via instant messaging clients, such as Slack and HipChat.

- **IT monitoring**: Incident notifications can be sent to various IT incident monitoring tools, such as BigPanda, xMatters, and so on, directly from Splunk whenever an issue arises.

- **IOT/M2M actions**: IOT/M2M devices can be switched off/on and alarm generation or any custom action by the device can be configured via scripts. Custom actions can also be performed using webhook (sending HTTP POST actions to URLs).

- **Custom actions**: Custom scripts or integration with any enterprise applications can help the alerting feature of Splunk to trigger any custom actions as per the requirement.

Splunk already had an alerting feature in the previous versions, which were capable of sending e-mail notifications whenever the specified condition was met. In Splunk 6.3 Enterprise, the custom alert action feature has been introduced, which makes Splunk alerts trigger an automate workflow in enterprise applications.

The following are some of the features of the custom alert action introduced in Splunk 6.3:

- Various third-party applications/add-ons directly integrate with enterprise applications

- UI-based configuration of settings and administration options can be set directly from the Splunk Web console

- Various enterprise-applications-based extensions can be developed and distributed to Splunk users for integration with Splunk

- Enterprise application add-ons/extensions are already available for the famous, most widely used alerting, incident management tools and thus can be directly integrated and used

The features

Splunk supports the following custom alert framework to use and manage custom alert actions:

- Custom alert actions will be made available as add-ons or extensions that can be directly used by configuring on Splunk.

- Configurations can either be done by a UI from the Splunk Web console or via the respective conf files. Features such as access control and add-on management can also be enabled for user configuration.

- We can explicitly invoke scripts (Python scripts and bash scripts) and can even pass information via tokens to the scripts.

- The configuration framework supports encrypting confidential information with the access method to read/write from the alert script.

- Splunk provides lots of enterprise application support for custom alert actions, such as BigPanda, ServiceNow, xMatters, HipChat, Slack, Hue Bulbs, Alert Manager, Insteon Home Automation Control, Jira, Yammer, and so on.

- The inbuilt plugins can be configured from the Splunk Web console by navigating to **Settings | Alert Actions**.

  The **Alert Actions** page will be visible with a list of installed alert actions along with the option to install add-ons/extensions from the Splunk app store. The following figure shows the **Alert Actions** page of the Splunk Web console:

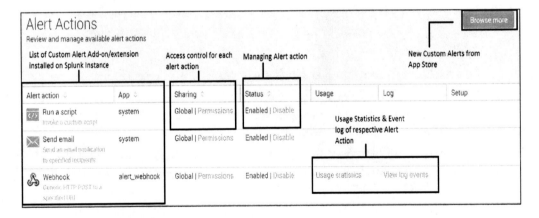

The **Custom Alert** page accessed via the Splunk Web console can be used to configure and manage alert actions that are already installed or new alert actions can be installed from the Splunk app store. The alert action panel also provides access to usage statistics and log events.

Implementation

Let's see how to create and use a custom alert action on the Splunk Web console.
Follow these steps to do so:

1. Write the search query on whose output the custom `Alert` action is to be
    defined on the Splunk search. Click on the **Save As** button and then on **Alert**:

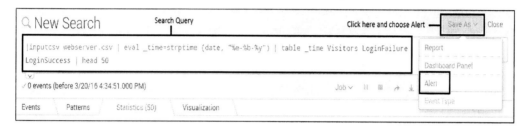

2. The **Save As Alert** screen pops up, similar to what is shown in the following
    figure, where various information needs to be configured. The first segment
    of **Save As Alert** is **Settings**, as shown in the following figure:

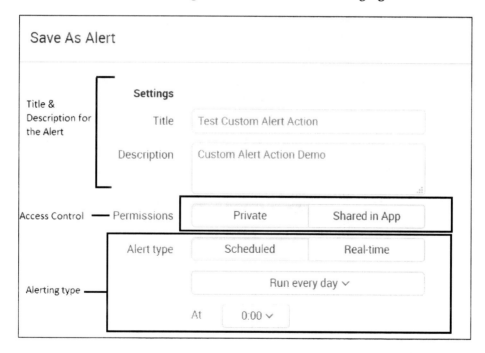

    ◦   The title and description of the alert can be specified as per the user
        to identify the alert

- ○ The access control option describes whether the alert is private or shared in an app and can be configured from here
- ○ The alert schedule describes whether a schedule is to be run every day, every hour, every month, or in real time, and can be configured from this section

3. The next section is **Trigger Conditions**. Here, when the preceding alert runs and the output is generated, then the condition can be specified in the trigger condition to do custom alert actions:

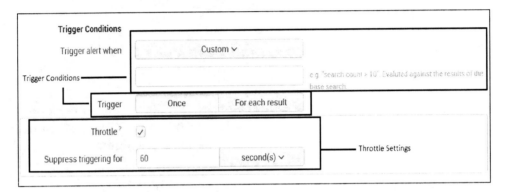

The alert condition can be configured by choosing one of the inbuilt options or a custom option can be selected where a user can specify the condition. Once this condition is satisfied, the configured custom alert action will be invoked.

There is also an option to throttle the trigger, which means that if a trigger condition is met, then for the specified time, the alert trigger will be suppressed to avoid duplicate triggers. The throttle condition can be enabled/disabled as per the requirement from the preceding settings.

4. Since we have configured the alert search, the trigger condition will configure the custom alert action. The alert action is the action that will be performed when the alert triggered condition is met. The last section of **Save As Alert** is **Trigger Actions**:

When we click on the **Add Actions** button from the **Trigger Actions** section, another pop up appears listing all the custom alert action add-ons/plugins installed in the Splunk instance:

5. The list of custom alert actions is available when we click on **Add Actions**, and then the user can choose one or more than one alert actions from the list. Each alert action selected can be configured from the same screen, and click on **Save** to create a custom alert action. The following screenshot shows three alert actions configured for an alert. Similarly, as per the required custom alert, actions can be chosen and configured:

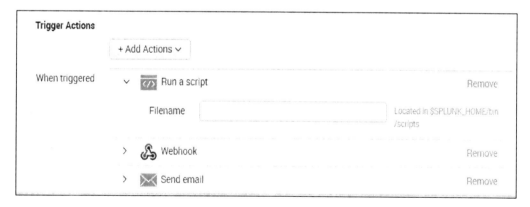

Example

Let's understand the use of the custom alert action with the help of a real-world example. Let's suppose that we have data from various payment gateways for credit cards on Splunk. Every second, millions of transactions take place from various sources, such as e-commerce portals, mobile devices, ATM/PoS transactions, and the log information from these sources is made available on Splunk.

Taking advantage of Splunk's custom alert action, the following are some of the use cases that can be implemented on the said data:

- **Fraud detection:** Fraud detection can be configured either on the machine-learning logic or correlation or outlier detection. Once the fraud detection search is ready, a custom alert can be defined whenever any such condition is met. The alert can be used to send an instant SMS or e-mail to the respective people. Run a custom script to inform the payment gateway in order to abort the transaction, and so on. Thus, the necessary action can be taken as required to avoid any loss to the business.

- **Automatic incident tracking:** Whenever the transaction fails due to any reason, such as an incorrect password, failure due to any hardware, network failure, and so on, the automatic incident will be logged in the incident tracking system to automate the fixing of the concerned issue.

Similarly, depending on the requirement and use case, a custom alert action can be defined, and the automation of workflow is achieved.

Summary

In this chapter, we saw various advanced dashboard customization techniques, which can be used on the Splunk dashboard. The customization methods learned in this chapter can be applied to build useful, highly functional, and dynamic dashboards on Splunk. Now, we will see how various tweaks and techniques can be used on Splunk to utilize its features efficiently. You will learn about a few features and tweaks of Splunk that can help us make quality analytics and visualizations.

10
Tweaking Splunk

We have already learned some important features of Splunk, creating analytics and visualizations, along with various dashboard customization techniques. Now we will learn about various ways we can tweak Splunk so that we can get the most out of it and that to efficiently. In this chapter we will learn various management and customization techniques for using Splunk in the best possible way.

In this chapter, we will cover the following topics in detail, along with example and uses.

- Index replication
- Indexer auto-discovery
- Sourcetype manager
- Field extractor
- Search history
- Event pattern detection
- Data acceleration
- Splunk buckets
- Search optimizations
- Splunk health

Index replication

Splunk supports a distributed environment. Now, when it is said that Splunk supports a distributed environment, what does this actually mean? What is the use of Splunk being deployed in a distributed environment?

Splunk can be deployed in a standalone environment and in a distributed environment as well. Let us understand what a standalone environment, a distributed environment, and index replication are.

Standalone environment

In a standalone environment, various components of Splunk, like the indexer or search head are available on a single machine, which handles everything from onboarding data on Splunk, indexing the data, analytics and visualization, reporting, and so on. Generally, standalone is used for development and testing purposes; it is not at all recommended for deployment scenarios.

Distributed environment

In a distributed environment, various components of Splunk (the indexer, search head, and others) are deployed in clusters. Deploying in a clustered environment helps to produce multiple copies of the same data for high availability and reduces the chances of data loss in case of hardware failures and disaster recovery.

Splunk is a big data log monitoring and analytics tool, which is the reason why Splunk should be deployed in a distributed environment. It helps in achieving real-time analytics on a Splunk distributed environment. So let us have a look at some of the terminologies of distributed components, which we will be using to understand a distributed deployment of Splunk:

- **Clusters**: Clusters are groups of Splunk indexers configured to replicate each other's data so as to have multiple redundant copies of all the data.

- **Master node**: Master node, also known as the cluster master, has the responsibility of managing the cluster. It is recommended to have one master node for one cluster. In Splunk architecture, the master node is shown using the following symbol:

Cluster Master / Master Node

- **Peer nodes**: Peer nodes are sets of indexers where the actual data gets indexed and is stored. There can be several indexers depending upon the replication factor to store multiple copies of all the data. The following image depicts the symbol for the peer node:

Peer Node / Cluster Peer

- **Replication factor**: This factor determines the number of copies of data that should be available in a cluster and thus, the replication factor can be said to be the fundamental level of a cluster's failure tolerance. The following image shows replication, with each box representing an individual replicated peer node of a cluster:

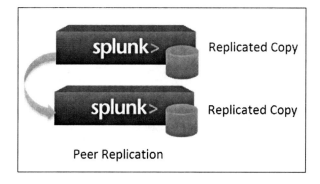

- **Search heads**: Search heads are responsible for managing and coordinating searching over peer nodes on the basis of the search factor. A search head is shown in the architecture of Splunk using the following depiction:

- **Search factor**: The search factor defines the number of searchable copies of data that should be available in a cluster. This factor can be used to understand the capability of a cluster to be able to recover its searching capability after any peer node's failure.

Replication

Now let us understand how searching actually happens in a distributed environment of Splunk, and some important scenarios.

Searching

The following image describes a single cluster of a Splunk distributed environment with the replication factor as three. As seen in the image, there are three peer nodes:

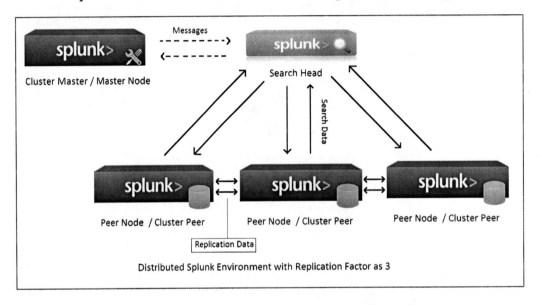

Distributed Splunk Environment with Replication Factor as 3

There are three types of communication in the preceding distributed cluster image.

- **Messages**: The cluster master communicates a list of peer nodes/cluster peers to the search head. The search head is always communicated with the list of peer nodes for searching.

- **Search data**: The search head distributes search queries to a peer node / cluster peer for search processing and then consolidates the result.

- **Replication data**: The peer node communicates with other peer nodes / cluster peers to keep all the nodes with an updated copy of all the data among each other.

Failures

How Splunk's distributed environment manages itself in case of failures to avoid performance issues and data loss is as follows:

- **Peer node / cluster peer fails**: Let us suppose we have a cluster similar to the one in the preceding example image. If any of the peer nodes fail or go down, the following is the mechanism performed by the various components of a Splunk distributed environment:

  1. The cluster master, which always keeps track of peer nodes detects the peer is down. It instructs another working node to act as a primary peer node.

  2. The cluster master now instructs the search head to use the redundant peer node for replication so as to meet the replication factor defined. Hence, a peer node, which is just kept for future use, is used and a full data replication starts on the new disk.

- **Cluster master fails**: If the cluster master, which gives commands to the search head itself goes down, then the following is the working flow of the cluster:

  1. The search head continues to run its normal functioning as per the list of search peer nodes last updated by the cluster manager.

  2. The newly arrived data may or may not have enough replicated copies, as the cluster master is not available to maintain compliance of the replication factor.

  3. Once the cluster master is back, it updates the search head and also starts replication for any unreplicated copies (if applicable) since its failure.

 Splunk does not charge separate license fees for replication; that means you can have replication enabled using your Splunk Enterprise license itself, where data duplication (sending data from one Splunk index to another index) is chargeable.

The Splunk Web console provides information regarding where the distributed environment can be found. In the Splunk Web console, click on **Settings | Distributed Management Console**. Using the distributed management console, various important information an be attained, like the number of available peer nodes, indexers for the given cluster, and from those, how many are searchable and how many are down. This section also gives information about the indexing rate, the amount of disk and license used, the number of searches and their types, and the system health status.

Thus, index replication should be used actively, using distributed Splunk deployment so as to avoid data loss in case of failures and for business continuity of real-time analytics and visualizations.

Indexer auto-discovery

Splunk 6.3 introduced a very usable and important feature for distributed environments. This feature simplifies forwarder management, which automatically detects new peer nodes in a cluster, and thus, load balancing is handled by itself.

Example

Let us understand the use of indexer auto-discovery using the following cluster example image. The following image shows forwarders sending data to peer nodes. The peer node list and other relevant messages are being communicated from the cluster master to the forwarders:

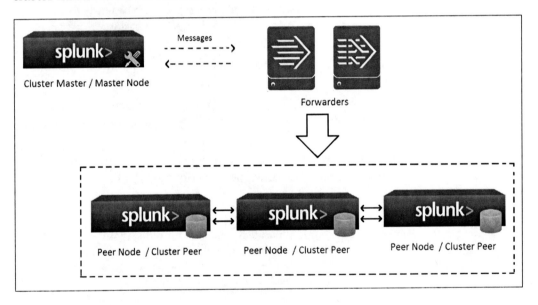

The following are the uses/advantages of indexer auto-discovery:

- There is no need for configuration on forwarders specifying the number of peer nodes in the given cluster. The forwarder is automatically informed with the updated list of peer nodes by the master. Thus, when a peer node fails or new peer nodes are added in a cluster, there is no configuration requirement on forwarders.

- There is no need to know the number of peer nodes when adding or removing a forwarder. Indexer auto-discovery needs to be enabled for a newly added forwarder and the cluster master takes care of the rest.

- The cluster master will be able to know the total disk space on each peer node, which can help to maintain load balancing. This information is communicated to forwarders and then the forwarders adjust the data sent to each of the peer nodes according to the disk space.

Implementation

Now let us have a look at how to enable and configure indexer auto-discovery in Splunk Enterprise:

1. The peer nodes are to be configured to receive and index data from forwarders:

    1. This can be enabled from the **Splunk Web console** | **Settings** | **Data** | **Forwarding and Receiving**. In the **Settings** page, under section **Receive Data**, a new port number to receive data from forwarders can be configured.

    2. Receiving can also be enabled by configuring the receiving port in the `inputs.conf` file.

2. Enabling indexer auto-discovery on the cluster master node can be done by configuring the `server.conf` configuration file on the master node.

    The following is a sample configuration to enable indexer auto-discovery on the master cluster:

    ```
    [indexer_discovery]
    pass4SymmKey = "Security_key"
    polling_rate = Number_btw_1_10
    indexerWeightByDiskCapacity = true/false
    ```

    The parameters used in the preceding snippet are discussed in the list that follows:

    - `Security_key`: It is a string which will be used to authenticate the cluster master and forwarders to enable secure communication.

    - `polling_rate`: It is the rate at which the forwarder polls the cluster master for the list of peer nodes. It can be defined as any integer value between 1 and 10.

- ° `indexerWeightByDiskCapacity`: If set to `true`, the cluster master fetches the disk capacity of all the peer nodes and communicates it to the forwarders for weighted load balancing.

3. Now, since the indexer auto-discovery is configured in the cluster master, forwarders are to be configured for index auto-discovery. The following is a sample configuration which needs to be configured in the `outputs.conf` file of every forwarder in the cluster to enable auto-discovery:

```
[indexer_discovery: Name_Index_Discovery]
pass4SymmKey = "Security_key"
master_uri = Master_Node_URI_with_Port

[tcpout: Group_Name]
indexerDiscovery = Name_Index_Discovery
useACK=true
```

The parameters used in the preceding snippet are discussed in the list that follows:

- ° A unique string (`Name_Index_Discovery`) which we will be using in `indexerDiscovery` of `tcpout` to identify the cluster master. This is useful in case more than one cluster has indexer auto-discovery enabled.

- ° `Security_key` is the same as that which is configured in the cluster master for authentication.

- ° `Master_Node_URI_with_Port` is the URI along with the management port of the cluster master from which the list of peer nodes is to be fetched.

- ° `Group_Name` is a unique name to define index discovery and acknowledge options. Any string can be defined as `Group_Name`, as per the user.

- ° `useACK=true` is an optional parameter; if defined and set to `true`, it enables indexer acknowledgement.

Thus, indexer auto-discovery should be enabled in a distributed environment of Splunk Enterprise so as to avoid reconfiguration and management of forwarders whenever there is any change in clusters or forwarders.

Sourcetype manager

Sourcetype manager is another very useful provision added in Splunk 6.3, which can be used to manage the sourcetype for on-boarding the data on Splunk. It can be used to manage (create, modify, and delete) sourcetype configurations independent of getting data in and searching within the sourcetype picker. We have already learned in the *Chapter 2, Developing Application on Splunk* about how to assign and configure sourcetype while uploading the data on Splunk.

Sourcetype manager enlists all the sourcetype configured in the Splunk instance along with the inbuilt default sourcetypes. The sourcetype manager can be accessed by navigating in the Splunk Web console to **Settings** | **Data** | **Sourcetype**.

Now let us learn what can be done from the sourcetype manager:

- **Create a sourcetype**: In previous versions of Splunk when sourcetype manager was not present to create a sourcetype, first we needed to add data to Splunk or else the `inputs.conf` file needed to be configured manually.

  Using the sourcetype manager, a new sourcetype can be created by clicking the **New Sourcetype** button on the top right of the page. This option helps to create a new sourcetype, along with configuration settings, as shown in the following image:

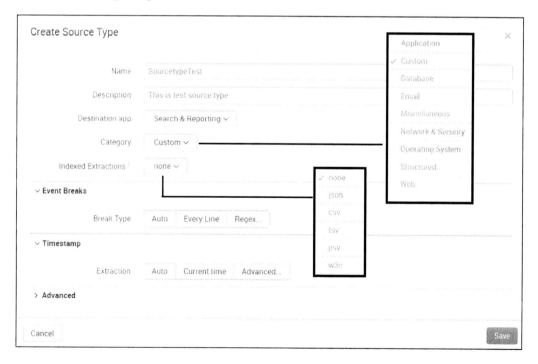

When creating a sourcetype, the following options can be configured:

- ○ The name and description of the sourcetype.

- ○ The app to which the sourcetype is to be associated by selecting the app name from the dropdown list.

- ○ The category can be chosen depending upon the source of the data so that pre-configured settings automatically get applied to the current sourcetype.

- ○ Indexed extraction for extraction of fields can be chosen in the respective format if the data is any of the predefined formats like CSV, PSV, TSV, JSON, or W3C.

- ○ Apart from choosing the pre-default options to apply pre-configured settings, manual settings can also be configured for event breaking, timestamping, and other advanced configurations, which will applied while uploading data on Splunk.

- **Modifying sourcetype**: Modifying various configurations can be done from the **Sourcetype Manager** page itself. Apart from the in-built sourcetype, the destination app can be changed along with category, event breaks, time stamping, and so on.

 Any change in sourcetype indexing parameters will not get applied on pre-existing data mapped for the given sourcetype. Only new data will get parsed in the modified format.

- **Deleting sourcetype**: In previous versions of Splunk, for deleting a sourcetype, there was no direct interface from the web console. It was done by running Splunk CLI commands. Now in Splunk 6.3, sourcetype can be deleted from the **Sourcetype Manager** page by clicking on the appropriate **Delete** button. Deleting the sourcetype could have adverse effects on the data associated with the sourcetype and also if any new data is associated with the sourcetype. Hence, deleting the sourcetype should done carefully.

Only sourcetypes which are created by a user can be deleted, the pre-existing default sourcetype available in Splunk cannot be deleted from the **Sourcetype Manager** page.

Field extractor

In Splunk, for any kind of analytics and visualizations, fields play a very important role. Splunk automatically tries to extract and make them available for use for known and properly configured data sources. Since there are a wide variety of sources for data, there could be many fields which do not get automatically extracted. Splunk also provides the Splunk command `rex`, which can be used to extract the fields, but this command requires a good understanding of regular expressions to efficiently extract fields from the data. So Splunk provides a very easy to use field extractor to extract fields using an interactive field extractor tool via the Splunk Web interface.

Accessing field extractor

Let us learn to access the field extractor to extract fields from the data, which in turn can be used to create analytics and visualizations in Splunk.

The field extractor can be accessed via the following options:

- **Splunk Web Console | Settings | Fields | Field Extractions | Open Field Extractor**.

- Using direct URL, by navigating to `http://localhost:8000/en-US/app/launcher/field_extractor`

  Where `localhost` and `8000` are to be replaced with, respectively, the IP address and web port of the user's Splunk instance.

- This option to access the field extractor is one the most useful and recommended ways of accessing the field extractor. It can be accessed from the result window of events when a search query is run on the web console.

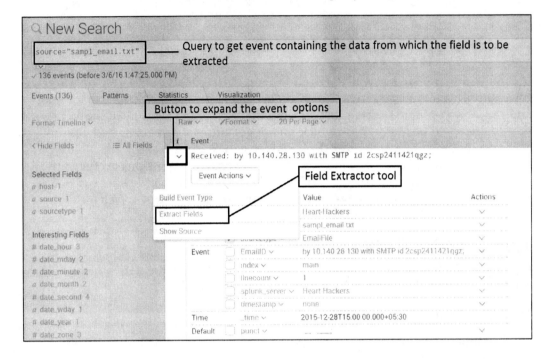

The preceding image shows an example to extract the field extractor tool, which can be accessed by taking the following steps:

1. Open a Splunk search page via the web console.
2. Query the data which has the value to be extracted as a field.
3. Click on the downward pointing arrow option of the respective event to expand the event options.
4. Click on the **Event Actions** button on the expanded window.
5. Then click on the **Extract Fields** option to extract the field from the selected data.

Using field extractor

Now, since we are aware of accessing the field extractor tool, let us see how to extract the fields using this tool. We will learn field extraction using the easiest and most recommended option, which is the third option explained in the *Accessing field extractor* section.

On clicking **Extract fields** via the third option, the following interactive screen appears. Even if the first and second options are chosen to access the field extractor, after selecting sourcetype, a screen similar to the following is shown:

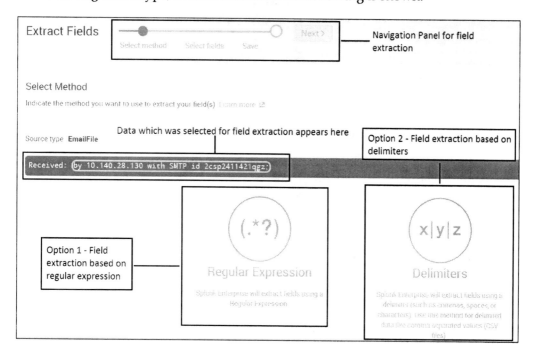

The preceding image has the following components:

- **Navigation panel**: The panel to proceed further and backtrack if required during the whole process of field extraction.

- **Data**: A subset of data of the selected sourcetype is shown, giving a choice of which option to choose (**Regular Expression or Delimiters**) for further field extraction.

    ○ **Regular Expression**: If the field which is to be extracted from the data is based on regular expression, then this option is selected, that is, field extraction using regular expression.

    ○ **Delimiters**: If the field which is to be extracted is from a structured file like CSV or TSV, then this option is selected.

Example

Let us have a look at field extraction using an example via the Splunk Web console. First we will learn field extraction using the first option as in the preceding image, that is, field extraction using regular expression, and then using the second option, or using delimiters.

Regular expression

Let us have a look at field extraction using regular expression. When regular expression is selected, then a screen similar to the following appears where we can extract the required fields:

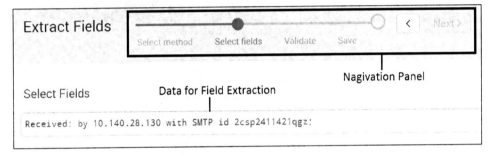

1. In the **Select Fields** where the data is shown, a set or subset of data can be selected to extract as a field. Let us say if the user wants to extract the IP address, then select the IP address and specify a name as required to get extracted. The following image describes the same:

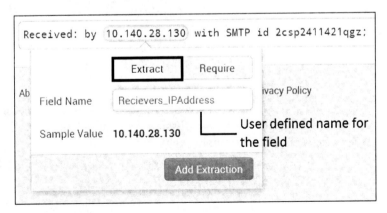

2. Click on **Add Extraction** and it will create a field as per the specified name and preview the value from the selected sourcetype, and verify and correct it if there is any discrepancy in extracting the value.

3. The following image shows the preview of the extracted field (**Recievers_IPAddress**):

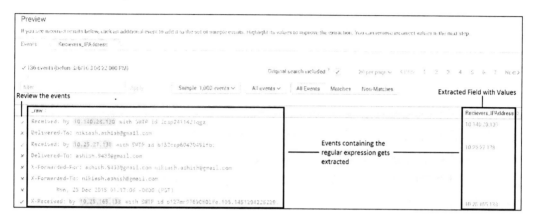

The **Preview** window has the option to select and deselect events to review any event which is wrongly extracted or any event which has a similar regular expression but is not extracted. Various options exist, like previewing matches and non-matches of fields from the data. The event selection sample can also be selected from the **Preview** window.

4. Once the required events are properly extracted, then click on **Next** to validate and save the newly extracted field.

5. The preceding procedure to extract the fields can be done for any number of datasets, and the required information can be extracted in the form of fields. Now let's suppose the user is interested in the IP address of only mails which were received in the inbox. Since the sourcetype will include all the data of the mail box, it will contain the IP address of various sent and received e-mails. So if any other conditions are to be specified while extracting the field, then it can be done here.

The following image shows how we can extract only the IP address of e-mails which are received in the mailbox:

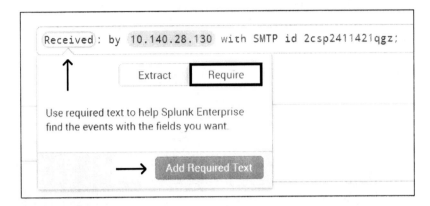

On selecting the **Received** option as shown in the preceding image, there are two options available. One is to extract similar data patterns in a field and another one is the **Require** option. It is used to instruct the field extractor tool to extract only those IP addresses (regular expression) where a received value is available. Thus, now the **Recievers_IPAddress** field will contain only those IP addresses where **Received** is available in the data.

Similarly, this tool can be used to extract fields based on requirements and can be used to build analytics and visualizations in Splunk.

Delimiter

When the delimiter is chosen while extracting the fields then a screen similar to the following appears:

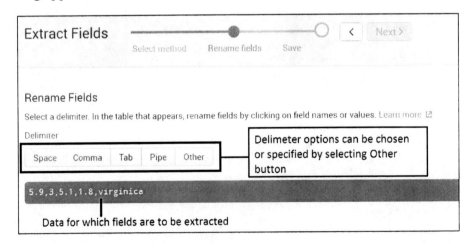

From the preceding screen, the respective delimiter option, when selected, automatically extracts all the data into fields; as per requirements, the field can be renamed and used. In the preceding example image, it is clearly seen that the data is comma-separated, and hence we will use a **comma** delimiter to properly extract the fields.

The following image shows the field extraction when the comma delimiter is selected for the preceding example:

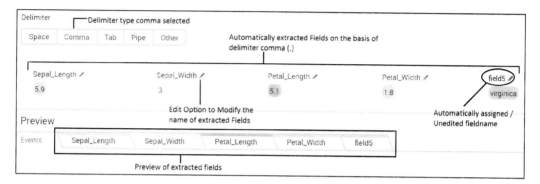

Thus, fields can be extracted on the basis of regular expression as well as on the basis of delimiter, as illustrated with the preceding example. Once fields are extracted, click on **Next** and then **Save** to make the extracted fields available for analytics and visualization. Permission to save extracted fields for any single app or for all the apps can be configured before saving right from the field extractor tool itself.

Search history

Search history is another useful feature introduced in Splunk 6.3 which can be used to view and interact with history of the `search` command. This feature can be used to get the complete list of search queries executed on Splunk over time.

The search history feature can be accessed via the Splunk Web console by clicking on **"Search & Reporting" App | Search**. It takes the user to the search summary dashboard with the option to run search queries.

The following image shows the search summary dashboard from where the search history can be accessed:

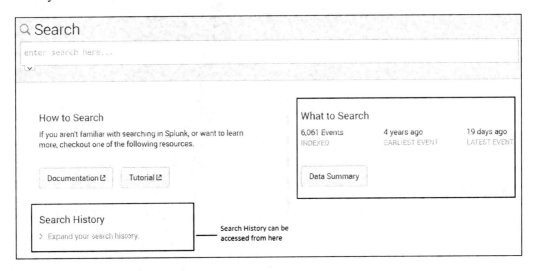

The **Search History** option enables the following information on the screen:

- The exhaustive list of search queries run on the Splunk instance along with the time of the last run
- The **Action** option to directly copy the respective search query in the **Search** bar so as to run the search query right away
- The **Filter** option to choose the list of queries shown on the basis of time defined in the time range picker or some specific word/string which can be configured in the text box

The following is a sample example screen of search history depicting all the preceding information:

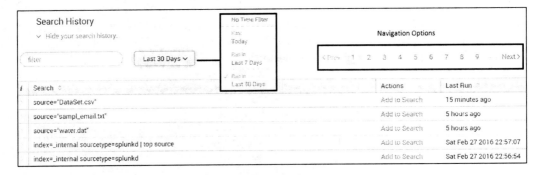

Event pattern detection

Event pattern detection is a feature in Splunk which helps in increasing the speed of analytics by automatically grouping similar events to discover meaningful insight in the given machine data. It helps users to quickly discover relationship, patterns, and anomalies in the given data, to build meaningful analytics on top of it.

In simpler terms, event pattern detection not only helps to find out the common patterns in the data but also highlights those events which are rare and could be anomalies. The event pattern detection feature of Splunk can be helpful in the following ways:

- Auto discover meaningful patterns in the given dataset
- Search data without the need to know what to search for
- Detection of anomalies, rare events, and so on

The following image shows a sample of data events when queried on Splunk. The sample data has mostly numbers in it, and if not much domain information is available about the data it would be difficult to get insight from it:

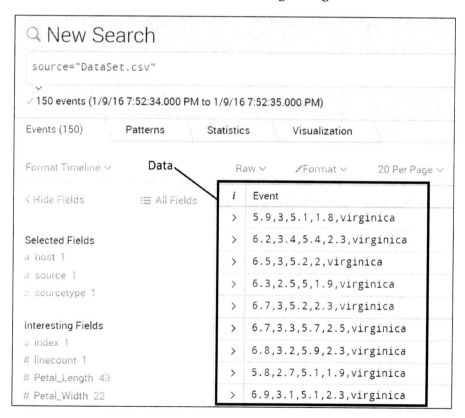

Now we will see how event pattern detection helps in getting quick insights from the preceding data. The following image shows the output of the **Patterns** tab for the preceding data:

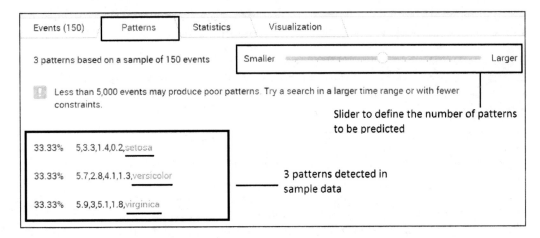

The **Patterns** tab output shows that the total data shows three different patterns, and those are listed in the output. Looking at the preceding output image, it is clear that the data has information about three different species. There is a slider tool available, which when moved to the **Larger** side tries to return a greater number of patterns, and when moved toward the **Smaller** end returns a smaller number of events.

Basically, sliding toward the **Larger** side shows those results as well which have a low percentage of common patterns, which could be of no use, and similarly, sliding towards the **Smaller** side will return only those event patterns which have a very high percentage of common patterns. Thus the slider can be adjusted and the best suitable for the respective data can be defined.

 Event pattern detection works well when the number of events is higher; thus, the warning message is shown in the preceding image.

Clicking on any identified pattern will display the detailed information about the pattern. The following image is a sample output of detailed pattern information:

In the preceding example output, the first pattern (highlighted) is selected and information regarding the selected pattern is shown on the right-hand side. The information includes the following:

- The number of estimated events which fit the criteria of selected patterns from the whole dataset
- The search query, which returns the selected pattern output
- The keyword used in the search query

The detailed panel also has the option to do the following actions:

- View the events on which this pattern is shown.
- Create an alert so that when such a pattern is detected in future, it is notified.
- Save the entered search query as an event type for future classification and while using analytics over data having a similar pattern.

Thus, event pattern detection can be used to derive meaningful insights from the data quickly and automatically.

Data acceleration

Splunk is a big data tool and hence, it is obvious that the reports and dashboards created on Splunk will have large datasets/events. So data acceleration is very much necessary to get real-time analytics and visualizations.

Need for data acceleration

Let's understand the need for data acceleration in reports and dashboards with the help of the following image. The following image is an example screenshot of a dashboard with many panels and thus, many searches. When there are many searches running concurrently in a report/dashboard then it takes time to show the analytics or visualization on the dashboard. Thus for real-time analytics, data acceleration will be required:

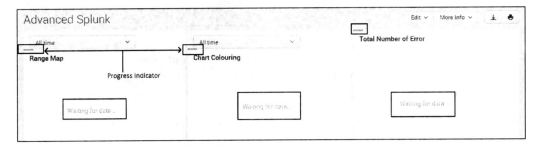

Splunk is a very powerful big data tool, so why does it takes time to populate the results on the dashboard/report? The reason behind why some searches complete quickly and some take too much time can be explained with the help of the following facts:

- Splunk is very fast at finding a keyword or set of keywords from millions of events.

  For example, searching `error=404` among millions of events.

- Splunk is not fast at searches having calculations on millions of events.

  For example, calculation of any mathematical formula, count, mean, median, and so on, on millions of events.

Hence, which kinds of searches should be included in the reports/dashboard can be decided by taking into account the preceding facts to get real-time analytics.

Data model acceleration

Let us understand how we can implement data model acceleration (also known as persistent data model acceleration) so as to speed up the data processing and data searching to give real-time analytics. Data model acceleration is an inbuilt tool in Splunk which adds a second layer to the data to increase the speed of a Splunk search on large datasets with millions of events in real time. Data model acceleration does not remove any functionality from Splunk basic searches but creates a schema of pre-defined fields:

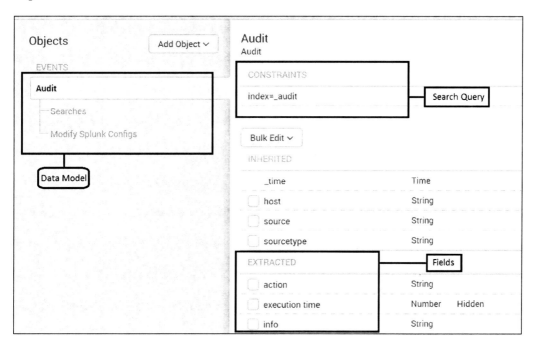

The preceding image is a snapshot of Splunk's inbuilt data model of the `Audit` index. The data model helps to create instant pivot charts as well as helping acceleration reports to get faster results. The data model is hierarchical in that at each hierarchy level, fields are extracted and kept ready for use for the next level in the hierarchy and so on.

Generally, in normal scenarios, the fields are extracted from the raw data during the search time, but when data model acceleration is enabled, the field extraction process happens during index time. So, search performance is optimized, as the fields are already extracted and available during searching, but this adds overhead during indexing and thus higher indexer utilization happens when data model acceleration is enabled. The extracted data model fields are stored in the **High Performance Analytics Store (HPAS)**, available on indexers as `.tsidx` files.

The data model can also be accelerated as shown in the following image. The option to accelerate the data model as shown in the following image can be accessed from the Splunk Web console by navigating to **Data Model | Edit | Edit Acceleration**:

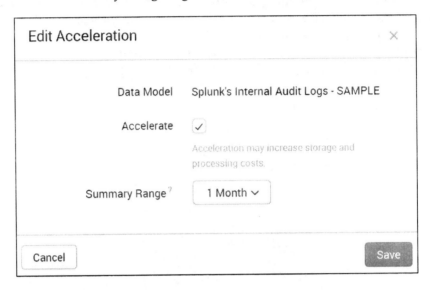

The following are the few limitations of data model acceleration:

- Only data model event hierarchy is accelerated
- Once the acceleration is enabled on the data model, it cannot be edited

Data model acceleration has been available in older versions of Splunk as well. In Splunk 6.3, which features an additional technique, parallelization, already learned earlier, helps in running two concurrent search jobs instead of one. Thus, more efficient and faster accelerations are possible as compared to older versions of Splunk. The data acceleration is due to the use of exclusive HPAS during the pivot and while using the tstat command.

Let us see how to check the status of data model acceleration from the Splunk Web console.

Navigate from the Splunk Web console to **Settings | Data Models**. The following image shows the sample of data model acceleration status:

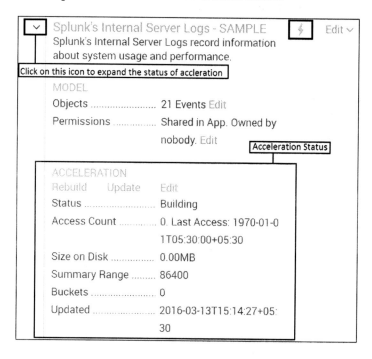

The data model's definition is stored in the respective model's folder or respective app directory `$SPLUNK_HOME\etc\apps\appname\default\data\models` in JSON format (`modelname.json`). The definition of the data model (JSON file) is stored on the search head.

Apart from persistent data model acceleration, which we have just studied, Splunk also has the capability to run ad hoc data model acceleration. The following is the scenario when Splunk automatically implements ad hoc data model acceleration:

- It is automatically applied to the Pivot UI.
- The acceleration happens at the search head, similar to persistent data acceleration.
- The summaries created for acceleration are deleted once the Pivot editor is closed.

Splunk buckets

The Splunk Enterprise stores its index's data into buckets organized by age. Basically, it is a directory containing events of a specific period. There can be several buckets at the same time in the various stages of the bucket life cycle.

A bucket moves from one stage to another depending upon its age, size, and so on, as per the defined conditions. The Splunk bucket stages are **Hot**, **Warm**, **Cold**, **Frozen**, and **Thawed**. Splunk buckets play a very important role in the performance of search results and hence they should be properly configured as per the requirements.

The following image shows the life cycle of Splunk buckets:

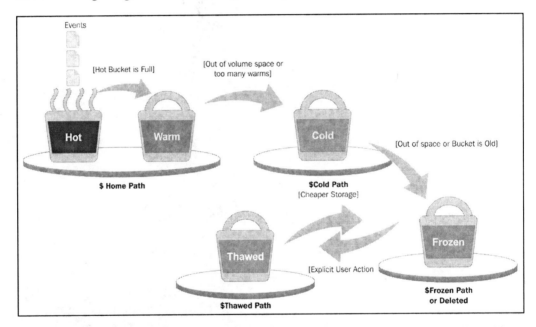

Let us understand the Splunk bucket life cycle, taking the above image as a reference. The Indexes.conf file can be modified to configure the aging and the conditions to move from one stage to another:

- **Hot bucket**: Whenever any new data gets indexed on Splunk Enterprise, it is stored in a hot bucket. There can be more than one hot bucket for each index. The data in the hot bucket supports both read and write. This is the only stage of the bucket life cycle where it supports write operations as well. Until and unless some specific conditions are configured, the data in the hot bucket cannot be backed up.

- **Warm bucket**: Whenever the hot bucket is full, it gets converted into warm bucket and a new hot bucket gets created. Unlike hot bucket, the data in the warm bucket only supports read and can be backed up. In terms of search performance, hot and warm Buckets are the same, with no effect on search performance. Hot and warm buckets are stored at `$SPLUNK_HOME/var/lib/splunk/defaultdb/db/*`

- **Cold bucket**: Once the warm bucket is full or the count of the warm bucket exceeds the configured number, the warm bucket is moved to the cold bucket. The storage type used for the cold bucket can be relatively cheaper as compared to that of the hot/warm bucket. The hot/warm bucket requires very high IOPS as compared to the data in the cold bucket and hence, relatively cheaper storage can be used for the cold bucket. Similar to the warm bucket, it supports both read and backup capability. The cold bucket is stored at `$SPLUNK_HOME/var/lib/splunk/defaultdb/colddb/*`

- **Frozen bucket**: On reaching the age limit or crossing the storage limit of the cold bucket, the cold bucket is converted into the frozen bucket. Frozen data does not support `read` operations and cannot be searched on either. Splunk, by default, deletes the frozen bucket but it can be configured to move to an archive as well. Archived data can later move to the thawed state.

Search optimizations

We have already learned data acceleration and the bucket life cycle in the preceding section. Let us now see how we can make the best use of search queries for better and more efficient results. Splunk search queries can be optimized depending upon the requirements and conditions. Generally, the search queries which need to be optimized are those which are used most frequently. Let us learn a few tricks to optimize the search for faster results.

Time range

We have already learned about Splunk buckets, which organize events based on time. The shorter the time span, the less buckets will be accessed to get the information of the search result. It has always been a common practice to use *All time in the time range picker* for any search, irrespective of whether the result is required for all of the duration or some limited duration.

So one of the best search optimization methods is to use the time range picker to specify the time domain on which the search should run to get the result. Since the time limit will be specified, only limited buckets will be accessed, irrespective of all the buckets and thus, faster and more optimized results will be obtained.

Search modes

Splunk has three search modes: **verbose, fast,** and **smart.** These modes are discussed as follows:

- The verbose mode is the slowest and most exploratory option, which returns as much events information as possible.

- The smart mode, depending upon the `search` command used in the search query, sometimes behaves like the fast mode and sometimes like the verbose mode.

- In the fast mode, field discovery is switched off and it is the fastest of all the modes. Dashboards and reports use the fast mode by default.

If the searches are done in the fast mode, the search results can be obtained three to five times faster than in the verbose mode.

Scope of searching

In Splunk, to access data we have index, source, and sourcetype. Index helps in locating the disk from which the data will be read. Source and sourcetype should be used to specify exactly where to look for data. Specifying the scope can result in up to 10 times faster results than not using the scope.

Let me explain the use of the scope and how can it accelerate the result of a search query using an example:

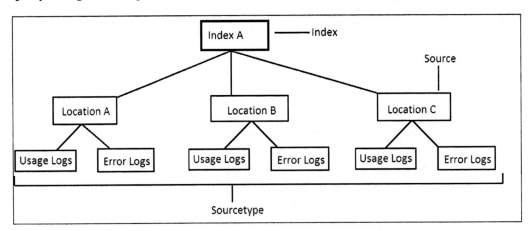

In the preceding example image, we have one index (**Index A**), three sources (**Location A**, **Location B**, and **Location C**) and two sourcetypes (**Usage Logs** and **Error Logs**):

- Now let us suppose if the result is required for only the usage logs of all the sources (locations), then the search query should be as follows:

  ```
  Index= "indexA" sourcetype= "usage_logs"
  ```

- If usage_logs of only **Location A** are required, then the source should be as follows:

  ```
  Index= "indexA" source= "locationA" sourcetype= "usage_logs"
  ```

Similarly, only the data should be searched for which the result is required and hence, since the amount of unnecessary data searching is removed by using scope (index, source, and sourcetype) the search will be efficient and faster.

Search terms

When specifying the scope of searching using index, source, and sourcetype, the following precautions should be taken to accelerate the search results:

- Avoid using the following search:

  ```
  Index= "abc" foo | search bar
  ```

  Instead, the preceding search query should be Index= "abc" foo bar.

- Avoid using NOT as far as possible:

  ```
  Index= "abc" sourcetype= "errorlogs" NOT error=404
  ```

  The preceding search query should be reformatted for faster processing as:

  ```
  Index= "abc" sourcetype= "errorlogs" AND (error=400 OR error=401
  OR error=403)
  ```

- Combine multiple instances of rename and rex together:

  ```
  ... | rename A as "I am A" | rename B as "I am B"
  ```

  The preceding search query has two instances of rename; those two should be combined as shown in the following. It should be noted that rename should always be added at the end:

  ```
  ... | rename A as "I am A", B as "I am B"
  ```

- Fields should be used before `stats`, for `table` command preferably, as shown in the following:

```
Index= "webserverlogs" | stats count by error | search error=404
```

The preceding search query should be replaced by the following query for faster processing:

```
Index= "webserverlogs" error=404 | stats count by error
```

- Subsearches (`append`) should be avoided for faster processing. The following example shows how an append can be avoided. Subsearches should strictly not be used for real-time searches:

```
Index= "locationA" | eval variable=locA | append [search index=
"locationB" | eval variable=locB]
```

The preceding search query can be replaced by the following for faster and more efficient performance:

```
Index= "locationA" OR index= "locationB" | eval variable=case
(index== "locationA", "locA", index== "locationB", "locB")
```

- Use `rename` instead of `eval` wherever possible. Using `rename` instead of `eval` doesn't make any difference in results, but it has been observed that `rename` is faster than `eval` sometimes:

```
... | eval abc= "This is test statement"
```

The preceding `eval` statement can also be written as follows:

```
... | rename abc as "This is test statement"
```

Thus by making efficient use of Splunk search queries, it can be optimized for accurate and faster results.

Splunk health

It is very important to keep track of Splunk's health status. Splunk Enterprise keeps logging various important information which can be helpful in the various stages of Splunk usage. Splunk's log and Splunk Enterprise can be used together to keep track of Splunk's health and various other important measures related to Splunk Enterprise. The Splunk logs can be useful in troubleshooting, system maintenance and tuning, and so on.

The following activities can be tracked by using Splunk's inbuilt logging mechanism:

- Resource utilization and Splunk license usage
- Data indexing, searching, analytics-related information, warnings, and errors
- User activities and application usage information
- Splunk component performance-related information

Splunk logging ranges from a wide variety of sources like audit log, kvstore log, conf log, crash log, license log, splunkd log, and many more.

splunkd log

Of all the sources for Splunk logs, one of the most important and useful logs is splunkd.log. This log file has information of data input/output, errors, warnings, debugging messages, and so on. splunkd also contains log messages generated by scripted/modular inputs. splunkd (Splunk daemon) is the service which runs the Splunk server and hence the name of the log file.

The splunkd.log file can be found at $SPLUNK_HOME$\var\log\Splunk. The maximum size of a single splunkd.log file is 25MB and only the five most recent files are retained in the file system. The log messages of the splunkd.log file can also be accessed by the Splunk Web console via index=_internal. The Splunk Web console can also be used to access the log messages of remote forwarders and indexers from the search head in a distributed environment.

The logging of the splunkd.log file can be configured to the required log level as per the requirement by modifying the log.cfg file located as $SPLUNK_HOME$\etc.

Search log

The search log can be found on the indexer and search head, which keeps logs related to search queries run on Splunk. The search.log file can be found at $SPLUNK_HOME$\var\run\splunk\dispatch\search_id. The search.log file is generated as per the searches and hence each search will have its own log file.

This log file contains complete information regarding the respective search, along with errors and warnings. Similar to splunkd.log configuration, search.log can also be configured by modifying changes in log-searchprocess.cfg located at $SPLUNK_HOME$\etc.

Apart from `splunkd.log` and `search.log`, there are various other important log files, like `scheduler.log`, which can be used to debug scheduling related issues, and Splunk utility logs, which keep track of license usage database validations.

Splunk logs provide operational information about performance, warnings, and errors. The recent log files can be accessed through the file system, whereas the historical file can be accessed from the Splunk Web console via a Splunk CLI query. Thus, Splunk can be very useful in various scenarios of usage, development, and deployment of Splunk Enterprise.

Summary

In this chapter we have read about various features of Splunk which can be used to utilize Splunk for better, more efficient, and faster analytics. We have learned various tools like sourcetype manager, field extractor, event pattern detection, and so on. We also had a look at data acceleration, efficient search queries, and various other important tweaks of Splunk Enterprise. In the next chapter we will learn about enterprise integration of Splunk with various other analytics and visualization tools.

11
Enterprise Integration with Splunk

We now have enough understanding of how to use Splunk for analytics and visualization. In this chapter, we will go through how Splunk can be integrated with any present/legacy proprietary applications in detail along with examples. Splunk provides an **Software Development Kit (SDK)** on almost all programming languages, such as .NET, Java, Python, and so on. The SDK can be used to integrate with applications to get better, efficient, and faster (real-time) results in the applications. You will also learn how Splunk can be integrated with other tools such as R for analytics and Tableau for visualization.

The following are the topics that will be covered in this chapter:

- The Splunk SDK
- Installing the Splunk SDK
- The Splunk SDK for Python
- Splunk with R for analytics
- Splunk with Tableau for visualization

The Splunk SDK

An SDK plays a very important role in integrating the power of Splunk's real-time analytics and visualization in legacy/proprietary applications. Industries and organizations use some or the other tool to generate analytics and visualization. However, legacy/propriety tools may not be scalable to handle big data and provide real-time analytics, and hence Splunk comes to the rescue. It may not be possible to replace the current tools used in the workflow, and hence, the Splunk SDK can be used to integrate with the current tool to utilize the power of Splunk.

The Splunk SDK is available in almost all the programming languages, such as C#, Java, PHP, Ruby, Python, and JavaScript.

The following are the scenarios where the Splunk SDK can be useful:

- It can be integrated with current workflow tools seamlessly to utilize the power of Splunk's big data analytics and visualization in real time.
- An SDK can help in logging data in the Splunk server directly from the application; that is, rather than storing the logs in a text file and then uploading data logs on Splunk, the logs can be directly sent on the Splunk server using an SDK.
- It can be integrated with other analytics and big data tools, such as R, Tableau, and so on.

Let's understand the use of the Splunk SDK with the help of an example. Let's assume that we have a banking tool that is used in ABC Bank to do all kinds of transactions, internal process management, inventory and asset management, and so on. The tool logs all the transactions in a database and is used for various purposes, such as fraud detection, fraudulent transactions, cash inflow and outflow, analytics, and various other insights required by the bank. The database logging mechanism can handle a few thousand to a few lac transactions in a day, but due to advancements in technology, the number of transactions and workflow has increased to millions of transactions per minute. If the bank continues to use the pre-existing legacy tool, then it would take hours to a few days to generate insight. Let's say that there was a fraudulent transaction, but what is the use of finding that when the loss is already done. Here, the Splunk SDK comes to our rescue, using which informed business decisions can be taken in real time. In these scenarios, the logs can be directly sent to Splunk using the Splunk SDK, and the generated analytics and visualization can be shown in the pre-existing application. Also, Splunk's capability of alerting, custom alert action, can be used to take critical business decisions automatically.

Installing the Splunk SDK

We already know that the Splunk SDK is available for most of the popular programming languages, but we will concentrate on the Splunk SDK for Python on a Windows OS in detail in this chapter.

The Splunk SDK is available for download from the Splunk website (`http://dev.splunk.com/sdks`) and the Splunk SDK for Python can be directly downloaded from `http://dev.splunk.com/goto/sdk-python`.

The SDK is for Python, and hence, Python should be already installed to use the Splunk SDK for Python. According to Splunk documentation, the Splunk SDK supports Python 2.6 or higher but does not support Python 3.

The Python SDK can be installed in Windows using Python's **Setuptools** or by downloading the Python SDK from the preceding link manually. The Python SDK can be installed from the Command Prompt as follows:

1. Download Setuptools from the Python website (`https://pypi.python.org/pypi/setuptools`) and in Command Prompt, navigate to the `Setuptools` folder and type Python `easy_install.py install`.

    Once the installation is complete, the next step is to run the following command in order to install the Splunk SDK:

    ```
    easy_install.py splunk-sdk
    ```

    The Splunk SDK for Python is installed and ready to use in Windows.

2. The second way of installing the Splunk SDK for Python is by downloading the SDK from Splunk's website. Then, navigate to the directory where the downloaded SDK is located via Command Prompt and run the following command:

    ```
    Python setup.py install
    ```

    It has been observed that while installing the SDK via this method, the dependency is automatically downloaded from the Internet. If for some reason, it couldn't be downloaded, the user needs to manually install the dependency by downloading it from the Python website.

The Splunk SDK can be installed via any of the preceding method, preferably the first method as it is easy and straightforward. Once the installation is done, the Splunk SDK for Python is available for use in Python.

Similarly, the Splunk SDK for the required platform can be downloaded and installed to integrate it with an enterprise tool.

The Splunk SDK for Python

We understood the use of an SDK and also saw the installation part of the Splunk SDK for Python. Now, we will see how the SDK can be used to integrate the power of Splunk's analytics and visualization.

Importing the Splunk API in Python

The following `import` statement will make the Splunk API available for use in Python:

```
import splunklib.client as client
import splunklib.results as results
```

The preceding two `import` statements make the API exposed using the Splunk SDK that is to be used in the Python code for integration.

Connecting and authenticating the Splunk server

The following image in the code snippet connects and also authenticates the Splunk server. The login details can be passed as a parameter when running the Python code or can be hardcoded in the code itself and can be saved in a `.splunkrc` file:

```
# Create a Service instance
global service

#The Server credentials are hardcoded here but can also be passed as a parameter
service = client.connect(host=localhost, port=8089, username=admin, password=admin)
```

Once the authentication is successful, the Splunk APIs can be used to send data on Splunk, enlist or run saved searches, run a search query on Splunk, upload files, create and delete indexes, and so on.

Splunk APIs

The following screenshots show the same code snippet that is used for various Splunk APIs and to perform various operations from the Python code itself.

Creating and deleting an index

The following code snippet can create and delete an index on Splunk via Python. In the following code, there are two functions (`CreateIndex` and `CleanIndex`) that can be used to create and delete a specified index as a parameter:

```
### Creates Index
def CreateIndex(INDEX):
    #If the index does not exisits, then create an Index
    if INDEX not in service.indexes:
        myindex = service.indexes.create(INDEX)

### Deletes the Index
def CleanIndex(INDEX):
    #If the index exisits, then Delete it
    if INDEX in service.indexes:
        myindex = service.indexes.delete(INDEX)
```

Creating input

The following snippet can be used to create a TCP input to accept the data coming on that port and upload it on Splunk that is mapped to a specified index and sourcetype. Information such as the port number, index mapped to this TCP input, and the respective sourcetype needs to be passed as a parameter while the function is called. Also, since the connection created is a `tcp` connection, it is hardcoded, but if a UDP connection is required, then `tcp` needs to be replaced with `udp` in the following code:

```
### Create TCP Input & Index
def CreateTCPInput(Port, INDEX, SOURCETYPE ):
    # Create a new TCP data input, if the specified port is not already defined
    if Port not in service.inputs:
        # Port, Index & Sourcetype is obtained as a parameter when function is called
        tcpinput = service.inputs.create(Port, "tcp", host=localhost, index=INDEX,
        sourcetype=SOURCETYPE )
```

Uploading files

The following code snippet can be used to upload files on Splunk by providing the INDEX and PATH of the file while calling the function:

```
### Upload File to Splunk
def UploadFileToSplunk(INDEX, PATH):
        # Retrieve the index for the data
        myindex = service.indexes[INDEX]

        # Upload and index the file
        myindex.upload(PATH);
```

Saved searches

The following code snippet helps in creating a **Saved Search** from Python:

```
### Create a Saved Search
def SavedSearch():
    # The search query for saved search
    myquery = "index=_internal | stats count by sourcetype"
    #The name of saved search
    mysearchname = "SDK Test"
    #If a saved search with identical name exisits, it delete and then creates
    if mysearchname in service.saved_searches:
        service.saved_searches.delete(mysearchname)
    mysavedsearch = service.saved_searches.create(mysearchname, myquery)
```

Splunk searches

The Splunk SDK is a great tool that supports modes for the search operation depending on the complexity of the operation. Following are the modes of search supported by Splunk via an SDK:

- **Normal mode**: In this mode, the search runs on Splunk and the code is returned with a search ID, with which it can poll for completion. Once the search is complete, the results can be displayed.

- **Blocking mode**: This mode is a synchronous call, and the code is blocked until the result is available and returned to the code.

- **One-shot search mode**: This is also a synchronous call, but it keeps on sending data, as in when it is available unlike that of blocking when the complete result is available and only then the results are sent.

The following code snippet can be used to run searches on the Splunk dashboard and return the results in the required format:

```
### Searches the Query and return the result in csv format
def Search():
    #The execution mode is set to Normal and the output mode as CSV
    normalsearch = {"exec_mode": "normal", "output_mode": "csv"}
    query = "index=_internal | stats count by sourcetype"
    job = service.jobs.create(query, **normalsearch)

    while True:
        job.refresh()
        stats = {"isDone": job["isDone"],
                 "doneProgress": float(job["doneProgress"])*100,
                 "scanCount": int(job["scanCount"]),
                 "eventCount": int(job["eventCount"]),
                 "resultCount": int(job["resultCount"])}
        status = ("\r%(doneProgress)03.1f%%   %(scanCount)d scanned    "
                  "%(eventCount)d matched   %(resultCount)d results") % stats

        if stats["isDone"] == "1":
            break
        sleep(2)

    result_stream = job.results()
```

This is how the Splunk SDK can be used to perform various activities to leverage the power of Splunk in the legacy/proprietary applications.

Splunk with R for analytics

We now have enough knowledge of Splunk's features and analytical capabilities; let's look at R and its capabilities. R is a statistically and graphically supported programming language for data analysis and data mining. R has extensive library support for statistical computing (linear/nonlinear modeling, clustering, classification, time series analysis, graphical plotting, predicting, forecasting, data mining, and so on).

Splunk, being a big data tool, can be integrated with R to leverage its advanced analytical capabilities for real-time insights. The Splunk app store had an app called *R Project*, but it is no longer available on the app store. The R Project app for Splunk can now be downloaded from GitHub (`https://github.com/rfsp/r/`).

The app can be installed on a Splunk instance like any other app downloaded from the Splunk app store. This app on Splunk exposes a new search command – r, which allows us to pass data from Splunk to the R-Engine for calculation and then pass results back to Splunk for further computation or visualization.

This R Project app makes seamless integration to run custom R scripts rights from the Splunk search console. This integration leverages real-time data analysis, data mining, and other statistical algorithm/packages of R to be directly used from Splunk. The following diagram shows how R Engine interacts with Splunk, which can be used by different stakeholders:

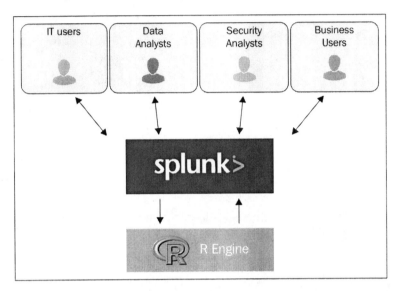

When an R command is executed on Splunk search, the data from the Splunk pipeline is saved as a .csv file. This CSV file is taken as input in R and runs the scripts to create another .csv file, which is nothing but the result of the script. The resulting CSV file is loaded in Splunk, which is used to create visualization or generate insights from the processed data.

The setup

The following are the steps to be followed to integrate the R app with Splunk:

1. Download and install the R app for Splunk from the GitHub link provided in the preceding section.

2. The R tool also needs to be installed, and it can be downloaded from `https://cran.r-project.org/bin/windows/base`. There is no compatibility issue with any version of R. The example and illustration in this chapter can be completed using the 3.1.0 version of R.

3. Once the R tool is installed, its installation directory path is required to be configured in the Splunk R app. Generally, the default path is `Program Files\R` folder in the drive where Windows OS is installed. The path in our example is `C:\Program Files\R\R-3.1.0\bin`.

   Note that the setup procedure is explained taking a Windows system as a reference, and the respective folder/path needs to be configured for the Linux/MAC OS.

4. Now, in Splunk Web console, navigate to **Apps | R Project | Setup**. A page similar to the following screenshot will be visible. Key in the path of the R tool installation and click on **Save**. This is the one-time configuration required to set the path of the R tool in the Splunk app for R.

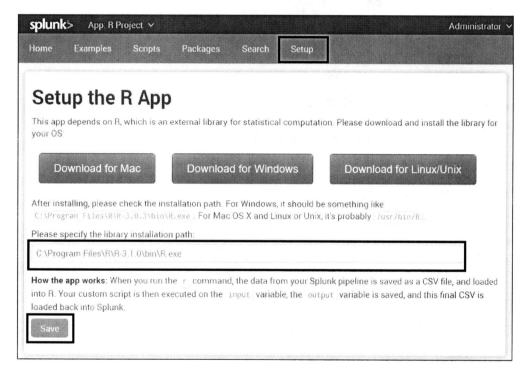

5. Now, once the path is configured, sections such as **Examples**, **Scripts**, and **Packages** of the app will be accessible to us.

6. Packages can be installed by navigating to the **Packages** menu. There are two ways of installing packages from the R Project app on Splunk. The packages can either be manually downloaded from the CRAN repository or can be specified in the textbox. Depending on the option selected, the specified packages will get installed and be available for use in R scripts.

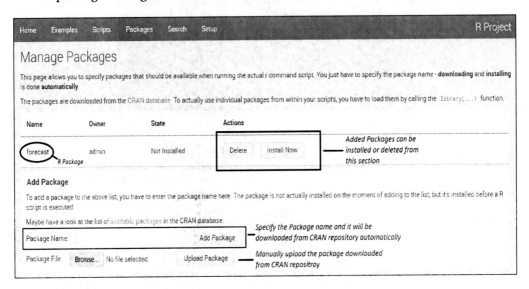

Using R with Splunk

Once we have set up the R app, we can use the r command for computation or to run custom R scripts from the Splunk search itself. The Splunk app for R comes with various examples to explicate the usage of R-Engine from Splunk via the R Project app. The examples can be accessed from the Splunk Web console by navigating to **R Project App | Examples**. Following are the steps for running custom R scripts with Splunk:

1. Run a search command that takes input from Splunk:

```
index=_internal |r "output=colnames(input)"
```

The preceding search command passes the result of index=_internal to R-Engine with the help of the input variable.

2. Run the R function on Splunk:

```
| r "
    gm_mean = function(x, na.rm=TRUE){
      exp(sum(log(x[x > 0]), na.rm=na.rm) / length(x))
    }
```

```
data <- data.matrix(input);
output <- apply(data, 2, gm_mean)
"
```

R-Engine by Splunk can be accessed using the R command in Splunk. Splunk's R Project app provides an interface to upload custom scripts that can be used along with the R commands. The script can be uploaded by navigating in the Splunk Web console to **R Project App | Scripts**. This web page of Splunk provides users with an interface to upload the script.

The uploaded script can be used along with the R commands to pass the value from the Splunk pipeline to the R script as input parameters, and then the result from R-Engine can be shown on Splunk to create visualizations and generate insight.

Although the **Splunk Machine Learning** engine is evolving day by day and now has the computation capability of complex algorithms, the R Project can be used to integrate any pre-existing scripts/algorithms right away with Splunk. This helps in achieving enterprise integration of pre-existing tools, scripts, or technology with Splunk.

Splunk with Tableau for visualization

In the preceding section, we saw how to use R along with Splunk to generate useful insight from the data using R libraries from Splunk itself. In this section, we will see how to use the processing power of Splunk and the visualization power of Tableau for interactive visualization.

Tableau is a very advanced, interactive, business-intelligent software. It helps in deriving instantaneous insights by data transformation into interactive visualizations. It has an easy-to-use drag and drop feature that helps in making highly useful dashboards in minutes. Splunk already has a pivot feature and ample visualization, but Tableau can be used to answer many unknown questions from the data.

With Splunk being a big data tool and Tableau being an excellent interactive visualization tool, their integration can be very useful to derive insight and take informed business decisions on time.

The setup

There are various variants of Tableau, and a suitable version of Tableau can be downloaded from its website (http://www.tableau.com/products), and this needs to be installed so that we are able to integrate it with Splunk.

Splunk's integration with Tableau requires the Splunk ODBC driver, which can be downloaded from the Splunk app store (`https://splunkbase.splunk.com/app/1606`). Proper care is to be taken while installing the ODBC driver, and depending on the Tableau version (32 bit/64 bit), a corresponding ODBC version needs to be installed.

Let's understand how the data from Splunk can be fetched in Tableau using the ODBC drivers to create interactive dashboards. The following screenshot shows the complete procedure of accessing data:

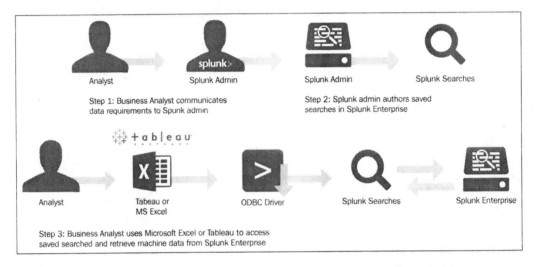

Tableau accesses data from Splunk via saved searches. Saved searches are search queries that are saved in Splunk Enterprise. Basically, saved searches are stored by the Splunk admin on the instructions given by business analysts. Now, an analyst can use Tableau and connect to Splunk using the Splunk ODBC drivers. The ODBC driver fetch all the saved searches from Splunk Enterprise in Tableau for the corresponding login. The saved searches then help to fetch the respective data from Splunk Enterprise, which can be used to create visualizations in Tableau.

Using Tableau with Splunk

The following is the procedure to connect Splunk from Tableau (in this example, Tableau 9.3 is used):

1. Navigate to **Tableau** | **Connect** | **To a server** | **More Servers…** | **Splunk**. A page similar to the following will appear. Fill in the corresponding details, for fields like **Server**, **Username**, and **Password** of Splunk to connect to it.

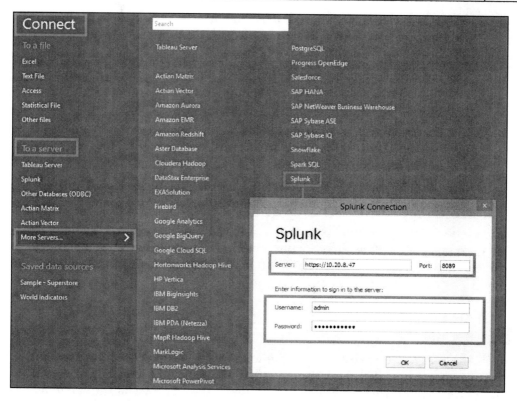

2. On successful authentication, Tableau will be able to communicate with the Splunk Server and fetch all the saved searches available for the login credentials used. The following screenshot shows saved searches fetched from the Splunk Server:

3. Select the **Saved Search** from the list on which analytics are to be done using Tableau. Once the **Saved Search** is selected, Tableau provides an option for the connection type, that is, **Live** or **Exact**.

4. The Live connection can be selected when the data in Splunk is updated every moment and the visualization to be created on Tableau should have real-time data.

5. The Exact connection is selected to fetch only the data that is available for the given saved search at that time. In this case, any change in data on Splunk will not be reflected on Tableau.

6. After the connection type is selected, click on the **Update Now/Update Automatically** button to fetch data from Splunk for visualization.

Once the preceding procedure is complete, Tableau can be used to create interactive visualization over the data fetched from Splunk. Thus, Tableau can be integrated with Splunk to use the power of visualization of Tableau for advanced analytics and better visualization.

Summary

In this chapter, you learned about the Splunk SDK, its setup procedure, uses, and enterprise integration of Splunk using Python. We also had a look at how Splunk can be used to integrate with R for analytics and Tableau for visualization. In the next chapter, we will look at the features introduced in the latest version of Splunk 6.4 along with examples and their uses.

12
What Next? Splunk 6.4

We already covered various aspects of Splunk 6.3 in the previous chapters in detail. We saw the implementation of various analytics and visualization along with the features of Splunk 6.3. Splunk recently launched an updated version: Splunk 6.4. In this chapter, we will glimpse at all the new features that have been added in Splunk 6.4 to enable better analytics and visualization. Along with the features, we will also see what all changes have been made in Splunk to make it more scalable, functional, and useful to the users. Splunk 6.4, the latest version of Splunk Enterprise comes packed with new features and customizations. The following are the key features that have been added/improved in Splunk 6.4:

- Storage optimization
- Machine learning
- Management and admin
- Indexer and search head enhancement
- Visualizations
- Multi-search management
- Enhanced alert actions

Storage optimization

Splunk 6.4 introduced the new **tsidx Retention Policy** feature, which allows users to reduce the storage requirements of data available in the cold bucket. The tsidx files are stored under indexers and are responsible for efficient searching in Splunk. Basically, the space taken by historical data available in the cold bucket can be reduced by approximately 50 percent by removing the tsidx indexing information. This can help in saving a lot of money every year that is spent on the storage of old/historical data. This policy can be modified by navigating in the Splunk web interface to **Settings** | **Indexes** in Splunk 6.4.

Machine learning

Splunk 6.4 has enhanced the *Machine Learning Toolkit and Showcase* app, which we already studied with an example in *Chapter 5, Advanced Data Analytics*. Splunk 6.4 comes with six new machine learning algorithms along with support to hundreds of algorithms of Python's data science library. Apart from this enhancement, the machine learning app has added the *Guided ML* feature that guides users step by step to build, test, and deploy machine learning models.

Splunk 6.4 has enhanced the `predict` command with features like these:

- A new algorithm for bivariate time series has been introduced, taking covariance between the individual time series into account for better and efficient prediction

- The `predict` command can be used to predict results for multiple time series at the same time and can also fill in missing data in the given time series

Management and admin

Splunk 6.4 comes with an enhanced distributed management console, which supports new topology views, search head clustering views, index and storage utilization, and performance views. It also has added support to grant restricted access to admins so that they can manage specific parts of Splunk deployments.

The following are some of the new features added in Splunk 6.4 under the distributed management console:

- **The HTTP Event Collector**: The management console enlists the entire **HTTP Event Collector input** classified on the basis of the authorization token. This feature enables the admin to understand and get insight of the data coming in via the `HTTP collector input` method.

- **Search statistics**: The console lists the heaviest/long running searches classified on the basis of users. This feature can be used to find out those searches that are causing overhead on Splunk servers.

- **I/O statistics**: The I/O utilization of bandwidth for Splunk instances is shown to take necessary actions whenever required. Along with this distributed console, it also provides options for threshold control. It can be used to control the CPU/memory, indexing rate, concurrency, and so on, and maintain the health of Splunk's distributed environment.

Indexer and search head enhancement

Splunk when deployed in a clustered and distributed environment is now introduced with various enhancements in Splunk 6.4 for higher efficiency and fault tolerance.

The following are the enhancements introduced in Splunk 6.4:

- The index now supports replication of data model and report acceleration summaries. Until Splunk 6.3, if the index failed, the data model and report acceleration summaries were required to be regenerated. In Splunk 6.4, depending on the replication factor, the data model and report acceleration will also be replicated to survive failures.

- In case of overheads or nonperformance of any indexer, the index can be quarantined. This feature restricts any new searches using this indexer, whereas any running searches will continue till the index search gets completed.

- The search head now supports replication of the search peer. This feature enables us to add any nonclustered indexers to a search head cluster. Search head enhancement in Splunk 6.4 also includes support for replication of a user, role, and password.

Visualizations

Splunk 6.4 has added support of 12 new advanced visualizations directly in the **Visualization** panel. Some of the new visualizations in Splunk 6.4 were possible in the earlier version of Splunk, that is, Splunk 6.3 using the D3 extension plugin along with the use of customized JS and CSS. Splunk 6.4 adds capability to create any new visualization that can be installed as a plugin directly and share it with other fellow Splunk users.

The following is the list of visualizations introduced in Splunk 6.4 that can be selected and used from the **Visualization** tab of the Splunk dashboard. When it is said that Splunk 6.4 supports inbuilt visualizations, this means that these visualizations can be directly downloaded from the app store, and the visualizations gets added in the **Visualization** tab.

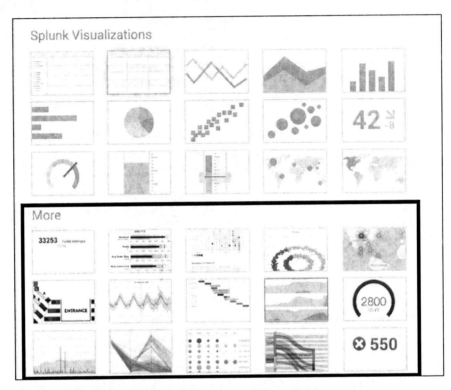

The following is the list of visualizations that we have covered in this book in various chapters of visualization using custom CSS and JS. In Splunk 6.4, these visualization apps can be directly downloaded from the Splunk app store and can be used from the **Visualization** tab of the Splunk dashboard. At the time of writing this book, not all the 12 visualizations apps are available on the Splunk app store, but they are expected to be there soon. The link for the apps is available on the app store.

The method used in Splunk 6.3 to implement these visualizations will still run in Splunk 6.4; it is just that instead of dealing with custom CSS and JS, it is now available as a ready-to-use app from the app store. The following is a list of these applications:

- Sankey diagram
- Punchcard visualization
- Calendar heatmap
- Parallel coordinates

The following are the visualizations that are newly introduced in Splunk, which can be installed as an extension and can be directly used from the **Visualization** tab from the Splunk dashboard.

- **Timeline**: The timeline chart is used to visualize data points over time. It depicts the value of a given parameter over time. This kind of visualization can be used to monitor network activities, climatic changes, and so on.

- **Status indicator**: The status indicator is a variant of single-value visualization. This visualization shows an icon and value together. Depending on the value, icon, color, and so on, it can be customized in this visualization.

- **Horizon charts**: The horizon chart is a suggested visualization that is used to compare data over time among many items within a category. It combines position and color to compare patterns of elements in a category over time. It can be used to compare indexes and scripts of share market, and so on.

- **Treemap**: Treemap is a widely used visualization that shows hierarchical data using rectangles and colors. It can be used to show hard disk space usage analytics, export/import of products, electoral data over different countries and states, and so on.

- **Bullet graph**: The bullet graph is a variant of bar chart visualization. It is very useful in showing the value of the variable along with its target value. It also shows whether the current value is good, bad, or satisfactory. Basically, it is a three-in-one bar chart that shows important information of three types of the factor in just one visualization. Let's say, the bullet graph can be used to show the sales along with the target for the given month. It also shows a scale of whether what has been achieved is good, bad, or satisfactory.

- **Location tracker**: Basically this graph visualization can be used to show information on maps. A device such an, automobile can be located on the map as per its reported coordinates.

Multi-search management

We have already seen how the post process was used to enhance the dashboard results based on a global search. Splunk 6.4 has enhanced multi-search management by adding a recursive search post process. Let's understand this enhancement with the help of an example:

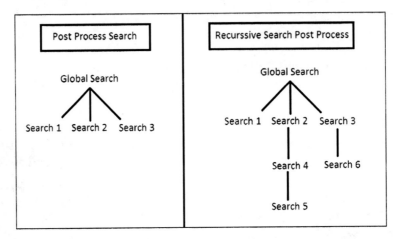

Until Splunk 6.3, multi-search management's post process search was based on a global search, that is, a global search is defined and then based on the result of the global search, other post process searches were defined. In the newly enhanced recursive search post process, we can use a search as a base search, which itself is derived from another search. As in the preceding figure, **Search 4** is based on the post process of **Search 2**, where **Search 2** itself is based on a post process of a global search.

We have already studied the post process search in this book; now, let's see how to implement the recursive search post process on Splunk 6.4. The following code snippet explains how the recursive post process can be implemented on the Splunk dashboard for optimized and fast processing of dashboard results:

```
<search id="globalSearch">
    <query>index=_internal | top sourcetype</query>
</search>                                          Global search

<search base="globalSearch" id="search_1">
    <query>search sourcetype=splunkd</query>
</search>                              Search 1 based on Global Search

<search base="search_1" id="search_2">
    <query>| stats count</query>
</search>                        Search 2 based on Post Process of Search 1
```

Using the enhanced multi-search management feature of Splunk 6.4, now the dashboards can be further optimized for enhanced performance.

Enhanced alert actions

We already covered custom alert actions in detail in *Chapter 9, Advanced Dashboard Customization*. In this section, you will learn what new features have been introduced in the Splunk 6.4 release.

Splunk 6.4 has a new feature to choose from the action list of alert actions, that is, it sends log events to the Splunk receiver endpoint. In the following figure, the option marked in the rectangular box is the newly added feature in Splunk 6.4 under alert actions.

This option helps users to redirect the alert log data to Splunk again under the specified sourcetype or index. The alert that used to either trigger e-mails, webhook, or any other defined custom action can also be sent on Splunk for analysis in future. This feature can be helpful for auditing alert scenarios.

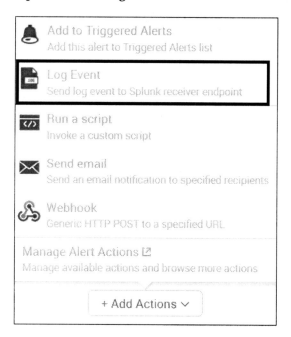

Let's understand the use of this **Log Event** feature in a custom alert. Suppose we have an alert defined to detect fraudulent transactions. Whenever such a transaction is detected, there is a support ticket lodged in JIRA and a custom script runs, which instructs the payment gateway to trigger another layer of authentication. Now, the alert data can be sent on Splunk under different sourcetypes, which can be used to determine and derive various insights relevant to the fraudulent transaction. This would enable us to restrict such activity in the future.

Thus, the **Log Event** option can be used in various scenarios as per the requirement under the custom alert action.

Summary

In this chapter, we had a look at the features and customizations introduced in the latest version of Splunk 6.4. We saw how these features and customizations can be put to use for better use of Splunk's capabilities. In this book, we saw how and where Splunk can be used to make sense out of machine-generated log data and how we can create analytics and visualizations in Splunk. You also learned how to customize dashboards, tweak Splunk, and how to integrate Splunk with analytics and visualization tools.

Index

Symbols

event configuration, data processing
character encoding 54

A

addtotals command 107-109
annotate action 117
anomalies command
using 115, 116
anomalies detection
about 115
anomalies command, using 115, 116
anomalousvalue command, using 117, 118
cluster command, using 118-120
kmeans command, using 120, 121
outlier command, using 121-123
rare command, using 123-125
appendcols command 86, 87
append command 85, 86
appendpipe command 87
app key-value store
about 14
collections, managing via REST 18
components 15-17
examples 18-20
replication 20
system requirements 15
uses 15
architecture, Splunk
about 2-4
index parallelization 5, 6
parallelization, need for 4
pipeline 3
processors 3

A (continued)

associate command
using 132-134

B

button switcher
about 233
example 233
implementation 233-236

C

calendar heatmap visualization
about 187
example 187
implementation 190
search query 188, 189
Call Detail Records (CDR) logs 44
charts
about 159
bubble charts 162-165
coloring options 159-161
overlay 161, 162
choropleth visualization 180
clean command 78, 79
cluster command
using 118-120
clusters 264
color modes
about 184
categorical 184
divergent 184
sequential 184
comma delimiter 279
comma-separated values (CSV) 41
contextual drilldown 168-170

capturing, ways 220
custom tokens 222
eval tokens 220
use cases 220
transform action 122
trending technique
trendline command, using 128, 129
x11 command, using 130, 131
trendline command
using 128, 129
tsidx Retention Policy feature 309

U

URL field value drilldown 171, 172
use cases, custom alert action
automatic incident tracking 262
fraud detection 262
use cases, tokens
conditional display 220
drilldown tokens 220
form inputs 220
search events 220

V

visualization
configuration settings 142-145
visualization grouping
about 239
example 240
implementation 241, 242
single-value grouping 240
visualization grouping 240
Visualizations tab, Splunk 6.4
bullet graph reference link 313
horizon charts, reference link 313
location tracker, reference link 313
status indicator, reference link 313
timeline, reference link 313
treemap, reference link 313

W

weighted moving average (wma) 128

X

x11 command
using 130, 131
xmlkv command 92, 93
xyseries command 109-111

CPSIA information can be obtained
at www.ICGtesting.com
Printed in the USA
FFOW02n1943100317
33340FF